The Other Side of Truth

The Paranormal, The Art of the Imagination, and the Human Condition

Paul Kimball

Redstar
Books

ISBN: 978-0-9916975-0-2

Published by Redstar Books, a division of Redstar Films Limited
www.redstarfilmtv.com/books
2541 Robie Street, Halifax, NS B3K 4N3

PRAISE FOR *THE OTHER SIDE OF TRUTH*

"New thinking such as that displayed in this book is sorely needed in the paranormal field. I have seen Paul's opinions greeted with open hostility on my radio show and elsewhere. Incredibly insane stories such as the U.S. President using a time machine to get to Mars don't garner half the vitriol that my good friend does. To me, that means he has something important to say that threatens the thoughtless. Good."
– Greg Bishop, host of *Radio Misterioso* and author of *Project Beta*

"*The Other Side of Truth* is a road-trip of physical, spiritual, and mental proportions that sees Canadian filmmaker Paul Kimball hot on the trail of what is commonly, and simplistically, referred to as the 'paranormal.' He demonstrates that there is nothing simple about matters such as UFOs, life after death, and synchronicity, and reveals through his own fascinating experiences that the journey in search of the answers can be a deeply satisfying one."
– Nick Redfern, author of *Final Events* and *The Real Men in Black*

"Paul Kimball's *The Other Side of Truth* shatters the bland, sterile image of the 'paranormal' foisted upon western society over the past thirty years. While this book won't give the reader any answers about ghosts, extraterrestrials, or the afterlife, it *will* inspire them to ask questions about the world and universe around them. Presenting one man's engrossing journey through the weirdness of our world and ourselves, Kimball's book fits nicely on a shelf with Jacques Vallee, William James, and Jack Kerouac."
– Aaron John Gulyas, author of *Extraterrestrials and the American Zeitgeist*

"*The Other Side of Truth* is a fascinating and entertaining examination of the paranormal. UFOs, ghosts, time travel, synchronicities and reincarnation are just some of the subjects covered in this thought-provoking book. Film-maker and musician Paul Kimball takes readers on a deeply personal journey, examining issues such as philosophy, consciousness, metaphysics and the nature of reality, fleshing out his insightful theories with details of some of his own bizarre experiences. Highly recommended."
– Nick Pope, United Kingdom Ministry of Defence (1985-2006) and author of *Open Skies, Closed Minds*

"It's a cliché, but Paul Kimball's *The Other Side Of Truth* is a 'must read' for the choir, the seekers and the doubters. His honest curiosity and skepticism – demonstrated over the years on my e-mail list and radio program – combine in what is an intriguing and easy read."
– Errol Bruce-Knapp, moderator of *UFO UpDates* and host of *Strange Days... Indeed* and *Mind Shift*

"After many years of research and adventures, and a whole lot of notes (or a fantastic memory), Paul Kimball has tried and tested all things covered under the 'paranormal' umbrella, from ghosts to UFOs to synchronicity. The end result is a truly entertaining, honest and eye-opening view of the mysterious world of unexplained phenomena."
– Dave Sadler, editor of *The Paranormal Review*

"In *The Other Side of Truth*, filmmaker Paul Kimball takes his questing intelligence on a trip with an intriguing destination: a better understanding of what constitutes the 'paranormal,' and a broader discussion of what constitutes 'truth.' Armed with a skeptical outlook but a remarkably open mind, Kimball takes the reader on a unique and entertaining journey through low and high culture – I love how he sweeps past the difference between the two – facts and feelings, and many remembrances of strange incidents in his own life, and arrives at a place that allows the 'paranormal' to breathe fresh air for the first time in many years."
– Ron Foley MacDonald, theatre / film critic and senior programmer of the Atlantic Film Festival

"If you are looking for a vivid glimpse into some of the most frequently asked questions and thoughts about the paranormal and the unknown, then this is the book for you. *The Other Side of Truth* is masterfully written by filmmaker Paul Kimball, who encourages the reader to open their mind to the possibilities presented by the paranormal. It's not just a good read, it's a necessary one for anyone with an interest in the spiritual world, UFOs, death, reincarnation, and any other subject your subconscious may bring to your attention. Be prepared to set plenty of time aside, for when you pick up this book you will not want to put it down."
– Kathleen Mendelin Marchbank, author of *Vamplitude*

"A glorious pastiche of things personal and things paranormal and transcendental. I can't do justice to the contents of this book; it is fecund with information and insight that readers will savor and have to think seriously about."
- Rich Reynolds, *The UFO Iconoclasts*

"If you are interested in a ride into the unknown, then this book is for you. Whether it's UFOs, ghosts, or other mysteries, Paul Kimball offers a fair and critical examination of the paranormal and explores the many questions of life. After reading this book you will certainly be better prepared to answer the fundamental question that challenges humanity each and every day: What is Truth?"
– Rev. Kyle Wagner, B.A., MDiv. Anglican Church of Canada

For Reg & Betty Kimball

CONTENTS

Acknowledgments

I like to say that the journey is the destination. If true, then one always needs good company on the trip. These folks have been my fellow travelers over the years in one way or another, although they may not have realized it.

Reg & Betty Kimball, Jim Kimball, Sharon Kimball Gough, Linda Wood, Peter Black, the late Mac Tonnies, Greg Bishop, Nick Redfern, John Rosborough, Christina Cuffari, Colin White, the late Gil Latter, Dave Salloum, Jeff Sullivan, Will Fraser, Dave Sadler, Aaron John Gulyas, Andrew Mark Sewell, Ron Foley MacDonald, Meagan Crane, Denise Djokic, Kris Lee McBride, Brittany Babakioff, Walter Bosley, Findlay Muir, Jeff Drake, Sandy MacLean, Sigrid Hudson Bishop, Susan Stothart, the late Patrick Christopher, the late Karl Pflock, Stanton Friedman, Brad Sparks, Rich Reynolds, Kathleen Mendelin Marchbank, Tony Morrill, Errol Bruce-Knapp, Shahid Dadabhoy, Geoff Morrison, Glenn MacCulloch, Evangelo Kioussis, Veronica Reynolds, Holly Stevens, Benjamin Stevens, Stephanie Steele, Katie Martin, Kate Mullan, Carly Street, Joseph Gallaccio, David Jalbert, Gary & Nancy Hill, Christine Boss, Lee Thompson, Ann MacKenzie, Barry Moody, the late Gordon Watson, James Farmer, Burkhardt Kiesekamp, the late C. J. Bartlett, the late James L. Stokesbury, the late Gabriel Fischer, the Gough kids (Emily, Matt, Alex, and Will), Dana & Bob Tonnies, Kelly McKeigan, Chris MacKenzie, Heather Schmidt, Mark Winkelman, Len MacKeigan, Nan MacDonald, Wayne Paquet, Michelle Aalders, Tall Poppies, Julia's Rain, Jeff Forbes, Antony Shearn, Tarek Abouamin, Lorrie McAllister, Andy Stephenson, Steve Mera, Graham Simms, Geof Petch, Mark Victor, Melissa Clattenburg, Dale Stevens, Tim Crawford, Tim Binnall, and Zachary Orgrot.

Last, but not least, the immortal Jack Kerouac, who wrote, "I saw that my life was a vast glowing empty page and I could do anything I wanted."

Truer words were never written.

Foreword by Greg Bishop

The Dadaist Paranormal School

It is clear, then, that the idea of a fixed method, or of a fixed theory of rationality, rests on too naive a view of man and his social surroundings. To those who look at the rich material provided by history, and who are not intent on impoverishing it in order to please their lower instincts, their craving for intellectual security in the form of clarity, precision, "objectivity," "truth," it will become clear that there is only one principle that can be defended under all circumstances and in all stages of human development. It if the principle: anything goes.[1]
– Paul Feyerabend

The UFO subject is far more interesting than lights in the sky, people from other planets, or simple hoaxes and misidentifications. Many are surprised about the verifiable connections between UFOs and other tabloid fodder such as psychic phenomena, ghosts, and liminal creatures like Bigfoot.

Most people who claim to be researchers in these subjects are often insular about their particular areas of interest, sometimes to the point of open hostility when the similarities are noted. "Ufologists" (a misleading term for an unregulated discipline) routinely bristle at the mention of any strangeness outside of supposed aliens. They have been fighting a 50-year battle for respectability, and that other "junk" might make them look silly.

What they don't seem to realize is that the vast majority of the

[1] Paul Feyerabend, *Against Method: Outline of an Anarchistic Theory of Knowledge* (London: New Left Books, 1975), 27-28.

public, particularly the arbiters of reality (primarily the media and academia), think it's *all* silly. The public face of paranormal research has done itself few favors in this regard. The loudest and craziest person in the room nearly always controls the conversation, gets on the popular radio shows, or gets the big book or movie deal.

For many years, however, there have been a few voices amongst those who think deeply about the paranormal whose study of the subject has not been reducible to sound-bites or hackneyed expeditions conducted on television shows using night-vision cameras strapped to high-strung actors and so-called "experts" (whose mantra always seems to be, "Did you hear that?").

This iconoclastic group of paranormal enthusiasts and researchers, such as Nick Redfern and the late Mac Tonnies, has been quietly cheerleading the unheralded insights of UFO and paranormal researchers like Jacques Vallee, Jim Brandon, John Keel, Jenny Randles, Greg Little and Graham Hancock, as well as the pioneering work of scientists such as Dean Radin, Robert Jahn, Richard Strassman, and Hal Puthoff.

Most UFO buffs and paranormal fans have never heard of these people, who have recorded their insights in books that largely remain unread, mainly because they downplay or outright reject the aliens-from-other-planets idea. The scientific viewpoint of credentialed academics such as those mentioned above is also routinely ignored because it doesn't flatter the "new age" bias of most readers. It also seems that fewer people have the patience to wade through the entire text of a book anymore, which puts readers of the present volume in rare company.

Most people have self-imposed blinders on which keep them from seeing outside the narrow viewpoint of their own personal interests, experiences and opinions. Many are also unaware of the underlying sagas that have brought them, their societies, and humanity *in toto* to this point in history. Our past has taught us that almost nothing happens in a vacuum, and the present is the result of a tangled fabric of interconnected and often disparate stories. The paranormal is no different. As a trained historian, Paul Kimball points this out immediately in his introduction, and keeps us aware of it throughout his narrative.

We have always lived with an awareness of forces and influences that are not apparent to our five senses, observation over time, or simple deduction. Some of these forces were eventually found to have verifiable explanations, such as magnetism, electricity, the weather, the motions of planets, the flight of birds, and so on. Others, with a long history of anecdotal evidence, like meteorites or ball lightning, took longer to solve. Other more complex and esoteric elements of our world, such as those discussed herein, are still awaiting better methods and theories to explain them.

Those who are invested in a fixed way of looking at the world declare that since we have perfected all methods of verifying reality, then anything that does not conform to the current understanding of physical laws does not exist. The truly skeptical attitude would be to reserve judgment and declare certain issues "unproven." Anything else veers perilously close to belief, not science.

A few pioneering individuals, such as the membership of the Society for Scientific Exploration, actively use the scientific tools currently available to test issues such as ESP, reincarnation, psychokinesis, UFO sightings, and other "fringe" subjects.[2] They are aware of the pitfalls of belief and experimenter bias, as well as the issue of scientific peer pressure, the question of who pays the bills and what they want to hear, and the spectre of fundamentalist skepticism.

---

[2] The Mission Statement of the SSE states: "The Society for Scientific Exploration (SSE) is a leading professional organization of scientists and scholars who study unusual and unexplained phenomena. Subjects often cross mainstream boundaries, such as consciousness, ufos, and alternative medicine, yet often have profound implications for human knowledge and technology. We publish a peer-reviewed journal, host annual meetings, and engage in public outreach. While our Full members are professional or experienced scientists and scholars, Associate and Student memberships are available to everyone. Consequently, we have a diverse and active membership, who promote critical thinking and rigorous – yet open-minded – scientific exploration." *Society for Scientific Exploration.* www.scientificexploration.org/.

Then there are the rest of us, who look on and try to make sense of something that we are often told is not worth the time or effort to worry about. After many years of study, listening to paranormal radio shows and attending lectures, most either become disillusioned, or settle into some sort of belief system based on their hopes and wishes. There are a thoughtful few, however, who decide to treat the whole thing as a sort of journey of learning. Those are the voices worth listening to.

Paul Kimball is one of those people who have embarked upon this journey. The book you are about to enjoy is a detailed chronicle of his evolution from disinterested skepticism to a deep and inquisitive involvement in what is loosely called "the paranormal." During the course of his narrative, Paul examines the issues in terms of a creative viewpoint, or even as an artistic act. In light of this, much reported witness testimony of UFOs and other "paranormal" strangeness could actually be considered surrealist stories.

Paul Feyerabend (quoted at the beginning of this introduction) was a philosopher of science, and author of the landmark book *Against Method*, wherein he put forward the argument that no progress can be made under inflexible rules, especially those of the scientific method. In a 1972 letter to a friend, Hungarian philosopher Imre Lakatos, Feyerabend declared his allegiance to the ideals of the Dadaist artistic movement of the early 20th century. His words could be instructive to the paranormal researcher and fan alike:

> A Dadaist is utterly unimpressed by any serious enterprise and he smells a rat whenever people stop smiling and assume that attitude and those facial expressions which indicate that something important is about to be said. A Dadaist is convinced that a worthwhile life will arise only when we start taking things lightly and when we remove from our speech the profound but already putrid meanings it has accumulated over the centuries ("search for truth"; "defense of justice"; "passionate concern"; etc. etc.). A Dadaist is prepared to initiate joyful experiments even in those domains where

change and experimentation seem to be out of the question."[3]

Perhaps after reading *The Other Side Of Truth*, I will now finally declare myself a student of the "Dadaist Paranormal School." Maybe you will too.

New thinking such as that displayed in this book is sorely needed in the paranormal field. I have seen Paul's opinions greeted with open hostility on my radio show and elsewhere. Incredibly insane stories such as the U.S. President using a time machine to get to Mars or culinary recipes channeled from historical figures, don't garner half the vitriol that my good friend does. To me, that means he has something important to say that threatens the thoughtless.

Good.

---

[3] Imre Lakatos and Paul Feyerabend, *For and Against Method, Including Lakatos's Lectures on Scientific Method and the Lakatos – Feyerabend Correspondence* (Chicago: University of Chicago Press, 1999), 295.

Introduction

The Journey is the Destination

Get your motor runnin', head out on the highway, lookin' for adventure in whatever comes your way.[1]
– Dennis Edmonton, aka Mars Bonfire

A couple of years ago, I was asked by a friend in the United States to explain what I thought the word "paranormal" meant. I knew he held the opinion that the term only meant things such as UFOs, or ghosts, and I was also aware that he thought it was all a bit silly; indeed, he had given me friendly grief about my interest in the subject from time to time. But I also knew that he went to church on a fairly regular basis, and that he was a liberal Democrat who had voted for Barack Obama in the 2008 presidential election.

In answer to his question, I referred him to a 2008 *Newsweek* interview with Obama wherein the future President discussed his religious beliefs. Obama stated that he prays for "forgiveness for my sins and flaws, which are many, the protection of my family, and that I'm carrying out God's will, not in a grandiose way, but simply that there is an alignment between my actions and what He would want."[2]

I then sent my friend a copy of an interview Obama gave to *Christianity Today* in 2008, wherein he stated unequivocally, "I am a Christian, and I am a devout Christian. I believe in the redemptive death and resurrection of Jesus Christ. I believe that that faith gives

---

[1] Dennis Edmonton, aka Mars Bonfire, "Born to Be Wild," Perf. by Steppenwolf, *Steppenwolf* (ABC Dunhill Records, 1968).

[2] Lisa Miller and Richard Wolffe, "Finding My Faith," *Newsweek*, 21 July 2008.

me a path to be cleansed of sin and have eternal life."[3]

"So," I asked my friend the next time I saw him, after the election, "let me get this straight. You just voted – in an election for the most powerful office in the world – for a man who believes in a supernatural being, with whom he communicates via telepathy. This supernatural being also sent his only son to Earth to be tortured and executed, and then brought him back from the dead a couple of days later, all so that a prophecy could be fulfilled. And of course there's the whole "walking on water" thing, not to mention the "water into wine' trick, and the raising of the dead, and…"

I paused for effect, and then, as my friend began to frown, I delivered the punch-line.

"And you think I'm a bit goofy for having an interest in UFOs and ghosts?"

I think he finally got my point.

At a lecture about the paranormal that I gave at the 2011 Hal-Con science fiction and fantasy convention in Halifax, Nova Scotia, I began by showing photos of some of my favorite paranormalists, just to drive home the same point.[4] The first was Søren Kierkegaard, one of the great Western philosophers, whose work was devoted primarily to examining the relationship between man and God (who has to be considered the ultimate in allegedly paranormal beings). I followed Kierkegaard with Abraham Lincoln, a deeply spiritual man who claimed to have had a dream about his own assassination just three days before it happened.[5] After Lincoln, I went with William Lyon MacKenzie King, the longest-serving Prime Minister in Canadian history and the primary architect of our modern social welfare state. King regularly consulted mediums and spiritualists to try and contact,

---

[3] Sarah Pulliam and Ted Olsen, "Q&A: Barack Obama," *Christianity Today*, 23 January 2008.

[4] Suzy Riddler, "Paranormal Investigations with Paul Kimball at Hal-Con 2011," *Hexed: Sisterhood of the Supernatural*, 19 November 2011. http://goo.gl/qECKO.

[5] Ward Hill Lamon, *Recollections of Abraham Lincoln, 1847 – 1865*, ed. Dorothy Lamon Teillard (Lincoln: University of Nebraska Press, 1999), 113 - 117.

among others, his mother, Leonardo Da Vinci, and one of his predecessors, Sir Wilfrid Laurier.[6] Albert Einstein got a mention, if for no other reason than his oft-quoted maxim that "God does not play dice with the universe."[7] Finally, I added Obama, and the quotes noted above.

The difficulty in coming up with this little exercise wasn't trying to find serious people who took an interest in the paranormal; it was trying to whittle the list down to just a few.

The paranormal is the ultimate Rorschach test. In many respects, how we view things like UFOs, or ghosts, or the possibility of an afterlife, tells us more about ourselves than it does about the subjects themselves. The paranormal is about far more than the caricature of the crazy cultists drinking the poisoned Kool-Aid so that they can beam up to the mothership, just as religion and spirituality are about far more than suicide bombers flying hijacked planes into the World Trade Center or murderers shooting doctors who provide abortions. These are things at the very fringe of what is most definitely *not* a fringe subject.

It shouldn't come as a surprise that I have drawn parallels between the concept of "God" and things such as UFOs and ghosts; the real surprise is that more people have not. It's all paranormal, and it has been a defining feature of the human journey from the very beginning, deeply embedded in our philosophy and our religion, our stories, songs and our poems, and yes, even in our science. It's worth remembering that Sir Isaac Newton, the man considered by many to be the greatest scientist who ever lived, actually wrote more about religion and the supernatural than he did about science, without ever

---

[6] Allan Levine, *William Lyon MacKenzie King: A Life Guided by the Hand of Destiny* (Vancouver: Douglas & McIntyre), 250 – 259. King was friends with the famous medium Etta Wriedt (1860 – 1942), whom he met in 1932, and who visited him a number of times when he was Prime Minister. See "Henrietta 'Etta' Wriedt," Library and Archives Canada. http://goo.gl/hovPZ.

[7] Albert Einstein, "Letter to Max Born, 4 December 1926," in *The Born-Einstein Letters*, translated by Irene Born (New York: Walker and Company, 1971).

4

seeing a contradiction between the two. That doesn't mean he was right, of course, but it does illustrate that the "paranormal" isn't as outlandish as some people would have you believe.[8]

Henry Alline, Canada's first great evangelist and a Christian of a mystical bent, had a profound spiritual experience in the late 18th century that changed his life and set him on his short career as the leader of the first Great Awakening in New Brunswick and Nova Scotia.[9] Here is how Alline described what happened to him as he walked through the woods of colonial Nova Scotia in 1775. It was about as intense and transforming an experience as one can possibly imagine, and as such it's worth considering within the context of the term "paranormal":

O the infinite condescension of God to a worm of the dust! for though my whole soul was filled with love, and ravished with a divine ecstacy beyond any doubts or fears, or thoughts of being then deceived, for I enjoyed a heaven on earth, and it seemed as if I were wrapped up in God, and that he had done ten thousand times more for me than ever I could expect, or had ever thought of: yet he still stooped to the weakness of my desires and requests, made as before observed on the 13th of February; though I had no thoughts of it then, until it was given me. Looking up, I thought I saw that same light, though it appeared different, and as soon as I saw it, the design was opened to me, according to his promise, and I was obliged to cry out: enough, enough, O blessed God; the work of conversion, the change and the manifestations of it are no more disputable, than that light which I see, or anything that I

---

[8] Many of Newton's religious works can be found side by side with his scientific writings at *The Newton Project*. www.newtonproject.sussex.ac.uk/.

[9] George A. Rawlyk, *Ravished by the Spirit: Religious Revivals, Baptists and Henry Alline* (Montreal: McGill-Queen's University Press, 1984).

ever saw."[10]

He continued:

> I will not say I saw either of those lights with my bodily eyes,
> though I thought then I did, but it is no odds to me, for it was
> as evident to me, as anything I ever saw with my bodily eyes
> (-in my Life); and answered the end it was sent for.[11]

The phrase "though I thought then I did" should give one pause for thought. Did Alline actually see a light, and perhaps come in contact with an advanced non-human intelligence, which he perceived as "God" because he filtered the contact through the cultural morays of his time? While he was clearly speaking in traditional Christian metaphor, using symbols that were common and well understood in his time, it's important to understand that the experience itself was very real, at least to Alline.[12] This was not some dry recounting of an intellectual process whereby he had come up with a seemingly rational reason for believing in God. If you had put it to him that he had "made contact" with some non-human intelligence, he would have certainly agreed.[13]

Alline was so inspired by this experience that he embarked upon an evangelical mission to spread his "New Light" gospel even as he was

---

[10] Henry Alline, *The Life and Journal of the Rev. Mr. Henry Alline* (Boston: Gilbert & Dean, 1806), 35 – 36. http://goo.gl/nOuvv.

[11] Ibid., 36.

[12] Alline was familiar with the works of the great Christian mystics Jacob Böhme and William Law, and his own experience contains a number of similarities with theirs. For a full discussion of the "conversion" experience, see William James, *The Varieties of Religious Experience: A Study in Human Nature, Being the Gifford Lectures on Natural Religion Delivered at Edinburgh in 1901 – 1902* (New York: The Modern Library, 2002). 210 – 285.

[13] See also *The New Light Experience of Henry Alline*, directed by Evangelo Kioussis (Halifax: Redstar Films, 2000). Television. http://goo.gl/ZnYkc.

wracked by tuberculosis. The eight-year revival he led transformed the religious and social life of the Maritime colonies and eventually spread to New England, before he passed away in 1784 at the age of 36.

Did his conversion experience provide irrefutable evidence of the existence of God, or some other form of advanced non-human intelligence, whatever it might be?

Of course not. But that's the wrong question to ask.

Henry Alline was but a single ripple in the "ocean" of human experience, just as people who study UFO or ghost phenomena, or experiment with altered states of consciousness, are ripples on that ocean. They're all out there, on the water, looking for new horizons. By doing so, they are often considered outcasts. Alline, for example, was called the "ravager of churches" by many mainstream clergy in Nova Scotia once he commenced his Great Awakening, because he didn't play by their rules.[14] He was a revolutionary who embraced new experiences, ideas, and ways of thinking.

Whereas many people talk about the ocean, however, very few actually go sailing. Indeed, most do their very best to stay away from the water altogether, because they've been told that it's dangerous. They have their regimented, ordered view of the world, and in that world it's better to stay on terra firma, a place where unimaginative conformity is the perpetual "normal." They "live" in the strictest, biological sense of the word, but they aren't actually *living*.

This is a book for the living – for people who understand that the journey *is* the destination, and who are willing to embrace the revolution of thought that fuels the trip. It's essentially a conversation with myself about the paranormal, and its relationship to the human condition. There are no answers proffered within these pages, however. Instead, there are questions that I think we should all be asking, and possibilities that I think we should all be willing to explore. If you want a book that confirms a pre-existing belief system,

---

[14] D. G. Bell, *Henry Alline and Maritime Religion* (Ottawa: The Canadian Historical Association, 1993), 11.

whether your belief is that UFOs are aliens from Zeta Reticuli, or that ghosts are the spirits of your dearly departed grandmother, or that everything we call "paranormal" is complete "woo," then this isn't the book for you. I have no interest in preaching to the converted.

My primary goal in writing this book is to stimulate the imagination about what kind of non-human intelligence might be "out there" beyond the realm of our current understanding, and how and why it might be interacting with us. If such an intelligence exists – and for the sake of argument I'm going to work on the assumption that it does – then I think there should be some sort of pattern to its behavior. It's this proverbial "signal" within the "noise" that I will attempt to identify and then amplify.

I discussed all of this with the late Karl Pflock in 2001 when I interviewed him for the documentary *Stanton T. Friedman is Real*. I asked him about what he called "the will to believe" as it related to UFOs, but his response applied to all aspects of the paranormal.

"What I mean by it is the desire for something to be true affecting one's judgment and assessment of the facts before you," he answered. "The poster on the wall in Fox Mulder's office that says 'I Want to Believe' is a representation of what happens to be a very real thing in UFO research. People want very much to believe whatever it is that happens to be their interest – alien visitation, abductions, et cetera. Unfortunately what happens is this leads them to ignore facts which are contrary to the things that they want to believe."[15]

Karl then made clear that this closed mindset did not just affect the true believers. "You have the mirror-image on the so-called skeptic side," he told me. "The CSICOP-ians, the Committee for the

---

[15] *Stanton T. Friedman is Real*, directed by Paul Kimball (Halifax: Redstar Films Limited, 2002). Television. www.beyonderstv.com/paulkimball-media/paul-kimballs-real-world-films/stanton-t-friedman-in-real/. Pflock died in 2006 of ALS after an interesting career. He was a former Marine, served in the CIA as an intelligence officer, worked as a political consultant, congressional staffer and lobbyist in Washington, D.C., and served in the Reagan administration as Deputy Assistant Secretary of Defense (Deputy Director) for Operational Test and Evaluation.

Scientific Investigation of Claims of the Paranormal. They start from the premise that 'they can't be, therefore they aren't.'[16] The true believers start from 'they must be, therefore they are.' So, those of us who are slogging through all this, and trying to follow the facts wherever they lead, are caught between these two extremes, and unfortunately are often defined by them."

For those of us in what my good friend Greg Bishop has called "the excluded middle," the way forward is to ignore the high priests of belief and / or disbelief who claim to have all the answers, and focus on the mystery that draws people to the subject in the first place. As will be seen throughout this book, it's my opinion that this isn't really a scientific endeavor with definitive answers so much as it is an artistic one, meant to fire the imagination with myriad interpretations, varied impressions, and the widest range of possible meanings.

Much of what follows is based on my own personal experiences, some of it is based on the experiences of others, and some of it is pure, unadulterated speculation, drawn from my own ideas about what our existence *could* be. But as Albert Einstein said, "I am enough of an artist to draw freely upon my imagination,"[17] and who am I to argue with Einstein?

So let us imagine!

---

[16] CSICOP changed their name to the Committee for Skeptical Inquiry (CSI) in 2006. See *The Committee for Skeptical Inquiry*, http://www.csicop.com. While they claim that their mission is "to promote scientific inquiry, critical investigation, and the use of reason in examining controversial and extraordinary claims," their way of thinking is for the most part not true skepticism, but rather the kind of disbelief that Karl talked about.

[17] George S. Viereck, "What Life Means to Einstein," *The Saturday Evening Post*, 26 October 1929, 117.

William Lyon MacKenzie King, Prime Minister of Canada from 1921 - 1926, 1926 - 1930, and 1935 - 1948. An ardent spiritualist, he used mediums to stay in contact with departed associates, his mother, and several of his deceased dogs, and was reported to have made frequent use of ouija boards and crystal balls. A survey of 25 historians in 1997 ranked him as the greatest Prime Minister in Canadian history. (Photo: Yousuf Karsh / Library and Archives Canada / C-027650 – public domain)

Chapter One

The Rubicon of the Imagination

Rationality is what we do to organize the world, to make it possible to predict. Art is the rehearsal for the inapplicability and failure of that process.[1]

– Brian Eno

Julius Caesar crossed the Rubicon in 49 BCE, an act of defiance that sparked the civil war which eventually led to the fall of the Roman Republic and the rise of the Roman Empire. He uttered his famous phrase "veni, vidi, vici" whilst sitting on a horse, and the legions that he led were armed with swords, spears, and similar weapons.

When the Roman Empire in the West fell in 476 CE, after five centuries as the pre-eminent power in the ancient world, it was to Germanic armies that wielded more or less the same equipment Caesar's legions had fought with. When Belisarius re-captured large parts of the Western Empire in the middle of the 6th century for Emperor Justinian, he too led armies that would not have seemed unfamiliar to Caesar.[2]

Thus, while there were certainly changes in tactics, and formations, and even to some degree materiel, the armies commanded by

---

[1] Brian Eno, *A Year With Swollen Appendices: Brian Eno's Diary* (London: Faber & Faber, 1996), 272.

[2] Lars Brownworth, *Lost to the West: The Forgotten Byzantine Empire That Rescued Western Civilization* (New York: Crown Publishing Group, 2009); Adrian Goldsworthy, *The Fall of the West: The Death of the Roman Superpower* (London: Weidenfeld & Nicolson, 2009).

Belisarius had not changed in any fundamental way since the period when the Empire had been created, six centuries earlier. This was typical of human technological development for most of our history. Change, when it came, was generally slow and fitful.

Change began to accelerate more rapidly after the Industrial Revolution began in the mid 18th century, but it was in the 20th century that the "game" truly changed. The British Grand Fleet commanded by Admiral Sir John Jellicoe was the foundation of Imperial might at the beginning of the First World War in 1914.[3] A single dreadnought would have been sufficient to defeat the combined fleets of the British, French and Spanish navies at Trafalgar just a century earlier. By the time that the Second World War ended in 1945, however, battleships were obsolete. Blockades and great naval battles between surface fleets were meaningless when compared with air power, as demonstrated by the sinking of HMS *Prince of Wales* and HMS *Repulse* by the Japanese in 1941, much less the development of atomic weapons and rockets by the end of the war, all of which came to the fore within less than two decades.

Technological change since then has increased at an exponential rate not seen before in human history. My home computer provides a good example. When I founded my film and television production company just twelve years ago, I bought desktop computers for the office and for my home that were near the top of the line, and which were specifically assembled for us by a local company. They each had 20 GB of hard drive space. The mass-produced computer I'm using as I type this in 2012 has 500 gigabytes of hard drive space, and is hooked up to a separate drive that contains another 500 gigabytes. On

---

[3] Robert K. Massie, *Dreadnought: Britain, Germany and the Coming of the Great War at Sea* (New York: Random House, 1991), and Robert K. Massie, *Castles of Steel: Britain, Germany and the Winning of the Great War* (New York: Random House, 2003). Just half a century later, a single nuclear-armed submarine could have obliterated the combined fleets at Jutland with a single missile, and without any of the thousands of doomed sailors having any understanding of what had caused the sudden blinding flash of light that was about to destroy them.

the shelf nearby is another drive with a terrabyte of space. The difference between the processing speeds is even more pronounced than the relative storage capabilities. I can edit an entire film on this computer, and post it immediately to various places on the Internet, or send it via FTP to someone in Asia, or Europe, things I couldn't have done a decade ago.[4]

This is really just the beginning, however. "Moore's Law" states that computer power doubles every eighteen months, an unheard of increase in technological power that permeates every level of our society.[5] Futurists such as Ray Kurzweil have stated that this model can also be applied to a wide variety of other technologies, in what Kurzweil called "the law of accelerating returns."[6] The future as imagined by science fiction writers in the 1960s is already beginning to look not just quaint, but archaic.[7]

All of this has a direct bearing on the paranormal, and any advanced non-human intelligence with whom we might be dealing. When I was in London in May, 2009, I attended a lecture given by theoretical

---

[4] The change can perhaps best be seen in classrooms. When I was a student in 1989 finishing my honors degree in history at Acadia University, there was only one computer in the entire history department, and no student that I knew had a personal computer, much less a lap-top or iPad. I had to pay the department secretary to type my thesis (on the origins of the Second World War in Europe), which I had written out by hand. Today, every student takes some form of computer to class.

[5] Michio Kaku, *Visions: How Science Will Revolutionize the 21st Century* (New York: Anchor Books, 1998), 28 – 29.

[6] Ray Kurzweil, *The Age of Spiritual Machines* (New York: Viking, 1999), 30 – 32. "The Law of Accelerating Returns: As order exponentially increases, time exponentially speeds up (that is, the time interval between salient events grows shorter as time passes)."

[7] For a look at what one analyst predicts the next hundred years or so might have in store for us, I recommend George Friedman, *The Next 100 Years: A Forecast for the 21st Century* (New York: Anchor Books, 2010). The odds are that Friedman will be wrong about the vast majority of his projections, having erred too far on the side of caution.

physicist Michio Kaku at the RSA.[8] He talked for approximately half an hour about his book, *The Physics of the Impossible*, and then there was a period of time for questions and answers. I raised my hand, because I wanted Kaku to elaborate a bit on what he had written about the prospect of communication with an extraterrestrial civilization.[9]

"You've written about the possibility that there's a galactic conversation going on that we're not part of, and that's far beyond us," I asked. "Two questions: first, what do you think might be the best way of tapping into that conversation, if it's taking place, and second, how soon do you think we might have the ability or knowledge to do so?"

There were a few snickers in the audience as I finished, but Kaku skipped a couple of other questions and went directly to mine. I think he appreciated that I was interested in a subject that he clearly takes seriously, and also that someone had actually read his book before coming to the lecture.

"Let me try to answer that," he said. "First, why don't the aliens visit us, and how do we contact the aliens who are out there? Well, if you're walking down a country road and you see an ant hill, do you go down to the ants and say, 'I give you trinkets, I bring you beads, I give you nuclear energy, I give you biotechnology - take me to your ant leader'? Or maybe you step on a few of them."

I remember thinking at the time that if there was anything that might make people more uncomfortable than the prospect of not being at the top of the food chain, it would be the idea that those further up the chain than us might be as inclined to step on the "ants" as we are, whether by accident or on purpose. I'm sure that explained the few nervous chuckles I heard from the audience.[10]

---

[8] The Royal Society for the Encouragement of Arts, Manufactures and Commerce, founded in 1754. www.thersa.org/.

[9] Paul Kimball, "Michio Kaku: A Galactic Conversation," *The Other Side of Truth Podcast*. http://goo.gl/iIijS.

[10] I also remember thinking Kaku's analogy was far too simplistic, based on my

Kaku smiled, and continued. "A galactic civilization that could soar through the galactic space lanes would consider us not too different from an ant hill. Now, let's say that there's a ten lane super highway being built right next to the ant hill. Would the ants know how to communicate with the workers? Would they know the frequencies that the workers use? Would the ants even know what a ten lane super highway was, or the purpose of a ten lane super highway?"

"Then you begin to realize," he explained, "that a galactic civilization is about a million years more advanced than us, and on that scale, their frequencies, their culture, their goals, are going to be very, very different from our little ant hill. So how will we make contact with these people?"

He continued for a bit by describing how we're going to detect many Earth-like planets in the years to come. This, he said, would be an existential shock for many people, particularly once they realized that those planets might contain life more advanced than our own. Then he delivered his punch-line.

"We don't know their frequencies, we don't know how they communicate. For example, when you send an e-mail, it's chopped up into many pieces and then re-assembled at the other end, because it was a military weapon. The message was chopped up because in the future Los Angeles may be destroyed, New York may be destroyed, and your e-mail will still get through because it's been chopped up into pieces. Let's say that an alien civilization does the same thing. They take a message, chop it up, and send it through many, many avenues to have it re-assembled at the other end. That's the most efficient and error-free way to send a message. If we were to listen in on alien signals, we'd hear nothing. We'd hear gibberish. So we could be teeming with intergalactic civilizations, and we're simply too

---

own personal experience. While I might not stop and try to have a conversation with ants, I've always found them fascinating, from my days as a youngster frying them under a microscope (Paul as the ant Satan) to today, where I simply stop to observe them from time to time (Paul as the detached ant God). Occasionally, I'll put a twig in their path to see how they react to it (Paul as the scientist ant God). While I might not be able to "talk" with them, I can definitely "communicate" with them.

stupid to know it."

As I left what was a thoroughly entertaining lecture, I thought to myself that it's quite possible Kaku is right. His views seem to reflect the overwhelming majority opinion amongst the scientific community. But given the way that our own development has gone over the past century, it can't be said that he is *certainly* correct. The technological developments necessary to get us to the stars may not be thousands of years away – they may only be hundreds of years away, or perhaps even less. We just don't know anymore. Indeed, Kaku himself has speculated that a Type-I civilization, which would be a truly planetary society, capable of travel within the solar system, and eventually perhaps even limited interstellar missions, could be achieved in as little as a century. A Type-II civilization, which would be capable of interstellar flight within our local region of the Milky Way, might only be eight hundred years or so beyond where we are now, according to Kaku.[11]

To put that in perspective, that's roughly the same period of time that passed between Caesar and Belisarius. To add even more perspective, imagine this: if you had told someone living at the end of the Spanish – American War in 1898 that in less than a century, the United States would possess bombs that could obliterate entire cities, launched not by artillery but by flying machines that could travel several times the speed of sound, all while men walked on the moon, they probably would have locked you up in a rubber room.

In short, predicting the future has always been a tricky thing, and that's never been more true than it is today.

Accordingly, I don't think it's unreasonable to speculate that a civilization in our nearby "galactic neighborhood" could have developed space-faring abilities before us, and made their way here at some point, without having to imagine the aliens as god-like beings so far in advance of us that we wouldn't be able to recognize them, or communicate with them at some level. I also think that it's not

---

[11] Kaku, *Visions : How Science Will Revolutionize the 21st Century*, 323 – 324.

unreasonable to imagine that they would have some degree of interest in us. Not in our technology, of course; indeed, probably not for anything in the physical realm in which we place so much stock.

It's therefore quite possible that Kaku has gotten his timeline wrong, and that the more applicable analogy might not be humans in relation to ants, but rather adult humans in relation to the youngest members of our species. After all, while an adult is obviously recognizable to a five-year old child, they have vastly different outlooks on the world, on life, and on each other. Nevertheless, the adult still takes a profound interest in the development of the child, particularly a wayward child prone to self-destruction.

Regardless of the comparative levels that we might be at in terms of development, Kaku has made the more fundamental mistake of viewing contact from the perspective of humans trying to participate in a conversation with an advanced non-human intelligence. The more logical way to look at it is from the perspective of the advanced non-human intelligence, whomever or whatever they may be, trying to make themselves understood at some level by us. Any contact is going to take place on their terms, and not ours.

When a parent wants to interact with a baby, for instance, they don't read *War and Peace*, or *King Lear*, in the hopes that the child will understand; rather, they tickle them, and say things like "goochy-goochy coo," and sing them lullabies. Eventually, when the child gets a bit older, the parents will progress to simple illustrated stories like those written by Dr. Seuss. I think we're a long way away from being able to read their version of Tolstoy or Shakespeare, but we might just be developed enough to see them spin the shiny silver ball they've placed above our crib, and listen as they softly sing their version of "Frère Jacques" to us. Maybe a few of us are capable of an even greater understanding. As we've seen in our own species, there are always some precocious children, such as Mozart, who outgrow the cradle more quickly than most.

The great 20th century drama critic George Jean Nathan once wrote that great art is as irrational as great music. "It is mad," he asserted, "with its own loveliness."[12] The same could be said, in many ways, of the paranormal, which almost always seems to possess an element of irrationality to it. This raises a fascinating possibility: what if the paranormal is a form of artistic expression by an advanced non-human intelligence?

For example, one can find similar displays of the lights often ascribed to UFOs in our own culture. Black light theatre is a wonderful example, which I have been fortunate enough to see in person whilst traveling in the Czech Republic. If one were to travel to Nevada for the annual Burning Man festival, one would also see various light displays; so too at almost any Fourth of July celebration, or more than a few minor league baseball games I've attended.

It stands to reason that an advanced non-human intelligence, whether they're from another solar system, another dimension, another time, or even from right here on Earth, may be doing something similar for us, which we perceive as paranormal phenomena. If our art is capable of as many manifestations as there are human beings with imagination and creativity, think of how much more an advanced non-human intelligence might be capable of achieving, particularly if they have the same desire to create as we do, but combined with a greater capacity and much broader experience.

This leads us to another intriguing possibility – that whatever is responsible for the paranormal (and there may be more than one actor involved) has the ability to create art within the subconscious of another species, as a form of communication and enlightenment and perhaps even entertainment.

I think that if we had a chance to interview the advanced non-human intelligence, it might say something like this, by way of introduction:

> Hello.
> While my species does not really have "names" as you comprehend them, you may call me Vincent, although we

---

[12] George Jean Nathan, *The house of Satan* (New York: Alfred A. Knopf, 1926), 18.

have had many such appellations in our long interaction with you.

We find your species to be most interesting, at least from an anthropological point of view, so we decided to make contact, many thousand of your "years" ago (*memo to humans* – your linear concept of time is extremely quaint, but then you are an extremely quaint species, which is why we like you so much).

We have found it best to present ourselves in ways that fit in with the cultural norms of your time. Accordingly, we have actually appeared in many forms (the burning bush was my favorite, with the UFO meme a close second).

We do this using a technology that is far, far beyond your comprehension. You would probably call it magic, or the supernatural. Your species is still confined to your physical reality, or at least what you perceive as "reality," but we operate on different "levels."

I guess the best way to explain it to you is that when we make contact, we do not do it in what you would consider the literal sense, but rather in a more figurative way, using what you call dreams, and the subconscious, and... well, it all gets rather complicated, I'm afraid.

Suffice it to say, we are far more interested in the mind and spirit than the body (that is what happens when you get to our level of development as a species), and so that is where we make contact. In a sense, we "speak" to you, across the vastness of space. Indeed, once you really understand how things work, you realize that space is not actually that vast after all.

The wonderful thing about this form of communication is that it allows us to participate in your development, and slowly help guide you to a greater level of understanding, not about technology but about yourselves on an individual basis which will hopefully one day add up in the aggregate for you as a species. When you have been around as long as we have, that is what really matters.

I have to admit that it has been a rough haul at times, but some of you seem to "get it," and so we keep trying. Two of my favorites have been Henry Alline and Hildegard of Bingen, but Bach and that McCartney fellow were also very open to the bigger picture, albeit in a different way. Mozart was "out there," even for us, but he was something truly special. And I admit that I have a soft spot for The Smiths, because there is indeed a "light that never goes out." As a result, we have not abandoned the effort.

One final thing. I know many of you spend an inordinate amount of time debating where we are from, to which I can only ask the following: does it really matter whether we are from Zeta Reticuli, or another dimension, or another time, or from your own planet?

Does it even matter if we are *you*?

This scenario is one that I find plausible for a number of reasons. It takes into account the wide range of described encounters with a possible advanced non-human intelligence throughout human history. It makes us *part* of the story, but not necessarily the *center* of the story. Most important, it places the paranormal in its historical context. It provides us with a tremendous opportunity to speculate not just about the nature of the phenomenon, but also about ourselves and our relationship to it.

Vincent may not have to actually travel from "there" to "here" in a physical sense – he and his kind may be able to make their presence known in other, far more subtle ways within the human mind. Who would be the most receptive people for this kind of communication? In my opinion, it would be those amongst us who have the greatest imagination, many of whom become artists of one sort or another.

Astrologer John Varley reported that his friend, artist and philosopher William Blake, had experienced visions since his childhood, including a vision of a ghost of a flea at a séance the two held in 1819. According to Varley:

As I was anxious to make the most correct investigation in my power, of the truth of these visions, on hearing of this spiritual apparition of a Flea, I asked him if he could draw for me the resemblance of what he saw: he instantly said, 'I see him now before me.' I therefore gave him paper and a pencil with which he drew the portrait... I felt convinced by his mode of proceeding, that he had a real image before him, for he left off, and began on another part of the paper, to make a separate drawing of the mouth of the Flea, which the spirit having opened, he was prevented from proceeding with the first sketch, till he had closed it.[13]

If there really is an advanced non-human intelligence behind the paranormal then I suspect it communicates with us through the kind of visions that William Blake had, particularly if it has developed a much greater understanding of how the mind works than we have. If this is the case, then I believe we would all have the basic ability to receive that communication in some form or another.[14] However, I don't think that the vast majority of us have the willingness to access it, largely because we're afraid of what it might represent, namely a loss of control. We want to "fit in" to society as it's structured around us. Unfortunately, by fitting in we may be missing out on something far more important and meaningful – the ability to be truly free. In other words, the "art" may be there, but we choose not to see it.

This state of affairs can perhaps be seen most readily within religion. The more experiential and mystical aspects of Christianity, for example, have always been suppressed by the mainstream churches, which really serve as little more than adjuncts to political

---

[13] John Varley, quoted in G. E. Bentley, Jr., *The Stranger From Paradise: A Biography of William Blake* (New Haven: Yale University Press, 2001), 377-78.

[14] For example, Paul McCartney famously claimed to have woken up from a dream with the melody to "Yesterday," one of his greatest songs; Steve Turner, *A Hard Day's Write: The Stories Behind Every Beatles Song*, 3rd ed. (New York: Harper Paperbacks, 2005), 83.

authority. This was a theme that Søren Kierkegaard spent his life exploring, and it led to his devastating critiques of organized religion. For Kierkegaard, faith was the most important task to be achieved by a human being, because only on the basis of faith could an individual have a chance to become a true self. It was a matter of individual subjective passion, and it couldn't be mediated by the clergy, nor could it found in a church.[15]

All of this reminds me of a conversation I had with my good friend Greg Bishop in January, 2011, wherein we discussed language, communication, and art. I mentioned the idea that "aliens" who are far more advanced than us might not actually be here on Earth in a physical way, but have the ability to send messages through space and time directly to our subconscious. Maybe, I said, we can't quite understand them yet, but they appear to us as dreams, visions, or some sort of phenomena around us.

"Might we be making contact," I asked, "with some sort of higher intelligence in that manner?

Greg thought about the question for a moment, and then replied as follows:

I think you've hit on the crux of the thing here. We don't give ourselves nearly enough credit for what we think our perceptions of UFOs are. Our co-creation of what we think UFOs are, I think we're a huge part of that equation, like more than fifty per cent. I'm not saying that there's nothing there. I'm saying there's definitely something there, but we've got so much psychological and cultural baggage that we can't hope to meet it on its own terms for quite a while yet. I think we will eventually, but we're always going to be

---

[15] Søren Kierkegaard, *Practice in Christianity*, ed. Howard Hong and Edna Hong (Princeton, NJ: Princeton University Press, 1991); Søren Kierkegaard, *The Essential Kierkegaard*, ed. Howard Hong and Edna Hong (Princeton, NJ: Princeton University Press, 2000). For a general look at mysticism within religion, see James, *The Varieties of Religious Experience*, 413 – 468.

co-creating with it our perception of what it is, if that makes any sense. We talk about these things, and we don't realize that the whole time we're involved in this huge trap of our own language. Our language traps how we think because it makes us think in certain ways. And then there's the state beyond language, where people will try to describe a mystical experience, or anything having to do with spirituality, or psychology, or a mixture of the two, and once again you're trapped by language. It brings to mind something that Dean Radin told me when I interviewed him years ago, and he was applying it to psychic research. He said that trying to do psychic research with the instruments that we have is like trying to kill a fly with a sledgehammer. That's how I feel about language sometimes when we're talking about this stuff – we're using sledgehammer-like language to try and talk about something that's very subtle, and maybe fleeting, and just not amenable to the tools we have to describe it, which is our language.[16]

"It's interesting," I responded, "because I think the most thoughtful conversations you can have are the ones that you have with yourself, because you're not bound by language in the same way that you are when you're trying to express yourself to someone else. There are so many things that can go on in your own mind when you're not constrained by language, and the filters that it creates."

"Yeah," replied Greg. "The only thing that I would disagree with you on, sort of, is that you said that when you're just talking to yourself, or dealing with your thoughts, then you don't have to worry about the language, but the language that you used to pull in all of those thoughts is still affecting how you deal with them. You're still thinking in probably a fairly linear fashion, because you're dealing with ideas that have been communicated to you by language. However, if there's any way to possibly get out of that it's by that

---

[16] Paul Kimball, "Greg Bishop – (Nothing But) Flowers," *The Other Side of Truth Podcast*, 28 January 2011. http://goo.gl/ymc3q.

personal thought process, or by speaking with people who are willing to use the shorthand of the things that you're talking about, and the ideas that you're kicking around, to express things that probably can't be expressed exactly, which is why you get excited when you meet somebody who is basically finishing your sentences, because you know that you have the same shorthand, and you can start dealing on a different level."

At this point we took a brief break from our conversation, and listened to a song by the Talking Heads. When the song ended, Greg went directly to the subject of communication and art.

"The other thing that came to mind when you mentioned non-verbal communication is art," he said. "It's the only way that we really get that anymore, because that's one of the few ways that we can communicate something to someone else without having to explain it. Just showing them this visual language will cue these feelings and patterns in their mind, and by communicating that to them it becomes personal to them as well, because you meet somewhere emotionally and intellectually at the same time. You're both contributing to it – the artist, and you as the person looking at the art, which gets us back to the UFO phenomenon. I think that's where a lot of the true non-verbal communication is happening."

Artistic expression provides us with the unparalleled potential to transcend the barriers to true communication that language and culture impose on us. It liberates us from the confines of the "here and now," and allows us to *imagine* and to *feel*. It's a shared experience that provides a vehicle for travel beyond the temporal boundaries of our linear existence.

The artist creates a work and then we then create our own interpretation. In the process we become a part of the work, and we also become artists ourselves. That the original artist may be long dead is irrelevant, because he or she is still communicating with us through their work.

Marcel Duchamp expounded upon the nature of this relationship when he stated, "Let us consider two important factors, the two poles of the creation of art: the artist on one hand, and on the other the spectator who later becomes the posterity. To all appearances the artist acts like a mediumistic being who, from the labyrinth beyond time and space, seeks his way out to a clearing."[17]

In order to receive the message we have to open ourselves up to all of the possibilities that a painting, photograph, poem, or song present to us. As always with art, what it says to me might not be the same thing as what it says to you. The true importance lies in the inner conversation that it inspires us to have with ourselves. This is why I consider art, in all its myriad forms, to be one of the highest of callings in a world desperately in need of *real* communication and a new Enlightenment. Albert Camus had it right when he wrote, "A man's work is nothing but this slow trek to rediscover, through the detours of art, those two or three great and simple images in whose presence his heart first opened."[18]

Filmmakers, painters and photographers know perhaps better than anyone the ability that images have when it comes to communicating an idea and spreading a meme. Indeed, some of the most powerful moments in my own films have come when I have used images to evoke a particular mood or feeling, sometimes in concert with dialogue, and sometimes without dialogue altogether. As the old saying goes, a picture is worth a thousand words.

Sound, particularly in the form of music, works the same way. For example, *Rusalka*, the classic opera by Antonín Dvořák, can move people simply by the power of the music and the performances on stage, even if the people watching can't understand Czech, the language in which it was written and is most often performed. When I saw a performance at the National Theatre in Prague in 2009, there were many times I simply stopped looking at the translation that was displayed on a screen above the stage because the music and the performances of the cast were enough to convey the meaning of what

[17] Marcel Duchamp, "The Creative Act," *Art News*, Summer 1957: 28 –29.

[18] Albert Camus, *Lyrical and Critical Essays*, ed. Phillip Malcolm Waller Thody (New York: Alfred A. Knopf, 1968), 17.

was happening to me, while at the same time allowing me to place my own interpretation on it. This is a perfect example of what William James was getting at in *The Varieties of Religious Experience* when he wrote, "Music gives us ontological messages which non-musical criticism is unable to contradict… there is a verge of the mind which these things haunt; and whispers therefrom mingle with the operations of our understanding, even as the waters of the infinite ocean send their waves to break among the pebbles that lie upon our shores."[19]

One of my favorite examples of this combination of imagery and music can be found in John Boorman's wonderful film *Excalibur*, which presented a highly stylized and mystical take on the ancient legend of King Arthur and the quest for the Holy Grail by the Knights of the Round Table. In Boorman's version, a curse descends upon Arthur and his Kingdom is plagued with famine and disease. He sends his knights on a quest for the Grail in hopes of restoring the land and Sir Perceval encounters Lancelot, now a sort of holy man who preaches to followers that the kingdom has fallen because of "the sin of pride." Perceval attempts to convince him to come to Arthur's aid, but Lancelot and his followers throw Perceval into a river. Perceval then has a vision of the Grail during which he finally comes to understand that Arthur and the land are one. This realization allows him to obtain the Grail, which he takes to Arthur, who is near death. Perceval gives the Grail to Arthur, who drinks from it and is revitalized.

"Ready my knights for battle," Arthur tells his brother Kay. "They will ride with their King once more. I have lived through others far too long. Lancelot carried my honor, and Guinevere my guilt. Mordred bore my sins, and my knights have fought my causes. Now, my brother, I shall be King!"

As Arthur and his knights leave Camelot and ride out into the desolate landscape of the surrounding countryside, Carl Orff's "O Fortuna" from *Carmina Burana* begins to play. An extended sequence

---

[19] William James, *The Varieties of Religious Experience*, 459.

follows during which the land returns to life as Arthur and his knights travel through it – flowers bloom, the grass turns from brown to green, the clouds part and the sun shines through in a scene that is all imagery and music, tied together in what is in my opinion one of the most powerful and moving sequences in film history. It fires the imagination and the passions of the viewer, and it drives home the point that we may all be linked together, and not just with each other, but with the universe as a whole.[20]

This idea of the paranormal as art also goes a long way to explaining why there have been so many variations over the years in terms of encounters. As Greg Bishop wrote in 2007:

> Whatever it is that is behind the UFOs (and other assorted subjects we assign to the category of the "paranormal") do not want to be pigeonholed. To those that pay attention, the "art exhibit" is ever-changing, and hits close to home: fear, joy, wonder, inquisitiveness, and of course sex are all part of the mix.[21]

We can see something comparable by examining how themes and variations work within music.

In 2003 and 2004 I produced and directed a television series called *The Classical Now* for Bravo here in Canada. The series featured some of Canada's best young classical musicians and composers performing and talking about their lives and their work. In one of the episodes we set up a segment where the host, Will Fraser, stood next to the piano as pianist Ian Parker explained how a single basic melody could be subtly modified by different composers to achieve an entirely new result.

"The one theme that I really love to talk about all the time," Ian stated at the beginning, "is the one that's the most borrowed, and that's the twenty-fourth caprice written by the violinist Paganini."

---

[20] *Excalibur*, directed by John Boorman (Orion Pictures, 1981). Film.

[21] Greg Bishop, "UFOs as a Cosmic Art Exhibit," *UFO Mystic*, 29 September 2007. www.ufomystic.com/2007/09/29/ufo-art-2/.

Ian then proceeded to play the short basic theme from the caprice.

"What most often happens with this melody," he explained, "is a set of variations will follow once it's stated. Composers such as Brahms, Rachmaninoff, Liszt, have all borrowed this melody, and written many variations on it."

Ian focused on the 18th variation in D major by Rachmaninoff, which was written for piano and orchestra.

"We always hear this piece when you're on hold trying to book an airplane ticket, or whatever it is, and many people ask, 'so, where did Rachmaninoff get this melody? It's clear that he borrowed Paganini's for most of the piece, but where did this one come from?' For the longest time, I didn't know what to tell them until someone finally told me to turn Paganini's original melody upside down, speed it up a bit, and change the key. This is how Rachmaninoff made the melody – he reversed Paganini's original, majored it, and then moved it up a couple of intervals."

"What about one of the pieces that you're playing in the show today," asked Will. "Does the B Minor sonata by Liszt have themes which work in this way?"

"Great example," replied Ian. "Very near the beginning, there's this diabolical suggestion in the melody, a really, really nasty, devilish little melody in the bass. And then quite soon in the piece, this beautiful, heavenly melody comes in. These are two completely different melodies, but I had a professor who asked me once, 'how are these melodies related?' I didn't see the relationship, and she said, 'Well, why don't you play the pretty one a little faster?' So I did, and then I realized it was the same melody. For the longest time I had been telling my audience that they were melodies 1 and 2, when in fact they were actually melodies 1A and 1B."[22]

If there *is* an advanced non-human intelligence behind the paranormal, it may utilize these same tools of imagery and sound to tell a story, or to convey a message, in a way that we are capable of

---

[22] *The Classical Now*, "Ian Parker," directed by Paul Kimball (Halifax: Redstar Films Limited, 2004). Television. www.youtube.com/watch?v=GHSobdjplco.

processing at the time, if not always completely understanding. And as with Ian Parker's example of Paganini, Rachmaninoff and Liszt, their "art" may change with the times, but the themes remain the same. Perhaps ancient reports of winged flying creatures such as dragons, or something like Ezekiel's Wheel in the Old Testament, are earlier versions of the same melody as the modern UFO meme, played to a different audience.[23]

As a former musician myself, I'm well aware that there is another aspect of this concept of variation in performance. I wrote a song called "Mysterio" that was very popular with local audiences in my hometown of Halifax, and which became a sort of signature tune for both of my bands. After playing it the same way for a couple of years, however, I decided that a new arrangement was needed in order to keep it fresh, both for us and for the audience. We eventually wound up playing it many different ways – slower, faster, longer, shorter, and then in different styles, from country to rock, folk, and even a sort of jazz version at one point. In part it depended on the audience, and in part it depended on our mood, but in many ways every time we played that song there was a co-creation of a new version.

Performance art in many ways goes even further than the power of images or sound. It creates a shared experience between the performer and the observer that is both immediate and unique, because no two performances are ever the same.[24] It also transcends the moment

---

[23] For a thought-provoking look at how ancient Biblical stories may represent contact with an advanced non-human intelligence from elsewhere in the galaxy, see Rev. Barry Downing's classic study, *The Bible and Flying Saucers* (New York: Marlowe & Company, 1968). I also recommend a short clip of an interview I conducted with Rev. Downing in 2001, wherein he discusses UFOs and religion, which I have posted on-line at: http://goo.gl/3wyOK.

[24] I attended a performance of the hit musical *Wicked* at the Pantages Theatre in Los Angeles in late 2008. At one point in the second act the character of Fiyero is supposed to run on stage and save Elphaba (the green witch). At the performance I saw, Derrick Williams, the actor playing Fiyero, stumbled and fell as he ran out on stage for the scene. You could see him smile, but then he pulled himself up and worked the fall into his performance without breaking character. The other actors went with him as he ad-libbed, and the result was a brilliant and unique moment of

because the participatory aspect on the part of the observer indelibly etches the experience in the memory. Actors and musicians who perform on stage know this better than anyone. Frank Zappa got it right when he stated, "Music, in performance, is a type of sculpture. The air in the performance is sculpted into something."[25]

I played so many gigs in the 1990s with my bands Tall Poppies and Julia's Rain that I lost count. While I can still listen to the albums we recorded, because there is a permanence to them, the thrill of playing live is something that only exists in my memory. A couple of those performances were videotaped, but watching them now isn't the same as having been there at the time. The crowd provided an energy that we fed off as musicians and that was then returned to them by a performance that increased in intensity as a result. It was a true symbiosis. Bruce Springsteen, legendary for his marathon live performances, described those kinds of moments in a 1975 interview. "This music is forever for me," he stated. "It's the stage thing, that rush moment that you live for. It never lasts, but that's what you live for."[26]

I did the same thing in 2007 when I adapted and directed for stage a version of Peter Weiss' play *Marat / Sade*. Coincidentally, a local university dramatic society staged a version of the play just two weeks before ours, so I went to see it with Kris McBride, one of the actors in my version. The students did a standard take on the play where the fourth wall remained intact and the text was treated as sacrosanct.

With my version I threw the original text into a blender and turned the play on its head. I added elements from pop music, Shakespeare, the war poetry of Wilfred Owen and Siegfried Sassoon, and myriad other sources, all designed to enhance the revolutionary themes. Then

forced improvisation that those of us there that night shared with the cast.

[25] Frank Zappa, *Music Quotes Homepage & Commentary*, ed. Richard and Bonnett Chandler. http://goo.gl/o42Vm.

[26] Jay Cocks, "The Backstreet Phantom of Rock." *Time*, 27 October 1975.

I surrounded the audience itself with the characters so that they were the "street" as the revolution formed around them and amongst them. In one corner, under a red light, I had Kris clad as a prostitute who would wander out into the audience and proposition people, even when she wasn't involved in a scene. The characters of Marat and Sade spent most of their time on stage, but when Marat delivered his speech to the National Assembly the actor left the bath-tub in which he spent the majority of the play, walked through the audience to a podium, and then addressed them as if *they* were the Assembly.

There was a scene I added where a General directly quoted the speeches of Patton and Montgomery from the Second World War about honor, loyalty and service. He then encountered a shell-shocked homeless Veteran, whom he brutally beat whilst they stood in the midst of the audience. I wanted the people who paid to see the show to not only hear about the revolution, but to feel like they were part of it in a way that would be relevant to our circumstances today. Not everyone "got" it, but that wasn't the point. I set out to challenge the audience as much as possible, to engage my own artistic impulses (and those of the cast), and to push the boundaries of our collective expectations.[27]

It's possible that an advanced non-human intelligence "feeds" off this interaction with "the crowd" in the same way that musicians and stage actors do – they perform, we respond, they ramp up the

---

[27] Ron Foley MacDonald, "A 21st Century Marat," *InfoMonkey*, 23 February 2007. http://goo.gl/Hr7wd. MacDonald wrote: "Director/Adaptor Paul Kimball and Le Theatre de Boheme have drifted sufficiently far enough away from Peter Weiss' famous play Marat/Sade for the production to distill the title down to 'Marat' and drop any pretences of resembling the famous Peter Brook production of the play. The result is a fascinating – and strikingly original – take on what can only be described as one of the great artifacts of 1960s anti-theatre [that] sports some very focused acting, along with quite a bit of inspired direction. By dropping most of the self-conscious bombast, adding pop culture elements from music by Aaron Copland and Ravel to snatches of World War One poetry to speeches from Shakespeare's Henry V and Francis Ford Coppola's script for the movie Patton, Kimball has loosened up the tightly constricting scripture of Marat/Sade... Ultimately, that makes it a much different and far more relevant play."

intensity, and the cycle continues. As is the case with all good artists, they change the work over time, and add different interpretations. They also create new works, and perhaps even entirely different genres. Just as I did years ago when I slung a Fender telecaster over my shoulder and hit the first chord on a song, or when I staged a brutal arrest scene in the midst of the audience in *Marat*, an advanced non-human intelligence could be seeking to elicit a reaction from us, and to even involve us as co-creators in their works of art.

This could be the true nature of "contact." Maybe they are finishing our sentences for us and starting new ones at the same time, subtly leading us into new and different ways of thinking, all through a form of artistic communication that exists in two places — at a level somewhere between our conscious and our subconscious minds, in dreams and visions, but also right in front of us.

The poster for my adaptation of Peter Weiss' *Marat / Sade*, which was a radical departure from Weiss' original script. Perhaps an advanced non-human intelligence constantly re-invents their "art" in similar ways, and for the same reason – to challenge both the audience and the artist. In the poster, from left to right, are Erin Lynch, Sandy MacLean, and Kris Lee McBride.

A filmmaker has many tools that can be employed to evoke a mood or an emotion without the need for dialogue. In this scene from my feature film *Eternal Kiss*, we used both lighting and wardrobe cues to underscore the essence of Christina Cuffari's character, a sexually and emotionally repressed lawyer who finds herself in the thrall of a vampire. A good actor also has their own non-verbal ways to make an impression on an audience, as Christina did by using her facial expressions and body language. I suspect an advanced non-human intelligence employs similar visual methods when communicating with us.

One of my favorite modern artists is Stephanie Steele, who hails from the small town of Louisbourg, Nova Scotia. Her work is eclectic, and sometimes contains themes with what I see as a hint of a supernatural feel to them. (Photo courtesy of Stephanie Steele)

Just a flower... or is it something more? Consider the interaction of the lines and the shapes within the petal. Wheels within wheels. (Photo courtesy of Stephanie Steele)

One of my favorite pieces by Stephanie, a collage of images making use of the word "art" with the message "Another Random Thought." In the seeming randomness, however, lies a pattern, at least to me – others may see something completely different. (Photo courtesy of Stephanie Steele)

The artist as part of the work itself. Notice how Stephanie tosses the "come hither" look back at the viewer, even as the "graffiti monster" is looking at her. Might not an advanced non-human intelligence insert itself into its art in a similar manner? Would we follow if it did? (Photo courtesy of Stephanie Steele)

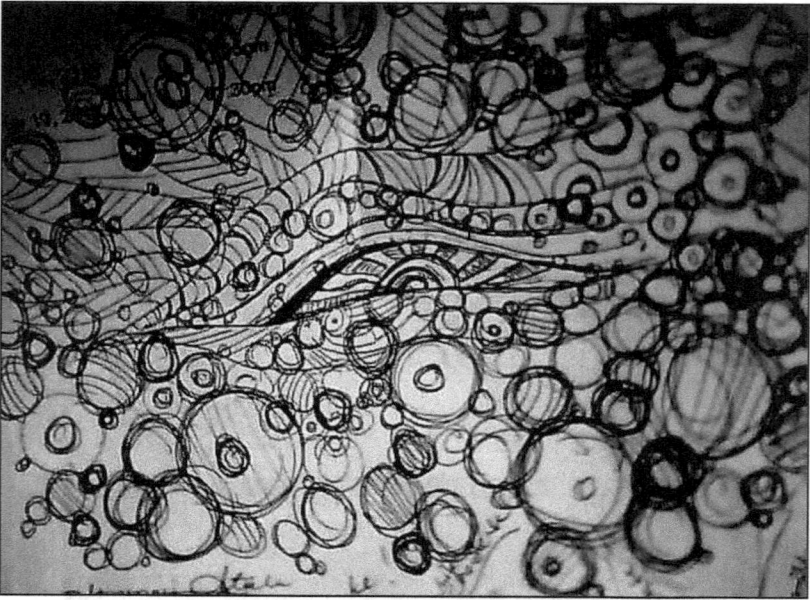

Of all the moving parts in this piece by Stephanie which one catches your attention first, and why? Each of us will have different reasons for coming up with a different answer; thus has the artist, through a single painting, underscored both our connectivity (we're all looking at the same thing), and our individuality (we're all seeing something different). I think an advanced non-human intelligence would interact with us in the same way. (Photo courtesy of Stephanie Steele)

Stephanie Steele

Stephanie's representation of the most intimate of human acts. I wonder if something similar happens when an advanced non-human intelligence interacts with us, the ultimate form of artistic co-creation. Do we become ravished by "God," as Henry Alline put it in the late 18th century, or by "aliens," as we might regard them today – and would it happen in the "real" world, or somewhere in our subconscious, perhaps even in our dreams? (Photo courtesy of Stephanie Steele)

Chapter Two

All That Jazz

It's the group sound that's important, even when you're playing a solo. You not only have to know your own instrument, you must know the others and how to back them up at all times. That's jazz.[1]
– Oscar Peterson

It's one of the great mysteries of our age: why do people continue to go see M. Night Shyamalan films?

In *Unbreakable*, Shyamalan took what I thought would be an interesting premise – an everyman discovers that he has superhuman abilities and becomes a reluctant superhero – and turned it into two hours of overwrought drudgery, made even worse by a final scene that was as hackneyed as it was predictable. In *Signs*, he used an alien invasion as a heavy-handed metaphor for our own times with a singular lack of panache or imagination. *The Village* was undone by glacial pacing and a completely preposterous resolution, with a "twist" ending that you could see coming from a mile away, like an 18-wheeler crawling towards you on Interstate 15 outside Barstow, California. *Lady in the Water* wasted the considerable talents of actor Paul Giamatti, which is akin to burning hundred dollars bills just because you can afford to do so. In *The Happening*, nothing actually happened, largely because Shyamalan "cast" *the wind* as the villain. And *The Last Airbender* was the worse big-budget film made in 2010, a cinematic abomination that actually had me looking back at the *Star Wars* prequels, and the character of Jar-Jar Binks, with a measure of

---

[1] Oscar Peterson, quoted at *Music With Ease*. http://goo.gl/6t2Ec.

fondness that I would never have thought possible.[2]

Shyamalan has been given hundreds of millions of dollars to make these movies, none of which will ever be confused with *Citizen Kane*. Nevertheless, people continue to watch them, and the films make a profit as a result. Even *The Last Airbender* made $319 million dollars at the worldwide box office (on a budget of $150 million dollars, although this doesn't include the advertising and marketing costs).[3]

All of which brings me back to my original question: why do people continue to watch these dreadful films?

The answer, it seems clear to me, is that most people continue to pay the price of admission to a Shyamalan film because they hold out hope that he'll replicate the magic of his one true success, *The Sixth Sense*. In that film, Bruce Willis starred as Malcolm Crowe, a child psychologist whose wife was murdered by one of Crowe's patients. A year later, Crowe encounters Cole, a troubled nine year-old boy (played to perfection by Haley Joel Osmett) who claims to see dead people. At first Crowe thinks Cole is delusional, but eventually he comes to believe that the boy can indeed interact with people who have died in order to help them complete unfinished business. At the end of the film, however, it's revealed that it was Crowe, and not his wife, who was murdered, and that the unfinished business was his failure to help the former patient who committed the crime. By helping Cole, Crowe is released from his own existential prison.

The film plays as a puzzle, and when the "twist" at the end was revealed it made sense to the audience even as it surprised them. A few audience members may have figured it out before the final "reveal" (although nowhere near as many as subsequently claimed to have seen it coming), but most became so immersed in the film that they didn't see the signs the filmmaker had planted along the way to

---

[2] The movie review site *Rotten Tomatoes* had *The Last Airbender* rated at 6%, which places it among the worst movies ever reviewed. "The Last Airbender," *Rotten Tomatoes*. http://goo.gl/kMSNV.

[3] "The Last Airbender," *Box Office Mojo*. http://goo.gl/eoZs8.

indicate that there was more happening than was readily apparent. It was a masterful concoction by Shyamalan, a sleight of hand which he has never come close to duplicating, despite what one can presume have been his best efforts. All these years later we continue to go to his films, hoping in vain that he'll find a way to thrill and surprise us once again.

The Sixth Sense is one of the more notable and successful examples of this type of storytelling in film history, but it's far from the only one. Indeed, other films of a similar type have gone even further than Shyamalan did in that they specifically refuse to provide a definitive resolution. Christopher Nolan's *Inception*, one of my favorite films of the past few years, managed to be that rare cinematic blockbuster which remained ambiguous even at its conclusion. I still debate with friends whether or not the main character Cobb made it home in the end, or whether he is still trapped in his own dream.[4]

This type of storytelling, regardless of the medium, is all about providing the audience with a mystery and seeing if they can spot the clues and figure out the pattern before the answer is revealed. In stories like *Inception* it's left up to the audience to determine their own ending, and ultimately their own meaning.

This fascination with mysteries, clues, and puzzles is deeply rooted in the human psyche. Every year, for example, someone in my family gets my mother a Sudoku book for Christmas because she enjoys them. She almost always gets a picture puzzle as well. Weeks later I'll pop by for a visit (and to scrounge for some homemade cookies) and discover the pieces of the puzzle spread over the dining room table. In college I played the video game Tetris so often that after I was done I would close my eyes and still see the colored pieces dropping into place.

And then, of course, there is the Rubik's cube, the most popular puzzle of them all. Introduced worldwide in 1980, it became a cultural phenomenon. In the three decades since over 350 million cubes have

---

[4] *Inception*, directed by Christopher Nolan (Burbank, CA: Legendary Pictures, 2010). Feature Film.

been sold.[5]

Puzzles are perhaps the ultimate form of co-creative art, and that seems to me to be the reason why we're so fascinated by them. They involve us in the most direct way possible. Someone else may design the puzzle and plant the clues, but we're the ones who must discover the pattern. In a 2009 interview with *Time Magazine*, Erno Rubik explained why his creation was so popular: "People like its beauty, simplicity and form. It's really not a puzzle or a toy. It's a piece of art."[6]

These puzzles serve as a metaphor for our own lives because most of us wonder whether there is a "pattern" to our existence. We look for clues that might provide an answer, or at least a hint. More than a few people think that at least some of those clues might be buried in our dreams, or revealed by events such as déjà vu or a series of strange coincidences.

Human history is replete with individuals who have been regarded as eccentric. One of them was an Austrian biologist, Paul Kammerer, a sort of mad genius who committed suicide at the age of 46 in 1926. Kammerer's passion (many would say "obsession") was documenting coincidences. He saw a pattern to them, and perhaps even a purpose or meaning, where others saw only random events.[7] This was a concept later expanded upon by Carl Jung, who referred to it as "synchronicity" – the notion that people see meaningful connections between the subjective and objective world.[8]

---

[5] Alastair Jamieson, "Rubik's Cube inventor is back with Rubik's 360," *Daily Telegraph*, 31 January 2009. http://goo.gl/2RwPu.

[6] William Lee Adams, "The Rubik's Cube: A Puzzling Success," *Time Magazine*, 28 January 2009. http://goo.gl/kSY5C.

[7] Paul Kammerer, *Das Gesetz der Serie* (Berlin: Deutsche Verlags-Anstalt, 1919). The book has never been translated from German into English. The German original can be found at: www.archive.org/details/DasGesetzDerSerie.

[8] See: C. G. Jung, *Jung on Synchronicity and the Paranormal*, ed. Roderick Main (London: Routledge, 1997), and *Synchronicity: An Acausal Connecting Principle*,

The idea that there might be a pattern to be found in at least some coincidences certainly has its critics. In 1958, for example, German psychologist Klaus Conrad coined the term "apophenia" to describe what he called the "unmotivated seeing of connections" accompanied by a "specific experience of an abnormal meaningfulness."[9] Where Jung saw the potential for meaning, Conrad saw psychosis.

But what if they were both right? In some people, it may indeed be a sign of mental illness, particularly if they fixate on coincidences to the point of obsession. But what about the average person who only notices coincidences when they seem to stand out more than the simple random events of our day to day lives? Are they psychotics, or are they perhaps, for whatever reason, getting a glimpse of those patterns Kammerer believed exist.

Even more intriguing is the possibility that these patterns, if they exist, may represent a form of contact with an advanced non-human intelligence. Christopher Nolan gave us *Inception* and let us figure out the ending. Erno Rubik gave us his cube and 350 million people moved the colored squares around, searching for the solution. Perhaps an advanced non-human intelligence has given us coincidences, as a sort of puzzle for us to solve, or a message to be deciphered?

A series of unusual events I experienced on a trip to Los Angeles in May and June of 2011 definitely made me think twice about the question of random coincidence versus meaningful synchronicity. I was house-sitting for a couple of weeks while Greg Bishop and his

---

2nd ed., trans. R. F. C. Hull (Princeton, NJ: Princeton University Press, 1981). See also Robert H. Hopke, *There Are No Accidents: Synchronicity and the Stories of Our Lives* (New York: Riverhead Books, 1997).

[9] Peter Brugger, "From Haunted Brain to Haunted Science: A Cognitive Neuroscience View of Paranormal and Pseudoscientific Thought," in *Hauntings and Poltergeists: Multidisciplinary Perspectives*, edited by J. Houran and R. Lange (Jefferson, NC: McFarland & Company, Inc. Publishers, 2001), 195 – 213. Brugger is a Swiss neuroscientist who posited that above average levels of dopamine increase the likelihood that a person will find meaning and patterns where there are none, and that this propensity is linked to belief in the paranormal.

wife Sigrid were honeymooning in Europe, and at different times while they were away my brother Jim and my friend Christina Cuffari joined me. I wrote about my experiences as they happened.

Here are the highlights, in "diary" form.

18 May 2011

Several years ago I was flying through O'Hare airport in Chicago on my way to Cedar Rapids, Iowa, to interview Kevin Randle for my documentary *Fields of Fear*.[10] Due to weather our flight was delayed for 9 hours. Anyone who has ever been to O'Hare knows that it's a huge airport, with multiple terminals, and within each terminal there are multiple concourses. The place is a bit like a giant rabbit warren, with all sorts of nooks and crannies, and it's an easy place to get lost. As I was walking through the airport who should I see but Will Fraser, the former host of my television series *The Classical Now*, and one of my closest friends. Will was on his way home to England for a visit from Mississippi, where he was studying for a graduate degree in English at the time. He was sitting in a coffee shop reading a newspaper when I noticed him out of the corner of my eye. If I hadn't been held over I would have missed him.

All of which is to say that I have a history of coincidences at O'Hare... which brings me to yesterday.

My flight to Los Angeles was through O'Hare, with a four hour stopover. Four hours is a lot of time to kill, and I didn't have any idea which gate my flight to LA would be departing from because it hadn't been posted yet, so I wandered around through several different concourses. After about half an hour of walking I grabbed a hamburger from McDonald's and found a seat at gate B6, totally at random. I ate my burger, listened to my MP3 player for half of the new *Mumford & Sons* album, watched a bit of news on CNN, and then walked over to the departures board to see if my flight had been

---

[10] *Fields of Fear*, directed by Paul Kimball (Halifax: Redstar Films, 2006). Television. http://goo.gl/SAHo3.

assigned a gate yet.

Indeed, it had – Gate B6. I stared at the departures board and pondered the odds of me sitting down at random in such a large airport by the exact gate to which my flight would later be assigned. I then went back over to the seating area at B6, reclaimed my seat, listened to some more music, and watched some more CNN.

Another hour went by and I still had an hour and a half still to kill, so I decided to stretch my legs again and get a copy of the *New York Times* to help me pass the rest of the time. I walked down to the Hudson News outlet by gate B16, bought the paper, and then moseyed out into the hall at the exact instant when an announcement came over the public address system to inform passengers that my flight had been relocated to a new gate – B16! As I looked over at the B16 stall next to me the information was posted on the board above the desk by the boarding ramp.

There was only one thing I could do when faced with this second coincidence. I sat down, cued up Golden Earring on my MP3 player, hit play for "The Twilight Zone," and settled in to wait for my flight.

<u>22 May 2011</u>

Continuing the run of coincidences on my current trip to Los Angeles, I had set up a meeting this evening at 7 pm with my friend Walter Bosley, a filmmaker, author and paranormal researcher. We were going to get together at the sprawling Farmer's Market here in Hollywood, but he was coming into town in the afternoon and asked if we could meet earlier to accommodate his schedule. I was fine with that, but my friend Christina Cuffari had already arranged to meet someone in Culver City at 11 am. She said she could get back to Hollywood and meet up with Walter and I between 2:30 and 3:00 pm at the Market, so I wanted to make sure that I was there no later than 2:45 pm, as she doesn't really know the area and I didn't want to leave her hanging there. I sent Walter an e-mail to let him know about this wrinkle, and I asked him to meet me at Greg's house at 2:00 pm, after which we could walk down to the Market and meet up with Christina.

2:00 pm came and went with no sign of Walter. I didn't have his cell phone number, and at 2:15 pm I decided that I had to head off to the Market to meet Christina. I sent Walter a Facebook message telling him what was up and letting him know that we would wait for him at the Market until at least 3:30 pm. I then hustled over to the Market (a 15 minute walk), and settled in to wait for either Walter or Christina.

After about ten minutes Christina showed up, and we each grabbed a coffee and sat down. Another twenty minutes or so passed and I was getting hungry, so I popped over to the Market Grill, one of the small eateries in the sprawling food court. I ordered a hamburger and fries, which the clerk told me would take about five minutes to get ready. I looked around and didn't see Walter, so I went back to our table and asked Christina if I could borrow her I-phone. I wanted to quickly check Facebook and see if Walter had responded to my earlier message.

I have never carried a cell phone of any sort, and I'm in no hurry to start. As I wrote on my profile at an on-line dating site once: "I don't own a cell phone (and probably never will), and I don't text or IM. While I'm very tech literate, to paraphrase Obi-wan Kenobi's views vis-a-vis lightsabers vs. blasters, I prefer a more civilized form of communication than 'how r u.' I also cherish the freedom to be out of touch with the world and far from the madding crowd whilst enjoying a vanilla milkshake, watching a film, walking around the Commons, having lunch... or just about anything else that's best done uninterrupted." In short, not being constantly "wired in" is my modern version of Thoreau's Walden Pond.

As a result, anytime that I use an I-phone and try to type on the "keyboards / pads" that they have I tend to muck it up, often more than once. In this instance, whilst trying to enter my Facebook user name and password, I made mistakes twice in a row. The third time was the charm, but the service on the phone was really slow so I told Christina that I was going to pop over to the Market Grill to grab my food, which I figured was ready. Just as I stood up and looked in the direction of the eatery who should walk into the very busy courtyard from the entrance besides the Market Grill but Walter.

After I introduced Walter to Christina and picked up my dinner, we all sat down and had a chat about the sequence of events that had to have happened for Walter to be entering the courtyard just as I stood up. For example, if I wasn't such a purposeful luddite I wouldn't have had the delay on the I-phone as I was trying to "connect" with Walter, and the timing would have been off.

Oddly enough, this wasn't the first coincidence on the trip that involved a restaurant. A couple of days earlier Christina and I toured Hollywood Boulevard with Greg Bishop. We walked all the way up and down the Walk of Fame and then visited Graumann's Chinese Theatre and the Kodak Center. After all of that it was time for lunch. We debated several choices, including the famous Pig & Whistle, but decided to maximize our time and just grab something relatively quick at one of the many spots in the Kodak Center itself.

We eventually settled on a Johnny Rockets, a chain diner, despite the fact that Christina is a vegetarian and Johnny Rockets is better known for burgers and fries than salads. Still, she was a good sport, particularly because she knows I love vanilla milkshakes, and they make a pretty good one at Johnny Rockets. But it certainly wouldn't have been her first choice, nor Greg's. Indeed, it obviously wouldn't have been mine either because despite myriad previous trips to the Kodak Center I had never once set foot in the Johnny Rockets there. But that day I did, with Christina and Greg in tow.

As we were leaving after lunch we stopped at the counter to pay, and noticed that there was a sign hanging on the wall behind the cash register. It read: "Christina Eats Here."

To paraphrase Humphrey Bogart's character from *Casablanca*: "Of all the restaurants in all the buildings on Hollywood Boulevard..."

27 May 2011

The run of coincidental weirdness continues on my West coast trip with what was the strangest experience yet.

Christina has returned to Canada, Greg and Sigrid are still in Europe, and my brother isn't here yet, so I'm footloose and fancy free. I got up this morning and decided that I would catch the bus and head out past Westwood to visit the Getty Center, which is perhaps my favorite place in Los Angeles. I spent the afternoon wandering through a wonderful series of art exhibits and sitting in the beautiful grounds listening to Vivaldi on my MP3 player. It's about as close as you can get to a Walden moment in Los Angeles.

After several hours I caught the bus and headed back to Hollywood. By the time I got back to Greg's house it was 6:00 pm and I was really hungry, having eaten only a package of M & M's up until that point.

I figured that my best option was to head over to the Farmer's Market to grab dinner and catch some Thursday night jazz. I decided to take a book from Greg's well-stocked collection to help me pass the time before the live music started.

At first I picked a compilation of John Shirley short stories, but at the last second I switched my choice and took another book which I had been meaning to read for quite a while.

More on that in a moment.

The Market was jumping when I got there and the tables in the area around the stage in the West Patio were packed. I wandered off to another section, where my favorite deli is located, and ordered a cheeseburger.

Now usually I just get it plain – burger and cheddar cheese and nothing else – but this time, because there were other options for the cheese, and because I was getting a bit bored with the "same old, same old," I decided to switch it up. I went with Swiss cheese, something I had never done before.

That's important.

The burger was going to take a couple of minutes to cook so I grabbed a beer from a nearby bar and took a stroll through some of the vendors' kiosks. After buying a couple of postcards for my niece and nephews I wandered back to the deli, picked up my meal, and headed back to the area of the Market where the jazz group was playing to see if I could find a seat there.

It was still packed but I spied a table at the back near an entrance that wasn't taken, so I moved as quickly as I could through the crowd to get it before anyone else noticed it was available. I sat down, reached into my knapsack and pulled out the book I had brought with me from Greg's apartment, placed it on the table, and began to eat my dinner.

The jazz was good, the food was better, and the beer was the best part of all after a long day of walkabouts and bus rides.

After a few minutes an elderly couple approached my table. There were three unused seats, and over the music the woman motioned to them as if to ask whether they were taken or not.

I smiled, nodded, and said, "They're all yours." She returned the smile, sat down with her husband, and listened to the jazz for a bit as I finished up my food. As the band came to the end of their set, the man stood up and headed off to get some food.

I'm a friendly sort, and I always like talking to people (it comes in handy in my line of work), so I looked over at the woman and asked whether she was from Los Angeles. As soon as she spoke, I knew that she was from further away than I was – her accent was definitely European, although I couldn't quite place it. Turns out she and her husband were from Switzerland.

I chuckled to myself – these random people who had sat down next to me were from Switzerland, and for the first time in my life I had ordered a hamburger with Swiss cheese on it instead of cheddar.

I asked her what they were doing in the United States, and she told me that they come here every second year to visit their daughter and then take a vacation.

"Oh," I said, "that's nice. Where does your daughter live?"

"Dallas," she replied.

I immediately looked at the book on the table in front of me, the one that I had grabbed at the very last minute instead of the collection of John Shirley short stories that I had first picked up. It was *Final*

Events by my good friend Nick Redfern, who lives in Dallas![11]

As I pecked away at my remaining French fries and listened to the jazz begin again, I was reminded of a quote by one of my favorite jazz musicians and composers. "Making the simple complicated," said the great Chales Mingus, "is commonplace; making the complicated simple, awesomely simple, *that's* creativity."[12]

I began to wonder if I had drifted into some sort of an alternate reality where "someone" was being very creative with me.

28 May 2011

Tonight, foot loose and fancy free in Hollywood, I wandered over to the Farmer's Market for dinner, after which I was planning on going to see *Thor* at The Grove theatres. Hardly living "la vida loca," I know, but my reputation as a "bad boy" is a bit overstated.

After I finished dinner I walked up to the theatre, took a look at the massive crowds inside, particularly the very long ticket lines, and decided to give it a pass. A Hollywood epic about the Norse god of thunder just wasn't worth spending two hours cooped up with the madding crowd. I wandered into the Barnes & Noble next door to read a few graphic novels and browse a few other sections of interest.

I spent about twenty minutes engrossed in *Superman: New Krypton, Vol. 3*, and then walked down a couple of aisles to the New Age section where I leafed through a few books, including Nick Redfern's new tome *The Real Men in Black*, and Mark Pilkington's *Mirage Men*, because I wanted to have another look at the section he wrote about my friend Walter Bosley, which Walter had informed me was inaccurate to the point of being libelous.

After about another twenty minutes I decided to head back to Greg's to catch the end of the Dodgers game on television. As I made my

---

[11] Nick Redfern, *Final Events and the Secret Government Group on Demonic UFOs and the Afterlife* (New York: Anomalist Books, 2010).

[12] Charles Mingus, "Creativity," *Mainliner Magazine*, July 1977, 25.

way to the escalator to the main floor I noticed the Philosophy section and walked over to see if they had Marcus Aurelius' *Meditations*. I lost my old copy whilst traveling about a year ago, and I've been meaning to pick up a new one ever since.

I found the book, flipped through it for a minute or two, and decided to buy it the next time I was in the store. As I was about to place it back on the shelf a scream from the adjoining aisle startled me. I looked around the corner of the shelves and saw three young teens in the Manga section laughing and carrying on quite loudly as they browsed some vampire books. I gave them a bit of a stern look, which did absolutely no good, and then I shrugged and turned back to the Philosophy shelves. Due to the distraction, however, my gaze focused not on the shelf where I found had *Meditations*, but the one above it, where a particular book immediately caught my attention: *The Duck That Won The Lottery*, by British philosopher Julian Baggini.[13]

As my friends are aware, for years I have traveled with a stuffed duck I named Zorgrot, who is sort of my film production company's unofficial mascot.[14] This trip to Los Angeles is no different. Unfortunately, I've been so busy since I got here last week that I had forgotten to take Zorgy out of my knapsack until this afternoon. Just before I left for the Farmer's Market, I had taken a few photos of Zorgrot and "Kitty," the cleverly named cat owned by Greg and Sigrid that I'm looking after while they're in Europe.

I thought it was a cute little coincidence that I had finally pulled Zorgy out earlier in the evening and now my attention had been drawn to a book with "duck" in the title, so I placed *Meditations* back on the shelf and picked up *The Duck That Won The Lottery*. I opened it at random to the first page of chapter 55, which is titled: "Chance wouldn't be a fine thing: The no coincidence presumption."

---

[13] Julian Baggini, *The Duck That Won the Lottery, and 99 Other Bad Arguments* (London: Granta Books, 2008).

[14] He's also supposedly an alien explorer from another planet, but that's an entirely different story for another day... or my therapist.

"Okay," I thought to myself, "what are the odds?"

Given the series of coincidences that I've experienced on this trip I decided to try a little experiment. I closed the book and put it back on the shelf. I wanted to see if this copy was somehow predisposed to open at the beginning of chapter 55. I picked it up and opened it at random a dozen times, and not once did it come close to the beginning of chapter 55. The three kids had distracted me just long enough so that I would notice *The Duck That Won The Lottery*, which I opened at random to the chapter on coincidences just that one time.

I put the book back on the shelf, and walked out of the store.

"Well, that was weird," I muttered under my breath.

On the way home I decided to pop into Canter's Deli on Fairfax Avenue to pick up some cookies for a snack later in the evening. I ordered six chocolate chip cookies and four little squares of some sort (they're tasty, but I'm not quite sure what they're called).

At Canter's the cookies aren't priced individually, but by weight, so the clerk weighed them and then rang them in. He turned to me and said, "That'll be three fifty five, sir."

Weird had just gotten weirder!

The antics of *three* kids had led me to notice a book with "duck" in the cover, which I then opened to *chapter 55*, about *coincidences*.

Then $3.55 for cookies, based on weight.

If the clerk had picked a couple of different cookies for me, the price would have been different.

It had to be *those* cookies.

3 kids? Chapter 55, about coincidences? $3.55?

I feel like I'm in the middle of a jam session with an unseen jazz trio, and I'm picking out the notes, but I can't quite figure where they're going with the melody – and as the famous Duke Ellington song observed, "It don't mean a thing, if it ain't got that swing."[15]

I'm a former rhythm guitarist, and I've always been about the

[15] Irving Mills and Duke Ellington, "It Don't Mean a Thing (If It Ain't Got That Swing)," Perf. The Duke Ellington Orchestra (Brunswick Records, 1932).

swing, so I'll keep at it and see if I can discover whether or not there's a meaning to this particular gig.

<u>6 June 2011</u>

Last night I joined my friends Walter Bosley and Greg Bishop, who has just returned from his European honeymoon, for an episode of Greg's independent radio show, *Radio Misterioso*, which we recorded live at the Kill Radio studio on Vermont Avenue in Los Angeles. About forty-five minutes in Walter and I brought up the run of coincidences that have been happening since I left for Los Angeles in late May, and I related the most recent one, which occurred while my brother Jim was in town a few days ago. [16]

One of the things that Jim wanted to do while here was take a drive up the Pacific Coast to Malibu and the beaches. I readily agreed, because I love that area. I came up with a little itinerary that included a stop at the Swingers restaurant in Santa Monica for lunch because it's one of the best spots I know of to get a vanilla milkshake in Los Angeles. I figured that from there we would drive up the Pacific Coast Highway, stop at Zuma Beach, and then head to Point Mugu where we could turn around and come back to the city via Interstate 5.

Seemingly apropos of nothing, I had gone on the Internet earlier that morning to check my Facebook page and my e-mail. After I was done I made my way to Wikipedia, which is a fun place to browse at random when one has some free time because it can lead one on interesting little "six degrees of separation" tangents of discovery. I once started with King Zog of Albania and wound up at Lauren Bacall! Last night I had watched a program on the History Channel that referenced the American Civil War, and as that was relatively fresh in my mind I decided to start with that terrible conflict and see where I wound up.

As I started scrolling through the main entry on the Civil War I ran

---

[16] Greg Bishop, "Synchronicity and Creativity," *Radio Misterioso*, 5 June 2011. http://goo.gl/hTqMo.

across the name of one of my favorite Presidents – Millard Fillmore. When people ask me why he's one of my favorite Presidents, I just smile and repeat his name: Millard Fillmore. How can you not like a guy with a name like that? It's the kind of name that a character in the old Looney Tunes cartoons would have had. As a result, I clicked on the link to Fillmore, read the page, and then followed some links from there to other material about him. By the time I was done I had spent an hour reading about this odd duck of a President, whose most memorable accomplishment was landing on almost every list ever made by historians of the worst Presidents.[17]

Jim and I set off on our day trip up to Malibu shortly thereafter. Like the Cylons of the re-imagined Battlestar Galactica television series, I had a plan, which we followed more or less to the proverbial "T" until we were getting ready to leave Zuma Beach and head up to Point Mugu. At this point I decided to ditch the plan and freelance, something I'm notorious for amongst my friends.

I pulled a map out of the glove compartment, took a quick look, and decided that it would be fun to take highway 126, which runs from the Pacific Coast Highway to Highway 101 through a valley with lots of orange groves. I had originally thought of going up on another route that circled through Ojai back to Interstate 5, which is a really pretty drive, but the reason that the 126 caught my eye was because I had never taken it before, and it went through a particular small town – Fillmore, California.

A small coincidence at best, but one that I couldn't pass up given the run of synchronicities I've been on. And then, almost as soon as we got on the 126, we saw a sign for the first exit as you drive north,

[17] Some trivia about Fillmore: He was the last member of the Whig Party to be elected President, he later joined the xenophobic No-Nothing movement, losing the 1856 Presidential election as their standard-bearer, he opposed Lincoln during the Civil War, and in a nice bit of synchronicity that I didn't realize at the time but which fits perfectly as I look back on that trip to Los Angeles a year later, Fillmore was President in 1850 when California became a state. See Benson Lee Grayson, *The Unknown President: The Administration of Millard Fillmore* (Lanham, MD: University Press of America, 1981).

which led directly to – Kimball Road!

As I related this anecdote on the radio show Walter slowly leaned back in his chair, listened with great concentration, waited for several moments afterwards as Greg and I bantered back and forth, and then pushed himself forward again and spoke slowly and purposefully into his microphone.

"I'll throw something else at you," he said, with a pause afterwards for effect. "You were on Highway 126. When you add up the digits in the highway number it comes to nine, and nine is a very esoteric number with special properties that no other number has."[18]

Greg chimed in with a comment about Whitley Strieber and his use of the number nine, and then Walter added that it was obviously a special number where baseball was concerned, and that baseball is a mystical game, a sentiment with which I have always agreed, although up until that point only in the figurative sense of the word "mystical."

"Now, this is freaky," I interrupted. "As you said that, I was just about to tell a baseball story from the game last night."

Both Greg and I are die-hard baseball fans, and whenever I'm in

---

[18] When you look into the history of the number nine in religion, philosophy, and mythology, you find that it has occupied a special place in many different cultures. For example, as the highest single-digit number, it symbolizes completeness in the Bahá'í Faith. The number 9 is also revered in Hinduism, where it is considered a complete, perfected and divine number because it represents the end of a cycle in the decimal system, which originated from the Indian subcontinent as early as 3000 BC. The first nine days of the Hebrew month of Av are collectively known as "The Nine Days" (*Tisha HaYamim*), and are a period of semi-mourning leading up to Tisha B'Av, the ninth day of Av on which both Temples in Jerusalem were destroyed. Nine was a significant number in Norse mythology as well: the all-father Odin hung himself on an ash tree for nine days to learn the runes. In the Christian angelic hierarchy, there are 9 choirs of angels, and there are nine levels of hell. Finally, Ramadan, the month of fasting and prayer, is the ninth month of the Islamic calendar, and in Islamic belief God has 99 names. See Annemarie Schimmel, *The Mystery of Numbers* (Oxford: Oxford University Press, 1993), 164-179; also "Mystic Attributes of the Number Nine," *New York Times*, 7 September 1895.

town during baseball season we try to catch some games, whether with the Major League teams in town or at the many minor league teams scattered around southern California. This trip had been no different.

"As you know," I continued, looking directly at Walter, "we went to see the Rancho Cucamonga Quakes last night, and we called you from the highway on our way out there to see if you wanted to join us, because you live in San Bernadino, which isn't far away."

"Yeah, but I couldn't make it," Walter replied.

"Right," I said. "But guess what? One of the relief pitchers used in the game was named Josh Walter. Not *Walters*, which would be a far more common surname, but *Walter*."

Greg and Walter then proceeded to have a discussion about coincidences versus synchronicity and whether there might be any meaning to it while I checked on my camera to see if there was any relationship to the number nine and the pitcher, Josh Walter. His uniform number was 38, which didn't fit, but then as I scrolled through the photos I had taken at the game I saw one of the scoreboard when he came in to pitch. It displayed his Earned Run Average, perhaps the most important statistic for a pitcher.

Josh Walter's was 4.05.

Add it up, and you had the number nine.[19]

Walter almost hopped out of his seat. "There's your nine," he exclaimed with a big smile on his face.

We continued on for a while with a friendly discussion about what Walter calls the "axis of circumstance, and the vector of desire," and how it happens at certain times in your life. Greg responded that the consciousness of the person experiencing a synchronistic event is just as important as the event itself, and that the events are always there but we usually don't notice them. Walter thought about that for a moment, and they came to an agreement of sorts in terms of their points of view.

---

[19] Walter's birth-date as listed on his Major League Baseball player page is *04/05/1985.* "Josh Walter." *Inland Empire 66ers.* http://goo.gl/KjQZI.

"You start seeing the fabric of reality, and how you fit in," said Walter at one point.

As Greg replied with an anecdote about how William Burroughs used to send writing students out to try and become more aware of their surroundings, I picked up a copy of John Fante's novel, *Ask the Dusk*. I had never heard of Fante before this trip to Los Angeles, but when Greg told me that Fante was one of his favorite writers, and a major influence on Charles Bukowski, who is one of *my* favorite writers, I decided to take a look. I immediately liked what I saw and so I brought Greg's copy of the novel to the studio with the idea that I would read from it on the show. I randomly opened it up as Greg was talking, and looked down at the page I had hit upon.

"Hold on!" I said as I broke in on Greg's train of thought. "I want you, Walter, to read the page number."

I handed Walter the book, he took a look, and then breathed an audible sigh.

"Ninety-nine."

We all paused for a brief moment, and then Walter said, "Welcome to my world."

"Somewhere in your subconscious," responded Greg, playing the Devil's advocate, "you can figure out where ninety-nine is, and then opened it up."

"I don't believe that," I shot back.

"I do," said Greg, "but I don't believe that it's meaningless. People will deal with concepts and include them in the creative process, and maybe they're not even aware of it. The concepts and the synchronicities are finding them."

I could see where he was coming from, and when he put it like that it made sense to me, particularly as I'm working on a screenplay that deals with the prospect of life after death, and free will versus pre-destination. And maybe that's what these past couple of weeks have all been about – opening my mind even further to the true nature of the world around us and the creative possibilities of existence.

Shortly after this exchange we started talking about politics and religion, a conversation which went on for about half an hour. One final coincidence (or synchronicity) was still waiting for us, however. Greg left to use the washroom, and I hijacked the show by playing *There is a Light Which Never Goes Out*, my favorite song by The Smiths.

When Greg returned, we all had a good laugh because Greg isn't a fan of their music. As he stopped the song from playing further, I once again picked up *Ask the Dusk* and opened it to a random page as I was paying attention to Walter, who was pontificating about something. When he finished his stream-of-consciousness soliloquy I looked down at the page and then shook my head in disbelief.

"Now remember," I said, "I had the whole '355' thing with the book at Barnes & Noble and then Canter's, and tonight it's been the number nine, so Walter, I want you to look at the book."

I held the book out to him so he could see the pages I had opened it up to, but didn't give it to him because he had the microphone in his nearest hand. "What pages did I open it up to? Fifty-four, which added together is nine, and fifty-five."

Walter nodded his head and smiled, because he had noticed something that I hadn't picked up on with regards to how I was holding the book open.

"You've got three fingers visible to me; therefore the three, five, five."

As I checked my hand and confirmed what he had said, Walter asked me to have a look at the pages and see if there was anything within them that might tie in with everything we had been discussing.

"The key is what's on the page," he said.

As I read the final paragraph on page fifty-five, which was the end of that particular chapter, we noticed a couple of things. The first was the fact that it talked about a mystery, which was exactly what we had been discussing all night. Then Walter chimed in.

"Okay, the first synchronicity is connected to me," he said, ignoring the 'mystery' angle that I had hit upon. "In that paragraph, there is something mentioned three times. I am a fan of Cary Grant, and in that paragraph Fante used the name Judy three times. 'Judy, Judy, Judy' – one of the lines Grant was best known for."

As Walter noted, it was another three to go with the fifty-five. Of course, Grant never actually said "Judy, Judy, Judy" in any of his films, but to me this perfectly illustrated the key point that it can be a fine line between perception and reality.[20]

Indeed, perhaps there isn't any line there at all.

As I walked out of the studio with Greg and Walter on our way to the House of Pies, a nearby diner where we always go after a show when I'm in town, I thought back to that first coincidence, or synchronicity, at gate B16 at O'Hare airport in Chicago.

If you assign a numerical value of '2' to the letter 'B' based on its position as the second letter in the alphabet, and then add it to 1 and 6, you get the number 9.

Now we're really swingin'!

<u>7 June 2011</u>

This is the last day of my three week long trip to Los Angeles, which has seen a weird run of coincidences. So it's only fitting that today saw the final truly weird coincidence, which was the most personal one of them all.

There has been a group of filmmakers from Halifax here in Los Angeles at a conference over the past couple of days (I'm not involved in the conference), one of whom is my friend Ben Stevens, the older brother of my *Ghost Cases* co-host Holly. I haven't seen Ben since the fall of 2010 when he left town for a gig in northern Alberta, so we decided to meet up at the Los Angeles Farmer's Market this afternoon (or as I have come to jokingly call it, the "Nexus of Synchronicity").

We met at noon along with Greg, who had worked with Ben in 2008 on my feature film *Eternal Kiss*. After coffee we made our way to The Grove because I wanted to get a picture of Lynda Carter, who was being interviewed for a TV show just outside the Barnes & Noble

---

[20] Nancy Nelson, "Judy Judy Judy," *CaryGrant.net*. http://goo.gl/NI3Tv.

(I remember her well as Wonder Woman, as does almost every man who grew up in the late 1970s). She showed up just after 2 pm, I snapped a few photos, and then we wandered off. Greg went back to his house to do some work, and I decided to walk up Fairfax for a couple of blocks to show Ben one of my regular hang-outs, Canter's Deli.

Ben had mentioned earlier that he would like to see the Walk of Fame on Hollywood Boulevard if I was game. It's quite a lengthy walk from the Farmer's Market, so he offered to pay for a cab. I had already been to the Walk of Fame on this trip with both Christina and Jim, so I was non-committal – one can get too much of a good thing. I also had some work of my own to do back at Greg's house, so I wasn't sure that it was the best use of my time.

As we walked up Fairfax, however, Ben and I were having such a nice chat that we just kept going. We hung a right onto Melrose, and headed towards central Hollywood. After about ten or fifteen minutes I realized that we were halfway to Hollywood Boulevard, so I decided to go all the way. It was very much a spur of the moment, last second call, in the same way my decision had been to travel on highway 126.

As we continued down Melrose, chatting away as friends do, I stopped paying attention to where we were until I looked up and saw that we were at La Brea, which is a cross street that leads up to Hollywood Boulevard (about ten blocks away). As I had never walked up La Brea before, but knew it intersected with Hollywood Boulevard at the beginning of the Walk of Fame, I figured it was the perfect way to get to our destination.

After a few blocks, I noticed a large statue of Kermit the Frog on the top of a building on the opposite side of the street, which I then recognized as Jim Henson Studios. I had driven past it before but didn't recall that it was on La Brea.

As anyone who knows me is aware, I'm a big Kermit the Frog fan, to the point where I've become well known back home for my impression of the legendary Muppet. For example, while on the set of *Eternal Kiss* Ben and I were filmed by another crew member one day goofing around during a break in production. At the end of the short clip I did my impression of Kermit at the request of the crew member shooting the footage.[21]

Naturally, I had to get a picture of Kermit, something I had never done before in all my trips to Los Angeles. I stopped, turned, and took the shot.

This was all a bit weird given the video of Ben and I from 2008, and that it was Ben and I who randomly made our way to La Brea today. But then things got much stranger when I glanced down at the sidewalk, something that I had absolutely no reason to do – indeed, something that I almost never do.

Of all the people who have seen me do my Kermit impression, *none* has enjoyed it more than my good friend Veronica Reynolds. She has asked me to do it so many times over the years, both for her and for others, that I've lost count. I recall one time where I was in a bar with several of Veronica's friends and she went out of her way to tell them that I did a great Kermit impression. I wound up "introducing" all of them the way Kermit introduced his guests on *The Muppet Show*.

So imagine my surprise as I stood on the sidewalk on La Brea, looked down, and saw a name carved into the cement exactly where I had stopped to take the Kermit photo. There was no plan to be there with Ben at *that* place, at *that* moment, taking a picture of Kermit while walking to Hollywood Boulevard from the Farmer's Market, something I had never done before.

The name?

Veronica.

By the way, referring back to that video of Ben and I goofing around on set on *Eternal Kiss* (which is the only video ever recorded of me doing my Kermit impression), there's one more factor, which is the question of how Veronica and I first met. It was years ago when she auditioned for and was cast in the original version of *Eternal Kiss*, which I had written in 2001 but didn't get around to filming until

---

[21] Paul Kimball, "Paul Kimball and Benjamin Stevens on the set of Eternal Kiss," *Redstar Films YouTube Channel*, 24 February 2009. http://goo.gl/O27Nc.

years later.[22]

The name of the character for whom she had been cast all those years ago was Elisabeth Langstrom.

In each of the two names for that character, there are exactly *nine* letters.

31 October 2011

Is an advanced non-human intelligence attempting to communicate with us through things like synchronicities? Could they be trying to inspire us to think in new and different ways about something bigger than ourselves? Perhaps they're providing us with clues about the true nature of existence, and our place in it.

Regardless of the nature of the experience, or how we choose to interpret what happens, it seems to be something that we all have in common. I doubt that there is anyone in this world who can honestly say they have never experienced a coincidence, or déjà vu, and that commonality may be the real point of the exercise. After all, the Rubik's Cube has 43,252,003,274,489,856,000 possible combinations on its six faces, but it has only *one* solution where everything fits together. Everyone who solves it will have found a different path to the same place.[23]

Who are we, and how do we all fit together? That's the question we need to ask, and the puzzle we spend our entire lives trying to solve. As Alice said in Lewis Carroll's classic novel *Alice in Wonderland*: "Dear, dear! How queer everything is to-day! And yesterday things went on just as usual. *Was* I the same when I got up this morning? But if I'm not the same, the next question is, 'Who in the world am I?' Ah,

---

[22] Her role was re-cast, against my wishes and at the direction of the distributor, when I eventually got the opportunity to make the film. She was crushed when she I gave her the news, and she wouldn't speak to me for over a year, which I completely understood.

[23] Jamieson, "Rubik's Cube inventor is back with Rubik's 360."

that's the great puzzle!"[24]

Robert H. Hopke, in *There Are No Accidents: Synchronicity and the Stories of Our Lives*, sees the artistic elements of synchronicity within a literary context. "The most essential and distinctive aspect of synchronicity is the experience of meaning upon which the coincidences are based," he wrote. "Through our ability to uncover and live out the individual meaning of what befalls us, we receive in a synchronistic event a reminder of an important truth: that our lives are organized, consciously and unconsciously, the way a story is, that our lives have a coherence, a direction, a reason for being, and a beauty as well. Synchronicity reminds us how much a work of art the stories of our lives can be."[25]

But how does this all integrate into *my* story?

Well, the last few years haven't been easy for me on either a personal or a professional level. Production on *Eternal Kiss* was a disaster that I was lucky to get through without going both bankrupt and mad. Some of it was out of my control, such as the financial crash of 2008 hitting just as we started filming, which wiped out our private American investment, or the craziness and corruption I wound up having to deal with in Shelburne, Nova Scotia, where we shot the film. But I made lots of mistakes on my own, the result of a combination of hubris and a desire to push my career forward at any cost, even when it came to relationships with friends.[26]

---

[24] Lewis Carroll, *Alice in Wonderland* (New York: Sam'l Gabriel Sons & Company, 1916), 10. http://www.gutenberg.org/files/19033/19033-h/19033-h.htm.

[25] Hopke, *There Are No Accidents: Synchronicity and the Stories of Our Lives*, 47.

[26] While I have trouble separating the film itself from the soul-draining experience of making it, others have been more positive. Long-time Halifax film critic and Atlantic Film Festival senior programmer Ron Foley MacDonald, for example, gave it the following review: "*Eternal Kiss* resembles Ingmar Bergman's mid-60s work, such as *Persona* and *Hour Of the Wolf* when that Northern European master mixed terse issues of identity with strong undertones of horror... Kimball's film emphasizes feelings of dislocation and looming desire. *Eternal Kiss* is an intense and personal trip into the Vampire world; it is as unsettling as it is engrossing." Ron

On a personal level, my long-term relationship of twenty years ended in 2007, although we remain best friends. My mother underwent life-threatening open heart surgery in 2008 (in the midst of me shooting *Eternal Kiss*, which provided another distraction). She survived, but it reminded me of the fragile nature of our lives. And then in October, 2009, Mac Tonnies passed away suddenly at the age of 34. He was one of my three or four best friends and a collaborator on various projects. His death threw me for a loop on a number of levels from which I still haven't quite recovered.

Maybe, just maybe, the run of synchronicities in May and June 2011 was there to remind me that we're all linked together, that I wasn't alone, and that my story, despite some rough chapters, is still being written. Maybe it was a reminder of the synchronicity of the people I love, which Hopke believes "lies not just in the amazing circumstances that make up our love stories but in the inner meaning we see and live in these stories of our lives."[27]

All of which brings me back to music.

I think our lives are a lot like jazz, the musical form that floats most often on a cloud of improvisation. Living is like that, too – it should be based on feeling, and on finding a groove, but most of all it should be based on enjoying the moment. As any good musician will tell you, however, no matter how brilliant a soloist might be as they improvise an inspired riff, the whole thing can be undone if they lose sync with the rhythm section around them. The greatest solo, the greatest moment of improvisation, is still always part of something bigger. In the end, maybe the purpose behind the puzzle of

---

Foley MacDonald, "Eternal Kiss: World Premiere," *InfoMonkey*, 4 April 2010, accessed 14 September 2012. http://goo.gl/m9Hqx. On the craziness and corruption I had to deal with, see Office of the Ombudsman, "Final Report: South West Shore Development Authority," Government of Nova Scotia, February 2010. http://gov.ns.ca/ombu/publications/2010-ombu-report.pdf. See as well Brian Medel, "Seacoast Assets on Block Today," *The Chronicle Herald*, 23 November 2011. http://goo.gl/fxifQ.

[27] Hopke, 93.

synchronicity is to act as a reminder of this common journey that links us together. As individuals, we're the notes – but all together, *we're the melody.*

As I write this section, it's now the 31st of October, 2011. I was working away at this book when my roommate, Linda, who was under the weather, asked me to run out and get her some groceries. I drove down to one of the local supermarkets and pulled into the first open parking space I saw in what was a very crowded parking lot. As I turned the engine off I noticed that the car parked in front of me had a vanity rear license plate.

It read *"Ghosts"*.

I paused for a moment and thought to myself, "Hey, that's weird." There are a couple of hundred thousand cars licensed in Nova Scotia, and only one of them has a license plate that reads "Ghosts," so the odds of running into that car in that place at that time are pretty long, to say the least.

I went into the store and did my shopping, came back out to the parking lot, stowed the groceries in the trunk, got in the car, and turned the key in the ignition. The radio, which I had left on earlier, was silent for just a split second... and then Ray Parker's "Ghostbusters" started to play. What made this really interesting to me is the part of the book I was working on when Linda asked me to get groceries. It was chapter three, about my ghost investigating experiences.

One more thing. It was Linda to whom I was engaged to be married from 1998 until 2007. Linda Wood.

Nine letters. Nine years.

I'm not quite sure what to make of it all. Like Cobb in *Inception*, however, I can't help but wonder if my top is still spinning. Or, in the words of Count Basie, "I'm saying to be continued, until we meet again. Meanwhile, keep on listening and tapping your feet."[28]

Is there meaning in all of this? None that I could demonstrate in a

---

[28] Count Basie and Albert Murray, *Good Morning Blues: The Autobiography of Count Basie* (Cambridge, MA: Da Capo Press, 1985), 385.

court of law, or to a panel of scientists – certainly nothing that I could replicate on demand. But there's meaning to me, and in the end, as with all great art, isn't that what that really matters?

Ultimately I think an advanced non-human intelligence would agree with Charlie Parker, who said, "Music is your own experience, your own thoughts, your own wisdom. If you don't live it, it won't come out of your horn. They teach you there's a boundary line to music. But, man, there's no boundary line to art."[29]

---

[29] Charlie Parker, "Charlie Yardbird Parker - Quotes," *Estate of Charlie Parker.* http://goo.gl/awuuv.

66

Christina Cuffari at the Johnny Rockets in the Kodak Center, May 2011. Note the sign.

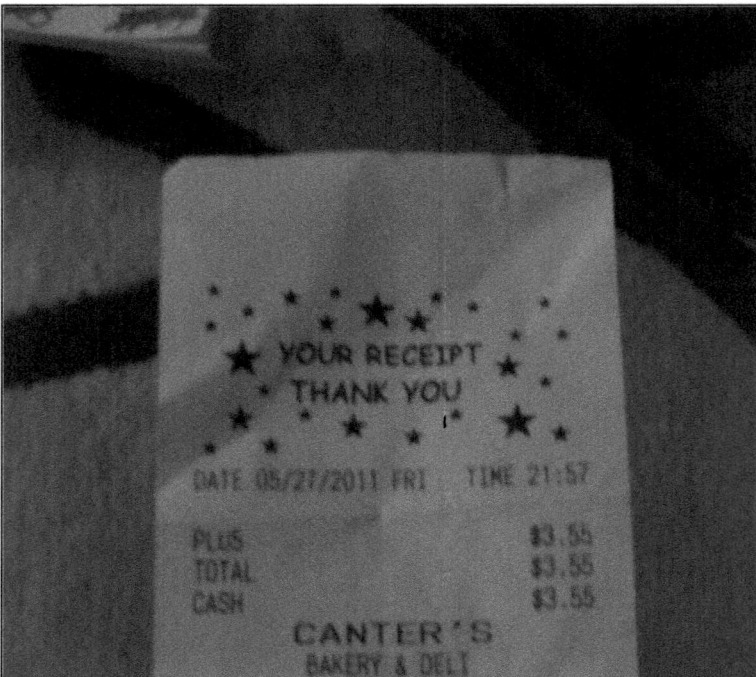

The receipt from Canter's Deli, May 2011.

The exit to Kimball Road off Highway 126, June 2011.

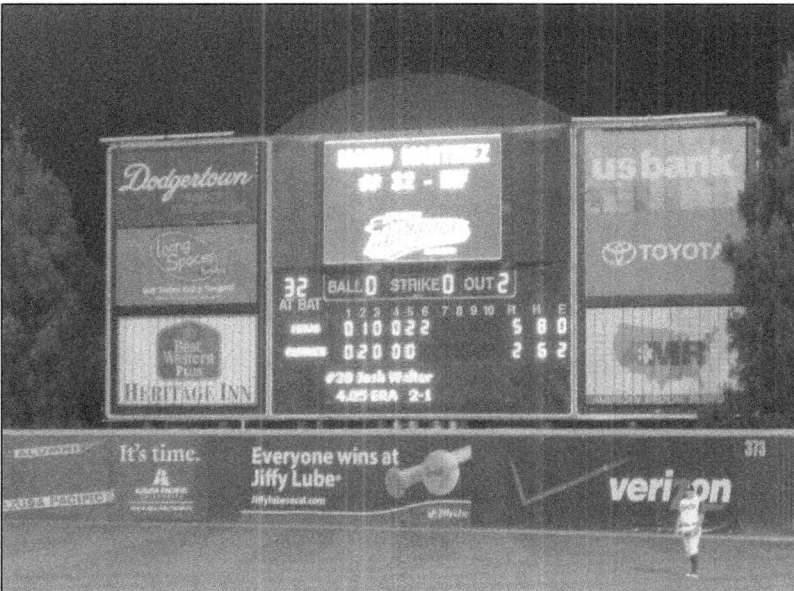

Josh Walter on the scoreboard at Rancho Cucamonga, June 2011. He was born on 04/05/85, and had an ERA of 4.05 entering the game that night.

My good friends Walter Bosley and Greg Bishop in the studio as we were on air on Greg's show Radio Misterioso. The synchronicities came fast and furious!

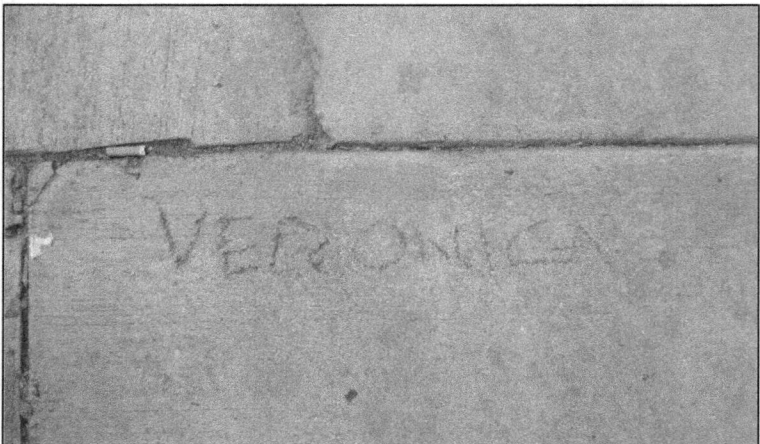

The name "Veronica" carved into the sidewalk on La Brea in Los Angeles, across from Jim Henson studios, June 2011.

Nick Redfern, Veronica Reynolds and I in Las Vegas in 2004 at a UFO conference.

Linda Wood in 2012. We remain best friends. Nine years. Nine letters. Maybe our relationship has nine lives, or nine different levels? Or maybe all of this was just a reminder of the people who matter to me. (Photo courtesy of Linda Wood)

Chapter Three

Things That Go Bump in the Night

I think of horror films as art, as films of confrontation. Films that make you confront aspects of your own life that are difficult to face.[1]
– David Cronenberg

When I was a kid my family used to go on vacation to Prince Edward Island, the small province across the Northumberland Strait from Nova Scotia. It was always an adventure because before the federal government built a massive bridge that connected PEI to the mainland in 1997 you could only get there from the mainland via one of two car ferries, and the Island itself had a magical, timeless quality as a result.[2] To a young boy from the city it was a rural paradise, full of mystery, like something out of a Hardy Boys novel.

PEI has always been best known for its pristine beaches, its potatoes, and of course Anne of Green Gables, but it also had a number of family-friendly attractions back then, small-town, low-budget "theme parks" like Rainbow Valley, where the highlights included things such as petting zoos and slides bigger than the ones you could find in your schoolyard back home. In the years since,

---

[1] "David Cronenberg," *They Shoot Pictures, Don't They.* http://goo.gl/i3FZn.

[2] One of the things that stood out in a positive way was the fact that you could only buy bottled soft drinks until very recently. Plastic bottles and aluminum cans were forbidden by the law. See "Islanders pop tabs as PEI's 'can ban' ends," CBC News, 3 May 2008. www.cbc.ca/news/canada/prince-edward-island/story/2008/05/02/can-ban.html.

much larger and flashier amusement parks have replaced most of these older gems from my childhood years, and I think that PEI lost something in the bargain. As a kid, we relied on our imagination; now the attractions do much of the imagining for you. Some people consider it progress, but I'm not one of them.[3]

In the 1970s, however, there was definitely a slower pace, and my brother and sister and I had all sorts of adventures because we had imagination to spare. One of my favorite places to visit was an attraction in Harrington, a speck on the map just outside the capital of Charlottetown. Looking back I realize that it was a pretty small-scale operation, even by the standards of PEI at the time, but it had the one thing that I remember above all others – a house of horrors!

In hindsight I realize that it was more of a "mobile home of horrors," but to a nine year old boy it seemed a lot bigger than it really was. I remember the first time we went there like it was yesterday. There were spooky sounds and music playing as we walked up to the "house," just like the kind my Dad still blares out the windows of his house on an old record player every Halloween from a well-worn K-Tel album he found in a bargain bin decades ago. The building just kind of sat there next to the parking lot. Some fake cobwebs were strewn around the entrance, and a skeleton as well, but there really wasn't a whole lot else. Nevertheless, it was all too real and frightening to me. For several minutes I refused to go in. Even after my Dad pointed out that my younger siblings had made it through unscathed I was convinced that I would go in and never come out.

I finally screwed up the courage to face both the monsters within the haunted "house," and the fear within me. As I recall, it wasn't the reassurance by my Mom and Dad that got me through the front door; it was my brother's taunting from the other side of the fence that

---

[3] See "Closed Canadian Parks: Rainbow Valley." http://goo.gl/K1X3t. Rainbow Valley was perhaps best known for its replica flying saucer gift shop. See "Futuro House – Home of the Future: The UFO Home of PEI, Canada." www.futurohouse.com/pei.html.

separated those who had gone through the building from those who had not. With one too many "'fraidy cat" jibes still ringing in my ears, I decided that I would rather face demons from Hell than spend the rest of the vacation listening to Jim make fun of me. So in I went.

And then out I came. It was as scary as I thought it would be, but I made it through in one piece (although I did scrape my elbow when I turned around suddenly as a witch puppet popped out from a wall). Before we left I went through again, but it wasn't nearly as frightening the second time around because I knew what was going to happen and therefore most of the anticipatory dread was gone. But my encounter with the "haunted house of Harrington" has stayed locked in my memory ever since, even as many others from my childhood have faded or disappeared altogether. It was the thrill that was scary, and the scare that was thrilling, the kind of experience that speaks to us all on the most primal of levels and is never forgotten.

The Maritime Provinces of Canada are famous for ghost stories, hauntings, demons, old hags, and various other tales of "creatures that go bump in the night," as well as some very interesting UFO stories.[4] I have many friends and family members who have related what can loosely be categorized as "ghost stories" to me over the years. The drummer of my old band grew up in a house where the walls dripped blood (among other strange things). When we were first dating in college Linda Wood showed up at my residence one night at 2 am shaking and in tears after a terrifying experience with a ouija board (she still won't go anywhere near one all these years later – when we were using one for *Ghost Cases* in 2009 she made me store it in the trunk of our car rather than in our house). Just the other day I got a letter from a woman in Dartmouth who is convinced that her house is haunted by ghosts tormenting her young son, asking me what she

---

[4] See, for example, Helen Creighton, *Bluenose Magic: Popular Beliefs and Superstitions in Nova Scotia* (Toronto: The Ryerson Press, 1968), and Helen Creighton, *Folklore of Lunenburg County, Nova Scotia* (Toronto: McGraw-Hill Ryerson, 1976).

should do about it.[5]

I also know a few people who claim to have seen a UFO. My good friend Ron Foley MacDonald, a theatre and film critic, was a young boy when he saw something fly over his home in Rockingham, Nova Scotia, in 1967, on the same night of the famous Shag Harbour incident.[6] All these years later he can still recount the story as if it had just happened.

A salt-of-the-earth family I know in Prince Edward Island once told me a story about what appeared to be a silvery, egg-shaped object surrounded by a bright light that appeared in a field near their house. It was witnessed by several family members for a minute or two and then flew away. They thought it was some sort of "forerunner." For those not familiar with the term, the Maritime folklorist Helen Creighton defined it in *Bluenose Ghosts* as a "supernatural warning of approaching events… usually connected with impending death."[7]

Even when someone around here has described something to me that most people elsewhere would categorize as a UFO case, like the egg-shaped object in the field noted above, they often place it within a more supernatural framework. If someone in New Mexico had relayed the story of the egg-shaped object, for example, they probably would have been interpreted as aliens.[8] In the Maritimes, however, it

---

[5] I recommended her son see a child psychologist instead of the alleged psychic / exorcist whom she wanted to call.

[6] For the definitive description of the Shag Harbour UFO incident, see Don Ledger and Chris Styles, *Dark Object: The World's Only Government-Documented UFO Crash* (New York: Dell Publishing, 2001).

[7] Helen Creighton, *Bluenose Ghosts* (Halifax, NS: Nimbus Publishing, 1994), 1. There was actually a death associated with this story – later on the same day that they saw the object in the field a neighbor was killed in a car accident on his way to a funeral.

[8] The famous Socorro, New Mexico "UFO" case of 1964, for example, involved an object that the key witness, police office Lonnie Zamora, described as roughly egg-shaped. See Jacques Vallee, *Forbidden Science: Volume One, Journals 1957–1969*

was viewed as a forerunner, but it just as easily might have been seen as a will 'o the wisp, or a phantom ship. As Creighton wrote, "The supernatural in Nova Scotia is… a part of our way of life."[9]

It should therefore come as no surprise that after several years of making films about the UFO phenomenon I finally got drawn into the world of ghosts.

In the Spring of 2008, just as I was beginning pre-production on *Eternal Kiss*, I was contacted by Dale Stevens, a fellow television producer in Halifax whom I had met while developing one of the myriad projects I've worked on over the years that never quite got off the ground.[10] Dale had come up with an idea for a series about ghost stories in the Maritime Provinces of Canada, and he had sold it to a local television network. He had cast four Nova Scotian ghost "investigators" as the hosts, but as he hadn't written, directed or headed up a production before the network wanted him to bring someone on board who had some experience. Dale knew about my interest in the paranormal and asked me if I wanted to get involved as his partner. As the series sounded like fun, and as it wasn't going to begin until after *Eternal Kiss* had finished shooting, I readily agreed.

Once *Eternal Kiss* wrapped production in October, 2008, I immediately turned my attention to the ghost series, which we had decided to call *Ghost Cases*. Each of the thirteen episodes would focus on an investigation of one particular location. We took the small crew and the four hosts to the town of Sherbrooke on the Eastern Shore of Nova Scotia, where there was a house and a library that were supposedly haunted.

As soon as we started filming, however, I realized that while the four hosts were nice people, and genuinely sincere about what they

(Documentica Research, 2007), 121-123, 130-131.

[9] Creighton, *Bluenose Ghosts*, 280.

[10] Coincidentally, I wound up shooting the film on a sound stage that was located in the de-commissioned naval station that had been at the center of the Shag Harbour UFO story. Or was it synchronicity?

did, they weren't quite what we were looking for. We wanted to highlight the personal experiences of our hosts, and we also wanted hosts who were a bit off kilter, a little quirky, and not quite what you would expect to see on your average, run-of-the-mill, bog-standard, "on every network in the world" ghost show. By the end of the three days in Sherbrooke I had decided to make a change, a decision with which the four hosts happily agreed as they had come to the conclusion that they weren't comfortable with the constraints that a half-hour television show placed on them.

With a tight shooting schedule ahead and set delivery dates for the first episodes only a couple of months away, Dale and I didn't really have time to open up a search for new hosts, so I hit upon what the character Baldrick in the old *Blackadder* television series might have called a "cunning plan" (or what some of my friends would have called "Paul's ego run amuck") – I would host the series, while continuing to co-write, co-direct and co-produce it with Dale.

Being well aware of my own limitations as an on-screen personality as well as the success of the male-female co-star dynamic that can be seen in shows such as *Moonlighting* and *The X-Files*, I convinced Dale that we should hire my good friend Holly Stevens to be my co-host.[11] I knew Holly had an interest in the paranormal, and she also had a degree in biology, which I thought added at least a thin veneer of scientific credibility to our efforts. I had worked with her on *Eternal Kiss* both as an actress (she had a small role) and as part of the production crew, and knew that she was a team player and a hard worker. As an aspiring actress she had the kind of on-screen experience and understanding of how a television series worked that a co-host required. Finally, there was little doubt that she and I had "chemistry" – many people who saw the show thought we were actually a "couple," which we weren't. Once you added all of this together, it was clear that she was the perfect choice to be the "beauty" to my "beast" – particularly as she shared my off-the-wall,

---

[11] Holly Stevens, *Holly Stevens*. www.hollystevens/ca.

no-holds-barred sense of humor!

Over the next seven months Holly and I investigated stories of ghosts, demons, and all sorts of other weirdness at thirteen unique locations in eastern Canada and England. I went into the process as an ardent skeptic about "ghosts" and "haunting," but after what I saw and experienced I came out of it much more open-minded to the possibility that there might be something genuinely "paranormal" to at least some of the stories. That's what happens when you encounter events for which you can't come up with a prosaic explanation, no matter how hard you try.

What follows are the most intriguing stories from the adventure that was *Ghost Cases*. Each of them altered my perception of the "paranormal," and my thoughts on the possible nature of an advanced non-human intelligence and its relationship with us.

The Case of the Haunted Graveyard

When I was a kid, maybe ten or eleven, I read a short story in which a young boy and girl wander into an old cemetery at night. They decide to play a game of hide-and-seek and the boy makes the mistake of walking around the church in a counter-clockwise direction as he searches for a hiding place. Because the church had been cursed this caused him to become invisible, as if he had run into a portal and shifted out of phase with the universe or something like that. The only way he could get back to our plane of existence was by walking around the church in a clockwise direction which would reverse the effect. As I recall, the boy eventually figured it out and escaped from the trap, but not before both he and the girl were frightened out of their minds.[12] Little did I know that three decades

---

[12] The fear of walking counter-clockwise in Anglo-Saxon culture dates back to 16th century Britain, where it was known as widdershins. The *Oxford English Dictionary* entry cites the earliest uses of the word from 1513, where it was found in the phrase *"widdersyns start my hair."* It was considered unlucky in Britain to travel in an anti-clockwise (anti sun-wise) direction around a church, and a number of folk

later I would find myself at a church in England where the truth would prove stranger than childhood fiction.

In order to broaden the international sales appeal of *Ghost Cases* I decided that we would film four episodes outside of Canada. Our first choice was Louisiana, and we had the locations and the trip booked, but we were turned away at the airport by US Customs, apparently because they don't like any competition for the dire ghost shows produced in the United States. Or perhaps they had read my Facebook postings critical of American foreign policy. They didn't really give us a reason.

Fortunately, I had met a good bloke named Dave Sadler when we were both speakers at a paranormal conference in Altrincham, England, a couple of years before. At the time Dave had made the mistake of telling me that if I ever needed any help from "across the pond" all I had to do was give him a call. With our American trip now a non-starter I definitely needed help, so I rang him up. He was more than happy to work with us, and two months later, largely thanks to his research and connections, we landed in England to film the four foreign episodes.

Dave picked Holly and I up at the airport, drove us back to our hotel in Congleton (a town about a half an hour south of Manchester), and introduced us to his fellow investigators from a group known as the Unknown Phenomena Investigation Association (UPIA).[13] This

---

myths make reference to this superstition. In the fairy tale *"Childe Rowland,"* for example, the protagonist and his sister are transported to Elfland after his sister runs widdershins around a church. There are also references to widdershins in Dorothy Sayers' novels *The Nine Tailors* and *Clouds of Witness*. See Rosemary Ellen Guiley, *The Encyclopedia of Witches and Witchcraft*, 2nd ed. (New York: Checkmark Books, 1999), 360; James MacKillop, Dictionary of Celtic Mythology (Oxford: Oxford University Press, 1998), 378-379; and M. M. Banks, "Widdershins: Irish Tuaithbheal, Tuathal," *Folklore*, Vol. 38, No. 1 (1927): 86 – 88. For "Childe Rowland," see Colin Bradshaw – Jones, comp., *World Folk Tales, Vol. 1* (Maesteg, Wales: World Folk Tales, 2006), 70 – 77.

[13] *Unknown Phenomena Investigation Association.* www.upia.co.uk.

somewhat motley but serious-minded crew included Steve Mera, an experienced investigator who would join Dave, Holly and I for all four episodes.

Thus began a week of all around strange happenings, the likes of which Holly and I had not quite run into before.

Our first stop was the White Hart Hotel in Uttoxeter, a location where a number of supposedly paranormal happenings had occurred, including the voice of a small child in the basement and a demon-haunted bedroom.[14] Dave was very skeptical – he thought that the hotel manager might be pulling a fast one in order to make a few bucks by billing the location for haunted tours. However, during our evening at the hotel a room that we had locked off and left a camera running in was found to have a substance that was subsequently confirmed to be blood spattered on a shower curtain. *No-one* had entered the room.

Then the manager took Holly and I down to the basement to conduct a "séance" in an attempt to contact the little girl that people had reported hearing. I thought the exercise was a bit daft so I excused myself shortly after we began, but Holly stuck it out. Nothing happened and after about half an hour she and the manager called it quits. Holly, however, had left her tape recorder running, and unbeknownst to any of us at the time it picked up what appeared to be the sound of a little girl crying out "no" just after Holly can be heard saying to the manager that it was time to head back upstairs.[15]

Our second location was another old inn, the Lion & Swan in Congleton, where we were also staying for the duration of our time in the area.[16] One of the stories about the Tudor-era location was that a painting stored in the basement was supposedly cursed – if anyone

---

[14] *The White Hart Hotel.* http://goo.gl/8iIqL

[15] The White Hart Hotel investigation can be seen in *Ghost Cases*, "The Case of the Demon-Haunted Inn," directed by Paul Kimball and Dale Stevens (Toronto: Breakthrough Entertainment, 2009). Television.

[16] *The Lion & Swan.* http://www.lionandswan.co.uk/.

touched it, someone close to that person would die. This story sounded impressive – and more than a bit dangerous – until I actually saw the painting, which was a cheap 60s knock-off of a half-clothed woman.

As Holly, Steve, and Paul Reeves (another member of the UPIA) investigated other areas of the inn, Dave and I set ourselves up in the basement with "Caroline" (the name we gave to the woman in the painting). Not taking things seriously, we mocked the story of the curse, and then I reached over, paused for dramatic effect, and grabbed the painting. After a moment I handed it over to Dave. We had a good laugh and then continued with filming our part of the investigation. Nothing happened in the basement and the entire evening passed uneventfully overall.[17]

When I wandered into the inn's dining room the next morning for breakfast, however, I was surprised to see that Reeves, who had been quite excited about coming with us to the next location, was not present. Dave and Steve, who both looked more than a bit shaken, explained to me that Paul's father had died suddenly the night before.

As Steve wandered off to tell Holly, Dave pulled me aside.

"Do you think…" he asked, and then his voice trailed off.

"No," I answered. "Absolutely not."

"Yeah," he said. "Pure coincidence."

"Right," I replied.

Despite our dismissal, neither of us seemed completely certain of ourselves as we joined the rest of the team in the dining room.

After we finished breakfast we made our way out into the English countryside to our third location near the small village of Shocklach close to the Welsh border. At the end of a lane which ran off a deserted country road we found St. Edith's, a small Norman church built in the 12th century, which makes it one of the oldest

---

[17] The Lion & Swan investigation can be seen in *Ghost Cases*, "The Case of the Cursed Painting," directed by Paul Kimball and Dale Stevens (Toronto: Breakthrough Entertainment, 2009). Television. Part 1 at: http://goo.gl/3G8e5; Part 2 at: http://goo.gl/mASvE.

ecclesiastical buildings in Cheshire.[18] Dave had been to the church dozens of times while Steve was visiting it for the first time.

As we walked around the grounds Dave recounted some of the strange things that he had experienced there over the years. He started with a story that involved a little girl who seemed to move through time by running around the church, which immediately caught my attention.

> A friend and I came to the site a few years ago. It was his first time, and he brought his young daughter with him. We wanted to talk about some things away from the prying ears of the child so we walked to the rear of the church. He lit a cigarette, took a drag of it, and asked her to go play. She ran to the opposite side of the church, and then as she went around one corner she automatically appeared around the corner closest to us, straightaway in an instant. I'm probably talking, for an eight year-old child to run that distance, about thirty seconds.

Dave followed up the "time slip" story with one about audio anomalies. He told us about how numerous visitors, including other members of the UPIA on a previous investigation, had heard the sound of horse's hooves on cobblestone and the neighing of the horses, despite the fact that there are no horses anywhere near the church and certainly no road that would sound like cobblestones. When Holly asked him what he thought might have caused the noises, he offered the following theory:

> There's a report from the 1800s of funeral processions coming to the church. At the time, obviously, it wasn't hearses but horse-drawn funeral carriages coming down the road.

---

[18] See "St. Edith's Church – History," *St. Mary's Tilston and St. Edith's Shocklach.* http://www.tilstonandshocklachchurch.co.uk/index.php/history.

After our walkthrough of the site I got the crew ready, set up the lights that we would need later in the evening, and then Holly, Dave, Steve and I began our investigation. As the sun began to set we split up and wandered through different areas of the large cemetery surrounding the church. Within a matter of minutes Steve saw Holly standing next to the church, where she looked out of sorts.

"Clear as anything," she told him when he went over to check on her, "I heard… I heard the horse's hooves."

"You heard the horse's hooves?" he asked.

"I heard the horse's hooves," she repeated. "I thought that was laughable because we had heard so much about them, but it was so clear, and so distinct, and so close."

She was laughing, but it was laughter to cover her nervousness. She looked over at Steve, who was examining the surroundings, and said, "It's very disconcerting to hear something that's not there." All that he could do was nod in agreement.

The sun tucked itself beyond the horizon shortly afterwards, at which point things proceeded to get even weirder. I had parked myself on a bench tucked up against the front of the church where I sat scanning the night sky. There was no-one else anywhere near me. Dale Stevens and the two-man camera crew were at the other end of the grounds filming an interview with Dave, and Holly and Steve were out by the car checking the monitors. And then I saw… well, here's what I had to say ten minutes later after I had excitedly called the crew over.

> So here's the crazy thing. I wasn't going to say anything, because I'm the skeptical member of the team, but I've been talking with Dale and he and I have seen the exact same thing at different times and in different places. Trained as a lawyer, as an historian, what I want is confirmation and now I have it. What Dale described, and what I've seen, I would describe it almost in a science fiction sense as if a door opened and a shape formed. It was totally black and surrounded by the night sky, which was slightly illuminated by the moon and a

82

town off in the distance. As soon as it was there it was gone, maybe two or three seconds afterwards. What makes it really weird is that it appeared exactly over the spot where I was standing two hours ago, filming a segment where I was discussing Holly's experience. The way my mind works, it was like a trans-dimensional door opening or something, full of blackness, as if the sky was totally blacked out.

Dale and I seeing the black void in the sky at different times and in different places set off a rapid-fire succession of anomalous events. First, the batteries in our sound-man's equipment completely ran out of juice despite the fact that he had just put brand new ones in the equipment twenty minutes before. Steve also experienced battery drains on his flashlight; he had to change them four times that night.

Then Steve reported seeing some unusual moving lights behind the church. As he explained it to me later:

I was actually situated in the back of the church, along with an infra-red camera, and I saw this light appear across a tomb. So I went around the corner of the church to look for somebody and I couldn't see anybody there, so when I actually brought it to your attention, trying to rationalize the experience, I thought that maybe somebody further down in the lower graveyard may have been flashing a light around and maybe somehow it had caught a reflection and strayed up to the top end of the church where I was.[19]

We accounted for everyone's whereabouts at the time, and established that none of us could have been responsible for the lights. Despite Steve's initial attempts to rationalize his experience in the same way that I had tried to rationalize the black void he remained genuinely puzzled.

"We couldn't replicate it, so I can only presume that it was

---

[19] "Dave Sadler and Steve Mera," *The Paracast*, hosted by Gene Steinberg and Paul Kimball (Making The Impossible, Inc., 2010). Radio. http://goo.gl/WTgVf.

something unusual," he concluded.[20]

It was at this point that I told Holly I had also heard the horse's hooves earlier in the evening in a different part of the cemetery. As with the black void in the sky I think I was going through my own process of trying to rationalize it, and when I realized that I couldn't come up with an explanation I decided to tell her.

"Are you serious?" she asked me with a mixture of anger, relief and curiosity. "Why didn't you tell me?"

I started to explain off-camera, in a sort of stream-of-consciousness way, when I suddenly stopped talking and looked directly at her.

"Did you hear *that*?" we asked each other, at almost the exact same time.

It was the horse's hooves again, and this time we both heard them for five or six seconds.

None of our cameras or audio recorders picked up anything anomalous that night. But those of us who were there all know that we saw and heard things that were genuinely out of the ordinary.

As Holly put it, "What happened to us that night at the church? I still don't know. But we all saw and heard things that we can't explain – it's almost as if the whole night, something was playing with us."[21]

I still haven't been able to come up with an explanation for the events that occurred that night at St. Edith's church, or the previous evenings at the White Hart and the Lion & Swan, but I can tell you one thing – once the weirdness started to happen in Shocklach I made sure that every time I walked around the church I went in a clockwise direction.

Just in case.

---

[20] Ibid.

[21] The St. Edith's Church investigation can be seen in *Ghost Cases*, "The Case of the Haunted Graveyard," directed by Paul Kimball and Dale Stevens (Toronto: Breakthrough Entertainment, 2009). Television. Available on-line at: http://goo.gl/m9xwl.

Sergeant Hutchings, I Presume?

In 1942 a young Royal Air Force sergeant named Tom Hutchings was stationed near St. Andrew's, New Brunswick, a small village near the border with Maine that looks like something straight out of a Stephen King novel. He left a dance one night with a pretty local girl named Bernice Connors who was found murdered the next day. Hutchings was convicted of the crime and hanged. He spent his final days in a small, dark, cold cell in the jail, within earshot of where his executioners constructed the gallows.[22]

By all accounts Hutchings was a model prisoner in his final days, passing the time quietly. He made his way to the gallows without a struggle and had nothing to say by way of a final statement.

Unfortunately for him, however, the gallows hadn't been built correctly. Instead of the quick death that he might have been expecting, it took Hutchings eighteen minutes to be pronounced dead. Ever since, people have reported strange occurrences in the jail, and in his cell in particular, which led to speculation by the locals that the gruesome nature of his death had somehow trapped Hutchings' soul in that spot, destined to haunt it for all eternity.

Given the circumstances it seemed to me that his old jail cell would be an obvious spot for an episode of *Ghost Cases*.

As a result, in February, 2009, Holly and I found ourselves in St. Andrew's, sitting in the cell at the jail trying to make contact with Hutchings. Just for good measure, and on the theory of "in for a penny, in for a pound," I came up with the bright idea of trying to antagonize the spirit of Hutchings by bringing along a noose that was on display at the jail as a "trigger" item.

For a laugh, as much to amuse Holly as anything else, I placed the noose around my neck as we were locked in the dark cell by the crew. Holly and I sat next to each other on the remains of Hutchings' old bunk, with an EMF meter to Holly's right, and out of my sight, as we

---

[22] "Murder of Bernice Cecilia Conners (1923 – 1942)," *Pennfield Ridge Air Station.* www.rootsweb.ancestry.com/~nbpennfi/penn8b1ConnorsMurder.htm.

waited to see what would happen.

After almost thirty minutes Holly and I hadn't experienced anything other than the winter cold and some pleasant conversation. It was at this point that I decided to turn off the low-level camera light we had set up in one corner of the cramped cell.

I took the noose off my neck and plunged us into almost total darkness, with only the barest, almost imperceptible hint of moonlight coming through the slit of a window in the wall of the cell.

Within minutes, I felt Holly shudder beside me.

"Oh, fuck…" she whispered.

Holly is about as level-headed as they come, and definitely doesn't frighten easily, so for her to utter a profanity out of the blue was an indication of just how shaken she was.

"That's weird," I answered. I turned to Holly and said, "I was sitting here and all of a sudden I felt this cold go around my throat, like colder than the cold, the freezing bitter cold that's in here anyway. I haven't felt that since I was in here, and it went right around my throat."

I thought Holly had felt it too and that's what she had caused her reaction, but she had actually experienced something completely different (which she thought *I* was reacting to). In her case she saw a black shape move in front of her, and felt a "presence." Then she had looked to her right, and noticed that the EMF meter had spiked from zero to a full-on reading of activity.

We were both pretty spooked but we decided to stick it out in the cell a bit longer to see if anything else would happen, although we were no longer quite courageous enough to do so in continued darkness, so I turned our camera light back on. Just a couple of minutes later, it happened again.

Holly looked down at her EMF meter and said, "It's up again… it's up again…it's up….and it's gone." As she had looked away from me to see the EMF meter she hadn't noticed what I had been doing, but the camera definitely picked it up.

I turned to her and said, "I can't see the EMF thing. There will be camera confirmation on that, that just before you said that, look where my head went, back down, I felt the same…" I couldn't finish the sentence, because I was so shaken – it had been the same sensation of deathly cold wrapping around my neck.

"Are you serious?" she asked.

"Yup," I replied, as I recreated the action of my head pushing down into my chest so that my neck would not be exposed, sort of like a turtle. I kept my neck there as I said, "I don't actually want to expose my neck at the moment."

Holly was genuinely concerned. "I don't think I've seen you like this before, Paul," she said.

"Yeah, well I have this thing about strangling and necks and throats and stuff," I replied. "Maybe in another life I was hanged. The noose was funny, because the noose was no threat, but this – who knows?"

At this point we called out to the camera crew that we wanted out of the cell. They obliged, and we made our way out of the cell block and back to the offices in the building as fast as we could. It wasn't any warmer there but it sure felt a lot safer.

As we recounted what had happened inside the cell, Elaine Brough, who works as a guide on tours of the jail, told us that what we had experienced was pretty much exactly what other people had reported happening to them when they went into the cell. She hadn't mentioned this to us before we went in because she wanted to see if we would have the same experience without knowing what to expect.

Holly and I laughed nervously.

"Mission accomplished," I said, as I gave a final glance back at the cell of Tom Hutchings.[23]

The Baby in the Basement

In March, 2009, the *Ghost Cases* crew drove down to the western

---

[23] The St. Andrew's jail investigation can be seen in *Ghost Cases*, "The Case of the Haunted Jail," directed by Paul Kimball and Dale Stevens (Toronto: Breakthrough Entertainment, 2009). Television. An excerpt is available at: http://goo.gl/278Z3.

end of Nova Scotia, to the small community of Quinan, about a half an hour's drive from the town of Yarmouth. We hung a right off the rural highway that runs through the center of the community and after a few miles we came to a small, isolated farmhouse that's been owned by a woman named Darlene for thirty-three years. Unexplained occurrences had been happening for decades, but when Darlene's daughter Shelley moved in with her in September, 2008, they became even more intense and frequent. The strangeness manifested itself throughout the house and surrounding property, but three areas in particular seemed to be the most active.

The first was the basement, where Shelley and Darlene described being pushed by an unseen force as they walked down the stairs and experiencing intense cold once they were in the room itself. The second area was Darlene's spare room on the second floor. She claimed that she would hear footsteps on the stairs leading to the room and that when she entered it she felt a malevolent presence. Finally there was the field behind the house. Both Darlene and Shelley described the sensation of someone watching them when they were out there, and Shelley told us that, "Whatever it is, I won't come out here at night. I won't stay out here. I don't want to be out here. It's not nice."

No matter how many technological bells and whistles you employ when you're investigating an allegedly haunted location, from digital video recorders to thermal cameras, in the end I really believe that it all comes down to whether or not you have a personal experience because that's what we're all really looking for. Sometimes, however, that personal experience turns out to be more than you bargained for, and at Darlene's farm that's exactly what happened to me.

On the surface the investigation began in the same way that it always did – Holly and I arrived with the camera crew, met with the owner of the location, got the back-story on what was supposedly going on, and then set up our gear and prepared to film. But at this particular location something was a bit different from the beginning, and both Holly and I sensed it.

For one thing, the owners were genuinely afraid, which was something we hadn't really encountered on previous investigations. As Darlene described the basement to us she was visibly shaking.

"The basement is pure scary," she said. "You get the feeling when you walk into my cellar that somebody is there to grab you. Not only the feeling of coldness but just pure fear. Something's down there and it's gonna get me." When you see that kind of fear in someone else's eyes it can definitely have an effect on you as well.

There was definitely a real sense of isolation at the farm. The house is literally at the end of the road, out in the middle of nowhere, like something out of one of those horror films where people take a wrong turn and head down the one road to the one house that no-one should ever visit.

It's one thing to investigate a building like a hotel, where there are other people just a minute or two away, but it's something altogether different to spend a night in a supposedly haunted house miles away from anyone who might be able to help if you get in trouble. That plays on the mind, particularly when the owners of the property describe whatever it is that's going on as "evil."

As Shelley said, "I get the feeling that something wants to get me, to harm me and mine and I don't know how to protect me or others from it."

Presumably whatever wanted to do them harm would be just as eager to have a go at Holly and I.

Given that the basement was a key nexus of reported paranormal activity, I decided that I would spend time down there alone while Holly and psychic Kelly Muise were upstairs in the kitchen conducting a sort of séance to try and contact whatever spirits were in the house.

While I've never ruled out the possibility that some psychic phenomena might be real, I had never been a proponent of using a psychic in one of our investigations. However, Dale prevailed on me to make an exception at a couple of locations because he thought it would make for good television, so in order to be a team player I acquiesced.[24] The results wound up challenging all of my preconceived notions about both psychics and ghosts.

As I sat on the stairs in the frigid cold basement with the door tightly wedged shut behind me, I could hear the proceedings upstairs in the kitchen through the floorboards. No matter what I thought of using psychics, I was struck by the fact that at least it was a shared experience between Kelly and Holly (and our camera crew), while I was stuck in the basement alone. That definitely ratcheted up the creepy factor. I couldn't help but think that if there *was* a malevolent presence in the house it would probably go for me first, as opposed to the group upstairs, because that's what I figured I would do if I was a ghost with bad intentions. As a result I felt like a lone wildebeest, cut off from the herd by a group of hungry lions.

About thirty minutes after I began my watch in the basement, surrounded by dead spiders and cobwebs, I heard Kelly and Holly start to talk about a "murdered baby" in the basement. They were both encouraging the spirit in the house to make contact with me and show me where the baby was buried. This was a development I wasn't exactly in favor of – indeed, the digital video camera which I had set up to record whatever happened caught me talking to myself, saying repeatedly, "I don't want to meet the baby," and "don't come show me where the baby is."

And then *it* happened. Just after another exhortation from Kelly and Holly for the ghost to pop by and pay me a visit, the door opened behind me.

As a skeptic my immediate reaction was that it had been the wind, but I could hear when the wind was blowing – as it had been earlier (without moving the door, I should add) – and it hadn't been blowing this time. It was as still as the grave outside.

Adding to the mystery was the fact that the door didn't open easily as it wasn't a perfect fit for the frame and got caught along the ground

---

[24] I should note that I was never comfortable using the psychic in the show, so in the four episodes in which she eventually appeared I managed to make sure that Holly was always her on-screen partner.

as it opened. Not the kind of door, in other words, that was likely to be pushed open by a simple breeze.

I immediately went outside to investigate. My first thought was that one of our crewmembers was playing a practical joke on me, but there was nobody out there. No wind, no people, just the still of the night, and Darlene's dog, a rather disinterested German shepherd that was lying next to its house at least thirty feet away from the basement.

That was it for me. I was genuinely scared and had no intention of going back down into the basement. Despite the fact that it was well below freezing outside, I didn't want to interrupt the filming upstairs (scared or not, I'm a consummate professional when it comes to filmmaking), so I waited near the back door for another forty minutes until Kelly and Holly had finished their séance before I went inside. I told everyone what had happened, and I'm not sure they believed me, at least until we went downstairs, retrieved the camera, and played the tape. Sure enough, there was the door opening behind me at the same time as Kelly and Holly had been exhorting the spirit to go to me in the basement. We were all a bit shaken, and I could see Darlene and Shelley nodding their heads as if to say, "We told you so."

Stranger still is the fact that when we reviewed the data from the audio recorder that I had with me in the basement, we heard what sounded like a baby crying at the same time as the séance was going on and the door opened!

The next day we all headed out into the freezing cold towards the back field, where the house had originally stood, to conduct what Kelly called a "spiritual cleansing."

Normally I would have been in a joking mood because I'm very dubious about things like this, but given what had happened the night before I kept my mouth shut and simply observed the proceedings.

Perhaps it was by chance, but as Kelly was spreading what she described as "holy water" over the area some of it landed on me. I still wasn't sure if I had encountered an evil spirit in the basement the night before, but I have to admit it crossed my mind that maybe a little holy water wasn't a bad thing, just to be on the safe side.[25]

It would be easy to chalk this all up to coincidence. After all, that's the simplest explanation, and as a result probably the most comfortable one for people to wrap their minds around. The problem with simple explanations, however, is that they're not always the *best* explanations.

With the farm in Quinan and the baby in the basement, as well as the other cases I've discussed here, from the graveyard in Shocklach to the jail cell in St. Andrew's, and all points in between, I can't help but think that I encountered something extraordinary that challenges everything I thought I knew. But that's what great art does – it upsets our pre-conceived notions of both the world around us and ourselves, and forces us to look at everything in a different light.

Which is *exactly* why I seek out these experiences in the first place.

Little did I realize as we finished filming the last episode of *Ghost Cases* in England in May of 2009, that things were soon to get even stranger. What had been an impressionistic experience in confronting my fears up until that point was about to turn the corner into surrealistic abstraction.

---

[25] The Quinan farmhouse investigation can be seen in *Ghost Cases*, "The Case of the Baby in the Basement," directed by Paul Kimball and Dale Stevens (Toronto: Breakthrough Entertainment, 2009). Television. Available on-line at: http://goo.gl/1z4QA.

Holly Stevens and I in California, November 2008.

Yours truly at the Quinan farmhouse, 2009.

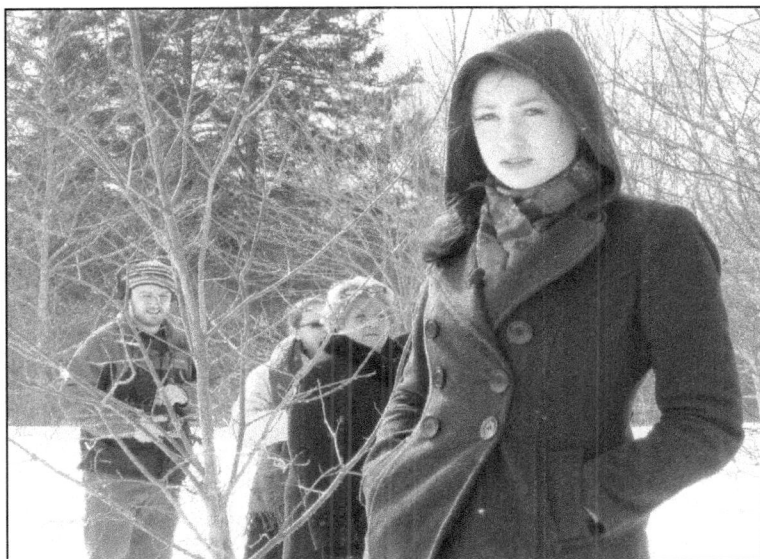

Holly in the field at Quinan. Behind her is psychic Kelly Muise.

The old Charlotte County jail, St. Andrew's, NB, 2009. The cell where Tom Hutchings spent his final days is at the end of the hall on the left.

St. Edith's church, Shocklach, 2009. I was sitting on the bench underneath the window when I saw the black void in the sky.

The White Hart Hotel, Uttoxeter, 2009.

The Lion & Swan, Congleton, 2009.

Yours truly directing *Ghost Cases*, with cameraman Aaron Gowlett, at Shocklach, 2009.

Holly Stevens, yours truly, and Dave Sadler, near Congleton, 2009.

Chapter Four

The Shadows of Český Krumlov

Find beauty not only in the thing itself but in the pattern of the shadows, the light and dark which that thing provides.[1]
– Junichiro Tanizaki

One of the fringe benefits of shooting a television series on the road is that you can always build a vacation into the process, which is exactly what Holly and I did in late May and early June of 2009 once we had finished filming the four episodes of *Ghost Cases* in the United Kingdom. After all, we were already there, which meant that we didn't have to pay for the airfare from Canada to Europe, so we took advantage of the situation. In many ways it had been a stressful eight months since we had begun production on *Ghost Cases*, much of it a carry-over from the *Eternal Kiss* shoot, so Holly and I were definitely looking forward to some time to decompress.

After we bid adieu to our good friends Dave Sadler and Steve Mera in Manchester we made our way south via London to the small village of Gillingham in Dorset, where we spent a couple of days with my old friend and colleague Will Fraser, who had hosted *The Classical Now* a few years back.[2] With Will as our gracious host and tour guide we visited the ancient sites of Stonehenge, Woodhenge, and Avebury, as well as Salisbury, where we all climbed to the top of the Cathedral

---

[1] Junichiro Tanizaki, *In Praise of Shadows*, trans. Thomas J. Harper and Edward G. Seidensticker (Tokyo: Charles E. Tuttle, 1988), 30.

[2] Will Fraser, "Bio," *Fugue State Films*. www.fuguestatefilms.co.uk/bios.html.

(and I also got to see the grave of former British Prime Minister Edward Heath, which I'm pretty sure I found more interesting than either Will or Holly did). I remember at one point, as we wandered about the Cathedral, that Holly made a joke about how we were still spending most of our time with dead people. We both had a good laugh.

After our stay in Gillingham Holly and I headed back to London where we saw five musicals in four nights (for those keeping score, the musicals were: *Wicked, Phantom of the Opera, The Lion King, Les Miserables*, and, on the spur of the moment, the final performance of *Joseph and His Amazing Technicolour Dreamcoat* at the Apollo Theatre, which blew the lid off the joint). We toured Buckingham Palace, Trafalgar Square, Baker Street, the British Museum, The Tower of London, and the Imperial War Museum, and also attended the lecture at the RSA by Michio Kaku that I discussed earlier.

From London it was off to Scotland, where I had studied in 1987 and 1988 whilst an undergraduate student. Back then I spent almost all of my time in the eastern part of the country at the University of Dundee and the surrounding region, so this time I decided to see what the western side had to offer. We flew into Glasgow, rented a car, and made our way up through Loch Lomond and Crianlarich to the Highlands, where we walked amongst the Three Sisters and Glen Coe, and then caught a ferry from Oban to the mystical Isle of Mull.

Three days on Mull based in Tobermory provided for some great whisky, a couple of castles, some ancient standing stones in Lochbuie and castle ruins at Aros, hill-walking galore, and a day on the Isle of Iona, which is one of those places that everyone should try to visit before they shuffle off this mortal coil.[3] I also made sure to visit every cemetery and burial ground that I could find because I've always been drawn to the history that one can discover there, and the connection you can make with the past. Luckily I had a great traveling companion who felt the same way, or was at least willing to indulge

---

[3] See *Isle of Iona Visitor's Guide*. www.isle-of-iona.net/.

what many other people might consider my ghoulish interest in the final resting places of the dearly departed.

Our trip back from Mull took us through Inverary, which was beautiful. We then spent two days and nights in Glasgow where we wandered the streets, poked about more old churches and cemeteries, drank some great beer, and unfortunately went to see *Terminator: Salvation*, a truly dire film. Still, that evening had a memorable moment. Before we went into our theatre in the multi-level cinema complex we popped by the bar for a beer. As we sat there chatting I noticed that there was a small black spot on my leg (I was wearing walking shorts). I took a closer look and discovered a heretofore unnoticed tick that I had picked up whilst hill-walking the day before. It was the second one on the trip; before we left Mull, the very nice lady who ran the bed & breakfast in which we stayed had removed another one that was… well, let me just say that it was too close for comfort for any man!

Having observed our host's technique for safe tick removal in Mull Holly said she would help me out. I figured it could wait until we got back to the hotel after the movie so we went in and found a couple of good seats. After five minutes of sitting in the theatre, however, I couldn't stop thinking about the bloodsucking little devil, so I asked Holly if we could get rid of it before the film started. We went out to the lobby where we quickly realized that we would have to use the child changing room given that she couldn't go into the male washroom and I couldn't go into the female washroom (a lesson I once learned the hard way after a night of hard drinking in San Juan, Puerto Rico).

We waited until the coast was clear and then snuck into the room and locked the door. I can only imagine what the people who were walking by must have thought when they heard the following rather animated conversation coming from inside.

"Do you see it?"

"It's so small"

"I can see it from *here*, and you're kneeling right next to it – how do you *not* see it?"

"Okay, there it is. I've got it… I'll just give it a twist."

"Be careful!!

"Does that hurt?"

"Ow!!!"

When we eventually exited the changing room there was a small crowd gathered in the hallway, evenly split between those patrons who thought we were horrible people engaged in some sort of carnal escapade and those who thought we were really cool people engaged in some sort of carnal escapade. I admit that I did nothing to disabuse them of their notions as we went back into the theatre. For those who were unfortunate enough to join us for *Terminator: Salvation*, at least we had provided some entertainment.

As our time in the United Kingdom drew to a close we flew down to London and stayed overnight at Heathrow before our flight early the next morning for the final destination on our grand adventure, the Czech Republic. Neither Holly nor I had ever been on the continent of Europe before, so we had debated where we would spend our last week on vacation. Romania was a contender because we both thought hiking through the mountains around Cluj and checking out the land of Dracula would be great fun. Greece was also a place we considered, for more leisure-oriented reasons, as was Italy, but we eventually settled on Prague, which came highly recommended by a number of our friends back home who had been there.

I'm sure Romania, Italy and Greece would have been wonderful (and I plan to visit all three someday), but we made a good call with the Czech Republic, where we had an amazing time. We spent the first five days in Prague, walking around the city for hours each day. Part of the charm and romance of Prague is getting lost on a walkabout, and we certainly managed to "misplace" our bearings on more than one occasion. One local I chatted up while asking for directions congratulated me on being so far from where I thought I was and then told me that if you didn't get lost in Prague you hadn't really been there, which I thought was pretty zen.

We popped into myriad shops and cafes and restaurants, and toured the magnificent Prague castle, where the Kings of Bohemia, the Holy Roman Emperors, and the presidents of Czechoslovakia and the Czech Republic all held "court". We also attended enthralling performances at the State Opera (Prokofiev's ballet *Cinderella*) and the National Theatre (Dvorak's *Rusalka*, which I mentioned earlier), and I managed to catch a little black light theatre while Holly was doing some shopping for her mother.

While we were based in Prague, we also wanted to see some of the rest of the Czech Republic, so we took two day-trips outside of the city. The first sojourn was to Terezin because I wanted to visit the former concentration camp. It was a very moving place, and both Holly and I came away with a different perspective on our world after spending the day there. We also continued our habit of poking about in places where we weren't supposed to go when we opened a door and walked into a series of dark tunnels which ran underneath the fortress. Eventually we made our way out to what had once been the grounds on which prisoners were executed by firing squad. Only when we looked behind us did we notice the sign indicating that the tunnels were off limits, presumably for safety reasons.[4]

For the second day trip we hopped a train to Kutná Hora, where we immediately made our way to the famous Sedlec ossuary, which contains the skeletons of between 40,000 and 70,000 people (a wide margin of error, but at some point when you're piling up skeletons I imagine you lose count). It was definitely a creepy place, with skulls and bones placed everywhere. As we walked out I once again thought to myself that for two people who were trying to decompress from several months of ghost investigating we were certainly spending a lot of our time in places where you would expect a few ghosts might be lingering.

We had some wonderful goulash for lunch and then took a tour of

---

[4] For more information on Terezin, see Ludmila Chládková and Miroslava Langhamerová, *Terezin and Litoměřice: Places of Suffering and Braveness*, trans. Petr Kurfürst (Prague: Jitka Kejrova, 2003).

an old mine that was so dark and confined I was sure I was going to get stuck underground (having had a double portion of the goulash probably didn't help as I tried to navigate the tightest spots). I don't like dark, confined spaces, so it was definitely a "confront your fears" moment. Finally, we visited Saint Barbara's Church, one of the most famous Gothic churches in central Europe and a UNESCO world heritage site. Somewhere along the way Holly managed to get us lost. As with our rambles in Prague, however, her error in Kutná Hora led to something we wouldn't have otherwise seen – a beautiful field of tulips on the other side of town, far from the regular walking routes taken by tourists.[5]

Holly and I decided to spend the final two days of our trip in Český Krumlov, a small city in the South Bohemian Region of the Czech Republic best known for the fine architecture and art of its historic old town and the State Castle of Český Krumlov, second only to the castle at Prague itself in size and splendor.[6]

I love riding trains so I convinced Holly that we should take the four hour train ride to Český Krumlov instead of what would have been a somewhat shorter trip by bus. It was a bad decision. The train was old, which was great, but it was musty, which aggravated my hay fever. Opening the window made it even worse as it was the beginning of June and pollen was everywhere. I spent four hours with watery eyes, a runny nose, and more than one roll of toilet paper next to me by way of tissue paper. To her credit, Holly never once said, "I told you so." Of course, she spent most of the time sleeping, which is probably what I would have done if I had been her sitting across from a de facto Snuffleupagus.

I had booked us a double room at the Pension Ve Vezi, an inn shaped like a small wizard's tower about a ten minute walk from the

---

[5] For more information on Kutna Hora, see "Kutna Hora Regional Information Service." http://www.kh.cz/?l=en.

[6] "State Castle of Český Krumlov," *mesto Český Krumlov*. http://goo.gl/KrnH1.

castle and another five minutes from the old town.[7] Unfortunately, when we got there things went from bad to worse. The new owner of the inn, who had taken over after I made the reservation two months earlier, had placed us in a room with only one bed, and all of the other rooms were occupied. He apologized profusely for the error and assured us that he would switch us to the room with two beds that we had reserved the next evening, but this still left us in a bit of a quandary.

We could have moved to another inn, but it was late in the afternoon, we had just arrived in town, I was still suffering from hay fever, and we really liked the Pension Ve Vezi. After all, who wouldn't want to spend a couple of nights in a wizard's castle? We told him that the arrangements would be fine, and he reimbursed the cost of the difference in rooms and gave me a break on the total price by way of apology, which was a nice gesture that I appreciated.

Holly and I made our way up the winding staircase to our room. It was quite cozy, and would have been great for a couple, but we were *not* a couple, so someone was going to have to sleep on the hard floor. Holly offered to do so, but I am nothing if not a gentleman, so I insisted that she take the bed. With a smile on my face I assured her that as a *Star Trek* fan I fancied the idea of sleeping on a good, solid floor, just like a Klingon warrior would. I'm pretty sure that she didn't believe me, which might have had something to do with the way I kept looking down at the floor and wincing, but I was insistent and she eventually agreed.

As it had been hours since we had eaten we decided to take a walk through our section of town, past the castle, across the bridge that spans the Vltava River, and into the old town square, which was ringed with hotels and restaurants. Despite our grumbling stomachs we couldn't help but meander because there was so much to see. There were cubby-holes, narrow lanes, and winding side-streets that made Prague look like wide-open Los Angeles by comparison, and

---

[7] "Pension Ve Vezi," *Krumlov Hotels*. www.krumlovhotels.cz/ve-vezi_e.php.

we were drawn down more than a couple of alleyways by the sight of an interesting looking shop or building.

As we walked along, I turned to Holly and said, "Now *this* is a place where we should have come to look for ghosts."

She nodded, and then replied, "Maybe we'll see some while we're here."

I just shook my head, smiled and said, "I certainly hope not. I'm retired from ghost hunting." Before she could answer, I began to imitate Dave Sadler in a most exaggerated manner, and she broke out into laughter.

We eventually made our way to Lazebnicky bridge where we got a great look at the castle, which was perched precariously on top of a rocky outcropping like something out of a fairy tale. The bridge itself is fairly short, with statues of various religious figures on the sides, including a very impressive one of Jesus framed with the castle as a backdrop.

We found a nice restaurant in the town square and plunked ourselves down on the patio. A very friendly waitress came by and immediately made us feel at home. She recommended the goulash, which was fine by me. Holly and I each ordered what turned out to be really good Czech beer and settled in for a couple of hours of great food, people-watching, and conversation, during which we conducted a spirited recap of our zany adventures.

One of the subjects that came up was the question of whether she and I might be carrying any "negative energy" (for lack of a better term) from our ghost investigating. Perhaps even more ominous, we considered the possibility that by opening the door as we did time and again to "contact," maybe we had allowed something unwanted to come in and attach itself to us, something about which we had been warned by more than a few people we had met over the preceding months.

Holly had discussed this subject at our blog a few months previously when she wrote:

There's always a risk you'll get burned when playing with

fire, and the idea of a spiritual realm is definitely a metaphorical fire, if not a literal one. Paul and I have joked from the beginning about having to travel to Peru at the end of the series to be "cleansed," but perhaps there is more truth there then I initially realized. I've never doubted the significance the unknown can play on a person's physical, emotional, and spiritual well-being, and with that knowledge, I have entered the world of "ghost hunting" with my eyes wide open, so to speak. However, being aware of the unknown doesn't make one any better equipped to deal with it. With the number of completed episodes mounting, and unexplained experiences increasing, I've recently redirected my research back to this idea of "aura cleansing." Just in case.[8]

As the conversation continued I casually mentioned to Holly that I knew a priest back in Canada who was an expert on exorcisms, and that perhaps he could save us the price of a trip to Peru, or some of the other destinations we had considered for some sort of shamanistic retreat. She thought it would be a good idea, although she still wanted to test the transformative powers of ayahuasca.

"If it helps break down the walls we erect and allows our own minds to battle the demons we all have within us," she said to me, "then paranormal or no, I'm all for it." I agreed, even as I wondered whether some cheap Czech absinthe might do the trick just as well. Still, a trip is a trip, and all doors open to the same pathway of elevated consciousness, which is something I either heard Jim Morrison say once or read on the wall of a dingy bathroom in an even dingier bar in northern Alberta. But I digress...

As I chatted with Holly I thought about relating an anecdote from *Three Men Seeking Monsters*, by my good friend Nick Redfern. In chapter nine, the Bard of Birmingham recounted a meeting he had

---

[8] Holly Stevens, "Ayahuasca - Paranormal Investigator's Ghost Buster?" *Paul Kimball & Holly Stevens*, 10 February 2009. http://goo.gl/OgZlE.

with an alleged witch named Sarah Graymalkin. "You don't realize that while you are looking for these things," she told him, "believing in them and telling others about them who also become emotionally charged believers, they are manipulating you and your followers as a food source."[9] In the end, I decided to keep that tidbit of information to myself, particularly as our own "food sources" has just arrived.

Speaking of Nick, he and I had discussed the question of being "stalked" over margaritas in San Juan, Puerto Rico, in 2005. We were there investigating the legend of the chupacabra for my documentary *Fields of Fear*, and had just spent the day interviewing a number of people in rural areas who claimed to have seen the alleged vampire-like creature. One in particular stood out for me because he was convinced that the chupacabra was actually a demon from hell sent to torment him. I remember asking Nick as we sat on the hotel patio next to the Caribbean Sea whether he ever got worried about the forces that we might be dealing with.

Nick thought about it for a moment, then smiled and shook his head.

"Bring 'em on," he said defiantly.

I wasn't quite sure whether he meant the forces of evil, or another drink, as he had just finished his margarita.[10]

The interesting thing about the chupacabra, as I look back on our adventures in Puerto Rico, is that it easily fits within the "performance art" interpretation of the paranormal. I think the vast majority of sightings of the alleged creature have simple prosaic explanations, but there were some cases recounted to us that were far more bizarre than just a few chickens being attacked in a cage by what was surely a wild dog. For example, a man named Pucho and his family told us about seeing a strange, shadow-like creature that

---

[9] Nick Redfern, *Three Men Seeking Monsters: Six Weeks in Pursuit of Werewolves, Lake Monsters, Giant Cats, Ghostly Devil Dogs, and Ape-Men* (New York: Paraview Pocket Books, 2004), 113.

[10] Nick recounts our adventures in Puerto Rico in *Memoirs of a Monster Hunter: A Five Year Journey in Search of the Unknown* (Franklin Lakes, NJ: New Page Books, 2007), 207 – 231.

resembled a huge bird. His account was not all that dissimilar to what I experienced at St. Edith's church in Shocklach, and the link is made even more interesting by the fact that Pucho's sighting occurred next to a small rural church (The Church of the Three Kings). Pucho ascribed it to the chupacabra because that was the meme his culture had created as a sort of "one size fits all" explanation for weird happenings, whereas with my interest in science fiction my first thought had been some sort of Star Trek-like trans-dimensional void. But what we both described was more or less the same thing.[11]

With this on my mind Holly and I finished our dinner and then meandered through the streets of Český Krumlov for about an hour, during which time I noticed a toy store that intrigued me because all of the toys were made locally and by hand. I filed a mental note to stop by the next day and see if there was anything there that would make a good gift for friends or family back home, particularly my niece and three nephews.

By the time Holly and I made it back to the wizard's castle it was about 10:30 pm. We chatted for a little while as I tested the floor, which I discovered was every bit as hard as it looked. Holly gave me all but one of her blankets, which provided at least a bit of separation and cushion from the floor, although it was a far cry from the comfortable beds that I had gotten used to on the trip. Around 11:20 pm we turned out the lights, intent on getting an early start on our sight-seeing the following day.

Within a couple of minutes I realized two things. First, the less time I spent lying on the floor the better, because I'm definitely more Ferengi than Klingon. Second, my hay fever was still acting up, which added insult to injury (I think it was probably the dust on the floor). After a few minutes of trying to get comfortable, and not sniffle every five seconds, I gave up. I turned on one of the lights and told Holly that I needed to go for a walk to clear my sinuses. She asked me if I wanted her to come along but I said that I would be

---

[11] Ibid., 226.

okay. After all, how much trouble could I get in on a weeknight in a beautiful and peaceful town like Český Krumlov?

I wandered out into the night and stood in the small garden next to the inn. I let the cool breeze waft over me for a few moments which definitely helped clear up the sinuses. The area was completely deserted as I started to stroll down Pivovarská. I had my MP3 player with me and I was listening to some Radiohead as I passed several buildings on my left and trees on my right. After a few minutes I reached Latrán, the street which cut through the center of the town. I hung a left and headed towards Lazebnicky bridge across the Vltava River and the town square on the other side.

Despite not being very late, at least by my reckoning, there wasn't another person out and about, which I guess wasn't surprising given the fact that it was a Monday evening in early June, before the real height of tourist season hits the town. A few lines from an old song I had written years before but never recorded suddenly came to me as I took in my surroundings:

> The streets are quiet in this old town
> the bars are closed and the girls have gone home,
> The streetlights shine, from end to end,
> and I wonder about the message that they send…

As I ambled along, stopping to look into shop windows or down darkened alleyways, I played a little game that I often engage in whilst on a walkabout where I sort of experiment with time travel, at least as a concept. I look at a place further along on my route and take a moment to imagine myself standing there. I continue on until I reach that point, and then look back at where I was and remember myself from that time. Sometimes it almost seems like I can see myself in the future, and then in the past.

By the time I reached the Lazebnicky bridge I had worked myself into a routine of picking the two points and then walking between them, almost like I was attaching pitons one by one as I climbed a mountain. I imagined myself at the end of the bridge, attached my mental piton, and then started across. When I got to the other side I leaned against the railing, looked back across the Vltava to where I had been standing just moments before, and pondered where and how we all fit into the grand scheme of things.

The lyrics from another old song of mine intruded on my thoughts again:

Sly scissors separate the threads,
look to see if the time, it does fit,
as it slips through the needle.
Stare softly at this sudden leap of faith,
catch the wind and fly away,
no destination, just a landing.[12]

My gaze wandered down to the river. I picked up two small stones and tossed one into the water below. As I watched the ripples move out from the point of impact I thought to myself that in many ways the interaction between the stone and the water served as a metaphor for our lives. I threw the other stone into the river at a spot a couple of feet to the right of the first one and watched as the ripples from its impact eventually met up with the ripples from the first stone. Then I continued on to the town square, having indulged myself in enough philosophy 101 for one evening.

When I got there everything was closed and there still wasn't another person to be seen. I sat down on one of the benches scattered about the square and enjoyed the solitude, the location, and the crisp night air, which was invigorating. I spent ten minutes looking around at the various buildings and imagining the people who might have lived in them over the centuries. From time to time I glanced up at the sky to see if I could pick out a satellite or a stray meteor.

Then, as I was looking down the street towards Lazebnicky bridge, I realized that I was not completely alone after all. I turned my head

---

[12] Paul Kimball, "Horseshoe Heart," Perf. Tall Poppies, *Tall Poppies - All Points in Between* (2012). http://youtu.be/6WCFf3TC-eo.

and saw what appeared to be a man walking slowly across the square at about roughly the same pace I had been moving at earlier. He was perhaps twenty meters in front of me. Although the square was lit to a degree, the level of illumination was insufficient for me to get a good bead on him, particularly as he wasn't looking in my direction. I didn't really think much more about it as he reached the center of the square, and I turned my head in a different direction. A second or two later, however, I felt obliged to have another look at the man – when you're in a foreign country, alone in a strange town at night (no matter how peaceful it might seem), it pays to be careful. When I looked back to where the man had been walking, however, he was gone.

I surveyed the entire square but there was no sign of him. What made it strange to me was that he had been walking at a slow and deliberate pace, and he was nowhere near the edges of the square or any of the various hotel doors when I looked away for just a second or two. I hadn't heard anything that would have indicated he had suddenly run to a door and opened and closed it, even if he could have made it in time.

Maybe, I thought to myself, I had looked back towards the bridge for five or six seconds instead of just one or two, but I immediately ruled that out. I remember shaking my head and saying aloud to myself, "I know the difference between a quick glance over my shoulder, and a shift that lasts several seconds longer." Eventually I just shrugged and figured that it was time to head back to the inn for some shuteye because I was obviously starting to see things.

I stood up and gave the area a final, curious look. I thought back to Dave Sadler's story of the young girl and the "time slip" at St. Edith's church in Shocklach, and wondered whether something similar had just happened to me. Then I laughed, and asked myself what I would have said if someone had told me, just a year before, that I would be standing in the town square of Český Krumlov talking to myself about shadowy figures and time slips. I know that I probably would have dismissed the idea as ludicrous.

As I made my way down the street towards Lazebnicky bridge I decided to stop and have a look in the toy store I had noticed earlier in the day. I leaned up close to the window and surveyed the display. There were wooden cars with little mice driving them which I thought were cute and would make a perfect tongue-in-cheek gift for Linda, who has a pronounced phobia about mice.[13] As I moved closer to see if I could make out a price tag I once again saw something out of the corner of my eye. I lifted my gaze up from the wooden mouse, and over my shoulder I could clearly see the reflection of a shadowy figure in the shop window.

I immediately clenched both fists, stepped to my left, and turned around – not because I expected to meet someone from the Men in Black, or a demon, or anything like that, but because I thought I might be about to get mugged. Somewhere in my mind, as I turned to face whoever was standing behind me, I was kicking myself for having forgotten my standard operating procedure for walkabouts. I've spent years living in Halifax and taking long walks every night, and the one thing that I've learned is that the best way to stay safe is to stay focused on your surroundings. The five months I spent as an RCMP special constable in the wilds of northern Cape Breton in the summer of 1990 also taught me that you react defensively to an unknown situation first and worry about whether or not someone gets offended afterwards.

In one sense I need not have worried, because as I stared out into the street I found that I was still alone. But while the lack of a mugger was a relief, the situation I now faced created an entirely different set of concerns for me. I had definitely seen the reflection of someone in the window, only to turn around and find that there was no-one there who could have made that image.

For the first time I felt a very palpable sense of unease, mixed with a tinge of fear. The disappearing man in the town square had been one thing because he hadn't been right next to me, so it wasn't really a

---

[13] Her version of Hell would probably involve spending eternity in a room full of mice and ouija boards.

threatening situation. But a figure appearing in a window over my shoulder when there was no-one there was something else altogether.

As I left the toy store I quickened my pace a bit. I reached the bridge, and started to walk across. At about the half-way point, next to the statue of Jesus, I heard footsteps behind me. The sound was as clear as the horse's hooves had been in the cemetery at St. Edith's a month before. I came to a stop, and could feel my jaw locking, which is something I do when I'm nervous. Trying to play it as cool as I could under the circumstances, I turned around slowly.

The footsteps stopped. There was no-one else on the bridge.

And then I felt it.

A force on my shoulder, like a hand. Not hard like a blow being struck, but the kind of feeling I imagine you would get when a police officer walks up behind you and places a firm hand on your arm.

I pivoted at the same time as I took a step forward, away from whatever was behind me. I'm not a fighter, but I learned a couple things during my stint in the RCMP.

One again there was no-one there.

I didn't run, although somewhere deep in my soul I wanted to take off as fast as Dandelion, a particularly speedy rabbit character from my favorite novel, *Watership Down*.[14] But after eight months of myriad strange experiences my curiosity had come to equal my fear, at least to the point where I maintained a semblance of dignity as I got off the bridge.

With a brisk pace, and more than a few nervous glances over my shoulder, I walked up Latrán, hung a right on Pivovarská, and made my way back to our inn. By the time I got there I had calmed down a bit, although when I pulled the key for the front door out of my pocket I dropped it on the ground. My hand wasn't shaking, but it wasn't perfectly steady either.

When I got back to the room Holly was asleep. Normally I would have washed up and changed before going to bed, but I just closed the

---

[14] Richard Adams, *Watership Down* (London: Rex Collings, 1972).

door and lay down on the floor. I didn't care about how uncomfortable it was – I was just happy to be back inside with someone else in the room.

I thought about waking Holly and telling her about what had happened but I decided against it. I wish I could say that I let her sleep because it had been a long day, and as a gentleman I figured at least one of us deserved a good night's rest. The real reason, however, was that I didn't want to tell anyone about what I was already starting to think of as the "shadow man." As was the case at St. Edith's church in Shocklach, my natural inclination is to keep an experience like this to myself lest I seem like a fool to others.

I pulled out my MP3 player, turned it on, and put the headphones into my ears. I cycled through the music until I found Radiohead. I scrolled down through the songs and finally came to the one I wanted: "Where I End and You Begin". I hit play and leaned back to listen as Thom Yorke sang:

There's a gap in between
There's a gap where we meet
Where I end and you begin...
X will mark the place
Like the parting of the waves
Like a house falling in the sea
In the sea
I will eat you alive
There will be no more lies...[15]

As I lay there on the floor I noticed a narrow ray of light coming into the room from the small window. After a moment, I held my hands out in front of me and started to form shadow figures on the wall, as I thought back to a song lyric of my own from 1993:

A troubled shroud it calls out loud

---

[15] Radiohead, "Where You End and I Begin," Perf. Radiohead, *Hail to the Thief* (London: Parlophone, 2003).

> amidst the music and the singing,
> it is ignored
> by the guilty ones,
> condescend to turn around
> deduce the nature of this conversation,
> try to remember
> what you once were...[16]

We're all guilty of something, I thought, as I closed my eyes and tried to get some sleep. Maybe what we see on the outside is a reflection of what we have on the inside. In its own way, that notion was as disturbing to me as the possibility that I had actually encountered some sort of supernatural being.[17]

When we got up the next morning I had a sore back to go along with more questions than answers about my strange experience the night before, but I didn't mention either to Holly. It was the second last full day of our trip and there was much to see and do in Český Krumlov, so I didn't want to provide any unnecessary distractions.

After a quick breakfast at the inn we walked up to the castle, which is even more impressive once you get inside. We toured an art exhibit located in underground catacombs and climbed to the top of the castle tower, which tested my fear of heights just as much as the ascent to the top of Salisbury Cathedral had a couple of weeks earlier. The other highlight was a guided tour through a section of the interior of the castle where we got to see the antique furniture, paintings, and other artifacts from centuries past.

After the guided tour we wandered around the grounds for another hour or so and then made our way back to Latrán, where we

---

[16] Paul Kimball, "Guillotine," Perf. Tall Poppies, *Tall Poppies - All Points in Between* (2012). http://youtu.be/6WCFf3TC-eo.

[17] For a good look at the Men in Black phenomenon, which bears some resemblance to my experience in Český Krumlov, see Nick Redfern, *The Real Men in Black: Evidence, Famous Cases, and True Stories of These Mysterious Men and Their Connection to UFO Phenomena* (Pompton Plains, NJ: New Page Books, 2011).

proceeded towards Lazebnicky bridge. As I walked across the bridge I thought about my experience the previous night for a brief moment, but I was having such a good time with Holly that I didn't dwell on it. The toy store was open, and we both went inside and browsed for what was probably close to half an hour. I bought some small toys for my nephews and niece, and the wooden car with the mouse behind the wheel for Linda.

As we left the store Holly and I decided to split up. On our trip we had spent almost all of our time together (particularly in the evenings – my walkabout the night before had been my first such solo foray at night during the entire trip), but from time to time we had wanted to see different things so we would head in separate directions for an hour or so. In this case, Holly was on the hunt for some gifts for her mother, while I wanted to check out a book store I had seen earlier. We agreed to meet in an hour at the restaurant where we had eaten the night before, and headed off in our separate directions.

Almost as soon as I turned a corner down the side-street that led to the bookstore I saw something drawn on the wall of a building that made me stop in my tracks. Outlined in black was a giant eyeball with three lines that ran straight down from the center like legs, and two hooked lines that jutted out from the sides like arms, or tendrils. What I found most interesting, however, was the center of the eye, where someone had drawn what appeared to be the shape of a shadowy figure.

I thought it might be my over-active imagination so I took a closer look. As far as I was concerned, the center of the eye was definitely not the kind of thing that you would expect someone to place there if he just wanted to indicate the pupil. I took a photograph of the strange graffiti, and then made my way to the bookstore.

Holly and I met up as planned in the town square where we had another lovely dinner, after which we decided to find a bar and sample more of the local beer. As we walked back towards Lazebnicky bridge Holly noticed a sign hanging over a door. She skipped over and stood next to it in the way a *Price is Right* model stands next to a car in the final showcase showdown. A big smile crossed her face.

"C'mon," she pleaded. "This is perfect!"

I walked over and stared up at the sign. It looked like a piece of abstract art, and had just two words on it: Horor Bar.

Sometimes you just have to shrug your shoulders, and go with the flow. This was definitely one of those times.

We walked in and immediately descended a staircase to the cellar of the building where the bar was located. All you really need to know about the Horor Bar is that it looks like a dungeon out of a 1930s horror film, and it has a coffin for a table where patrons can sit and enjoy a beverage. In other words, it comes by its name honestly. I almost expected to see Bela Lugosi hunched over behind the bar, hissing "yes, master" as Basil Rathbone ordered a nefarious-looking drink.

The joint was sparsely populated when we walked in. While neither Baron Wolf von Frankenstein nor Ygor were present, my disappointment was immediately ameliorated when I saw the waitress leaning against the bar. Wearing a Lana-Turner-at-the-soda-fountain face, she was possessed of the kind of physical beauty that carves a permanent little corner in your memory as soon as you behold it, like a first kiss, or a magic hour sunset.

Standing across from her was an older man whom I pegged for either a regular or the owner. There were a couple of locals huddled together at one of the tables near the bar talking to each other in low whispers, and a group of three young Americans tucked into a corner table by the door who were much more animated.

The waitress came over and asked us what we wanted (at least I assume that's what she said, as she was speaking Czech). As soon as we replied in English, she smiled and said, "Ahh... more Americans," a statement which drew a few glances from the group of boisterous gringos in the corner.

"Nope," I replied good-naturedly. "Canadians."

Her smile disappeared in an instant, and she became very

apologetic.

"I'm so sorry," she said in English that, whilst broken, was a lot better than my Czech. "Many apologies."

I smiled and shook my head. I had seen this more than once in my travels. A few Canadians with low self-esteem get offended when they're mistaken for our southern cousins, and I suspected that she must have run across a couple of these obnoxiously defensive types at some point.

"No worries," I said in a cheerful tone. "Tonight we're all Czechs!"

She smiled again, broader this time, and asked us what we wanted to drink. I told her to bring us whatever she felt was their best local beer on tap, a gesture of confidence in her knowledge of the local scene that she clearly appreciated.

In a couple of minutes she returned with two very fulsome brews. As this was our last real night of the trip Holly and I were planning on making it a late evening, so I inquired when the bar closed.

"When the last customer leaves," answered the waitress with a friendly laugh.

"My kind of bar," I said, as she smiled and then moved off to check on the Americans.

Holly and I raised a glass to toast eight months of adventures together.

"It's been a wild ride," she said enthusiastically, and then took an approving sip of her beer.

"No kidding," I replied, as I tasted what turned out to be an excellent lager. I gave the waitress a wave of thanks and a nod to indicate that she had definitely made a good choice.

"Flirt," joked Holly.

"Absolutely," I countered.

"She's pretty," Holly commented, looking over at the bar.

I took another sip of beer and played it cool.

"Hadn't noticed."

"Well, if you want some alone time," Holly said, tongue planted firmly in her cheek "just let me know, and I'll take an extended bathroom break."

"Deal," I replied with a grin, but knowing full well that I wouldn't go beyond casual flirting.

As the evening wore on Holly and I descended into a state of happy-go-lucky inebriation as we conducted something of a retrospective of our time working on *Ghost Cases*.

"What would you say was the scariest experience you had," I asked at one point.

Her face tightened as she took in a deep breath.

"Churchill Mansion," she said quietly, and then exhaled, as if it had been a Herculean effort just to say the words, much less conjure the memory. There was no need for her to say anything else. I remembered *that* investigation very well.

Churchill Mansion is an old home in Yarmouth, Nova Scotia, that had been converted to an inn. It has a well-known reputation for being haunted, and we weren't the first television show that had filmed an episode of a paranormal-themed show there.[18]

The stories at the Mansion revolved around the original owner, Aaron Churchill, a famous seafarer and entrepreneur who was said to haunt the place with lascivious intentions towards any female guests, and his niece Lottie, who eventually suffered a mental breakdown and wound up in an asylum in Boston.[19]

On our first night there, Holly, the crew and I sat down with the owner, a gnome-like old-timer named Bob, who related to us all of the various stories surrounding the mansion.

"I don't really want to go on the record with this," Bob told us cagily, although I've always found that as soon as someone says something like that it means that they really *do* want to go on the

[18] *Rescue Mediums*, "Churchill Mansion," (Toronto: Lamport-Sheppard Entertainment, 2006). Television.

[19] Aaron Churchill was an ancestor of mine. Yet another small coincidence, or synchronicity. For a recounting of Churchill's exploits as a sailor see Michael Rafuse, "Aaron Flint Churchill," *Yarmouth and the Age of Sailing Ships*. http://goo.gl/51oNv.

record, so I always keep the camera rolling unless they specifically request that I turn it off (at which point I always oblige). In Bob's case, the persuasion came from a bottle of whiskey that he kept close by. After a swig or two, he continued. "One of the stories is that Aaron and Lottie had..." He paused, and swallowed hard. "A relationship." Churchill died in 1920, but Bob explained that in a small town like Yarmouth there were some stories that you just didn't discuss publicly, at least not with outsiders. I knew exactly what he was talking about because when I was stationed with the RCMP in northern Cape Breton, perhaps the most isolated region of Nova Scotia, we often had trouble getting people to talk about various crimes. They preferred to keep it "in house," and then let us pick up the pieces after they had served their own rough brand of local justice.[20]

"This is hard to do without getting into trouble," he said. "We feel that there was a special connection between Aaron and Lottie. She was brought up as his daughter, and maybe she even was his own daughter. Lottie I think thought a lot of Aaron in ways other than as her uncle. There was certainly a connection between the two of them."

Bob intimated that Lottie may have murdered a servant at the mansion, which he hinted was covered up. He then quickly moved on to other areas of the overall story, and we didn't press him further as we all shared in the free-flowing whiskey.

After a while Holly left the living room. I assumed she was going to the bathroom. A few minutes later I was feeling peckish, so I stood up and asked Bob if there was any food in the kitchen. He told me that I was welcome to rifle through the large and well-stocked fridge and take whatever I wanted.

As I turned the corner from the living room and headed down the hallway towards the kitchen, I saw Holly leaning against the wall. She had clearly been crying.

---

[20] This theme is a staple of Maritime fiction. See, for example, Vernon Oickle, *One Crow Sorrow* (Chester, NS: Bryler Publications, 2010).

"Hey there," I said without my usual sarcastic edge. "What's wrong?"

"Can I have a hug?" she answered with a quavering voice.

I'm not much of a touchy-feely type, but a friend in need trumps my naturally reserved nature, so I embraced her, and we just stood there for twenty seconds or so. Then she lifted her head, said "thanks," and we stepped away from each other. I didn't press for an explanation as she wiped the tears from her eyes. I just waited for her to get comfortable and tell me on her own time what was going on if she wanted to.

"He's here," she eventually said, her voice steadier, but still a bit uneven.

"Who is?" I asked.

"Aaron," she answered. "I can feel him."

"Is there anything I can do?"

She looked around her and shook her head. I could tell that she was getting her bearings again.

"I think I'll be fine," she said, and went back to the living room while I continued on to the kitchen. As I piled various types of deli meat onto a couple of slices of whole wheat bread I found myself hoping that Holly was all right, and wishing I could have done something more to help.

When we finally called it a night I went to my room at one end of the upstairs hall and Holly went to hers at the other end. Mine had originally been Aaron Churchill's room, and she wanted no part of that, so she wound up in Lottie's old room. The crew had positioned small digital cameras to monitor us as we slept, because allegedly paranormal activity had been reported in each room.

I managed to fall asleep in short order, only to be woken up about an hour later by Holly knocking on my door. In the episode, she described the circumstances as follows:

> I tried to fall asleep, but couldn't shake the feeling that there
> was someone else in the room with me. I was so spooked that
> I went down the hall and asked Paul if he would come up to

Lottie's room and keep me company while I tried to fall asleep.

I had never seen Holly quite so shaken before. She was almost on the verge of tears again, but there was something else at work, something that ran even deeper. I went back to her room (where we left the door slightly open, lest anyone get the wrong idea if they wandered by), and sat down on the second bed. We chatted for about half an hour and then she finally fell asleep. I nodded off shortly thereafter. All the while, the DVR camera kept recording, which gave us a record of what became a very strange and disturbing evening.

The camera recorded Holly tossing and turning in what she later described as one of the most restless nights she had ever experienced. She wasn't the only one who found the room uncomfortable, however; I was lying on top of the blankets and was woken up by an intense chill, after which I crawled under the covers for the rest of the night.

As Holly and I were trying to get a decent night's sleep in Lottie's room, the digital camera we had stationed in the hallway recorded the door to a crew member's room suddenly and violently opening and closing. There was no draft whatsoever that could have accounted for the savage force with which the door was moved.

Meanwhile, back in Lottie's room Holly was still having trouble sleeping.

"It was made even more disturbing," she later explained, "by the fact that I also couldn't roll over. It was as if there was a person in the bed next to me."

We both got a surprise when we reviewed the camera footage once we got home, because we discovered what appeared to be an unnatural indentation beside Holly in the bed as she slept, as if someone else was indeed lying there.[21]

---

[21] The Churchill mansion investigation can be seen in *Ghost Cases*, "The Case of the Haunted Mansion," directed by Paul Kimball and Dale Stevens (Toronto: Breakthrough Entertainment, 2009). Television.

I asked her about it all again as we enjoyed another beer at the Horor Bar.

"It was almost as if I could sense the presence," she recalled, as if it had just happened. "Remember the footage where I suddenly woke up shortly afterwards?"

I nodded.

"I could definitely feel something or someone in that room with me," she said.

I thought back to the strange shadowy figures I had run into the previous evening and the feeling of the hand on my shoulder as I stood on Lazebnicky bridge. I wanted to say something to Holly – to let her know that I understood exactly how she felt. But we all cast our own shadows, and we have to walk with them by ourselves, so I just nodded, took a sip from my beer, and changed the subject.

The answer most often given by people who believe there is a paranormal aspect to ghostly phenomena is that ghosts are the spirits of the dead who simply refuse to accept the nature of their situation, and so they remain trapped in a netherworld between this life and the next. To the disbeliever, on the other hand, ghostly phenomena are nothing more than a trick of light here, a coincidence there, and any one of a number of other prosaic factors everywhere else.

In the vast majority of cases I have no doubt that the disbeliever is right. Indeed, there were times whilst filming *Ghost Cases* where we uncovered clear evidence of a hoax, or a story that had simply spun out of control over the years. But when confronted with experiences like those that Holly and I had in multiple locations in 2008 and 2009, I'm forced to conclude that there's probably something more at work – something that reminds us of who we really are deep down inside.

I don't believe, however, that these unexplained experiences represent the spirits of the dead haunting us, at least not in the sense of "my dead grandma is sitting on my bed with me." There may indeed be something waiting for us beyond the grey wall that is death, a subject I will address in greater detail a bit later, but in my opinion it doesn't involve our being trapped in this realm of existence to wander the same hallway or haunt the same bedroom for all eternity. I can't imagine that the afterlife, should it exist, is so banal.

As far as I'm concerned we either die and that's the end, which is an outcome that has a certain poetry to it, or there is something much more interesting waiting for us. Even purgatory would involve something more than aimlessly puttering around your old house as a disembodied "spirit," unless of course we choose to posit that "God the almighty" has no more imagination than a reality TV producer.

Of course, there are those who think that ghostly phenomena are brought about by demons. But what is a demon, exactly?[22] Once you cut through the clutter and ideological detritus of thousands of years of religious dogma, myths and legends, a "demon" represents nothing more than an advanced non-human intelligence. Over the years it has suited organized religion, as a tool of social control for political authority (regardless of how that authority has been constituted), to present us with a Manichean view of good versus evil, and angels versus demons. God is on "our" side, which is of course the "good" side; the "demons" are on the other side. But that has been an interpretation, and as with all interpretations one must consider the circumstances and the motivations of the people who created it. As I look at it, it's an interpretation based solely on a desire, a need even, to keep people divided and shackled by fear, and to keep them from thinking for themselves.[23]

As far as ghostly phenomena goes, I think that as with UFOs one can reasonably speculate that at least some unexplained cases of the phenomena we ascribe to "ghosts" are brought about by an advanced

[22] For an interesting take on how some people within the UFO research community view "demons," see Nick Redfern, *Final Events*, 109 – 121, 201 – 205. Nick also discusses how demons might be related to the Men in Black stories in *Men in Black*, 221-233.

[23] One of my favorite Bob Dylan songs, "With God on Our Side," addresses this idea of "God" taking sides throughout our various wars. Bob Dylan, "With God on Our Side," Perf. Bob Dylan, *The Times They Are a-Changin'* (Columbia, 1964). www.bobdylan.com/songs/with-god-on-our-side.

non-human intelligence, interacting with us under a different guise but for the same reasons.

I'm a big fan of Cirque de Soleil. I've been to Las Vegas several times over the years and always go to see a Cirque show when I'm there. While they are all wonderful entertainment experiences, my favorite remains the original, *Mystère*. As the name implies, it's a mysterious and magical journey that touches upon all aspects of the human condition. I've seen it four times, and each time I've taken something different away from it.

The second time I saw *Mystère* I was with the actress Kris McBride, a friend who had narrated my film *Best Evidence*. We managed to get seats in the front row of the upper section of the theatre. There was a wall about four feet high between us and the walkway which separated the two sections. During the show there's so much going on that your attention wanders all over the place and you can sometimes lose track of the various performers who engage at different times directly with the audience. Anyway, as Kris and I were sitting there, watching a spectacular act on stage (I think it was the aerial high bar, but I can't recall), some performers had made their way out into the crowd. I remember them as "bird people" because to me their costumes had a distinctly avian character. You could see them crawling on the walls and slinking along the walkways and floors. Given what was happening on stage, neither Kris nor I paid them any real attention. To us they were like shadows, lurking at the corner of our awareness.

As the act on stage ended and the audience erupted into well-deserved applause, one of these "bird people" suddenly popped up from behind the wall right in front of us so that the performer's face was no more than seven or eight inches from Kris' face. The performer's appearance definitely startled me and the people sitting around us, but our response was nothing compared to Kris' reaction, as she grabbed my arm with a vice-like grip and let out a shriek of terror that could be heard throughout the theatre. I suspect that the Cirque performer had never encountered a reaction quite that visceral because he stumbled away from the wall in surprise and fell back onto the walkway.

He quickly regained his composure, gave me a concerned look as if to say, "hey, make sure your friend doesn't have a heart attack," and then he beat a hasty retreat to the opening at the end of the walkway which led backstage.

Meanwhile, Kris still had the vice grip on my arm, even as she was being consoled by a very nice elderly couple sitting next to her. For at least twenty seconds she was breathing rapidly and deeply, even as she kept muttering over and over again: "What the hell was that?"

She finally calmed down, although she remained on a bit of a manic high for the rest of the evening. Everyone in our vicinity had a good laugh about it all, including Kris after she had regained her composure.

Over drinks after the show she and I both agreed that while it had been scary for her at the time it was something that she was going to remember in a good way for the rest of her life, just as the memory of the house of horrors in Prince Edward Island has remained with me for decades.

"I felt so alive," she said as she took another sip of her drink. "It was real."[24]

That's exactly how I felt in the cemetery at Shocklach, the jail cell in St. Andrew's, and on the streets of Český Krumlov. I'm willing to entertain the possibility that those experiences could well have been a form of performance art by an advanced non-human intelligence

---

[24] Kris is one of the most creative people I've ever met. She had the lead role in the first run of *Doing* Time in November, 2007, and did a wonderful job, but like Veronica Reynolds she was replaced in one of the lead roles for *Eternal Kiss* because the distributor didn't think she had enough experience. I handled it all very poorly and she hasn't spoken to me since, which I greatly regret (I also don't blame her). A mutual friend told me that she moved to western Canada a couple of years ago and directed me to Kris' writing blog. I wasn't surprised in the least to see that her work was very good. Wherever her journey takes her, I wish her nothing but success and happiness. See Kris McBride, *The Best New Blog on the Internet*. http://bestnewblog.blogspot.ca/.

designed to appeal to one of our most primal emotions: fear. In doing so, perhaps that intelligence is giving us greater insight into the full range of human experience and thereby helping us to a more complete understanding of ourselves.

Then again, like the filmmakers who created hits such as *The Blair Witch Project*, *Paranormal Activity*, and *The Exorcist*, or even the Cirque performer Kris and I encountered, they may just want to entertain us (and themselves), and see how far we're willing to go in the face of the unknown.

H. L. Mencken believed that the one permanent emotion of what he called the inferior man is fear – fear of the unknown, the complex, and the inexplicable.

"What he wants above everything else is safety," Mencken wrote. "His instincts will incline him towards a society so organized that it will protect him against all hazards, and not only against perils to his hide but also against assaults upon his mind – against the need to grapple with unaccustomed problems, to weigh ideas, to think things out for himself, to scrutinize the platitudes upon which his everyday thinking is based."[25]

It's a point of view with which I have always agreed, and something I wrote about in "All Afraid," one of my first songs as a young musician.

> What are you so afraid of,
> What has brought you to this state?
> Where are your natural emotions?
> You're such a sad, sad thing...[26]

An advanced non-human intelligence would understand that reality is far more complex than we can imagine. Many things may remain

---

[25] H. L. Mencken, *Prejudices: Second Series*, (London: J. Cape, 1921), 76 - 77. Available on-line at: http://goo.gl/Ks4XP.

[26] Paul Kimball, "All Afraid," Perf. Tall Poppies, *Tall Poppies - All Points in Between* (2012). http://youtu.be/6WCFf3TC-eo.

inexplicable even to them. But they would also understand that safety isn't an option if one is to progress. Fortune, after all, favors the bold. But we have been taught to fear the unknown, to the point that we live in a world where fear seems to be the guiding principle. We have become the "inferior man" of whom Mencken wrote.

Perhaps an advanced non-human intelligence has built a "haunted house" and opened the doors to all of us, to see if we can understand our own fears, confront them, and overcome them. If this is the case, then there's only one question that we really need to answer.

Do we have the courage to enter, or will we let our shadows of our fear continue to haunt us?

The castle at Český Krumlov, 2009.

Town square in Český Krumlov during the day, 2009.

Holly enjoying a local beer at dinner; behind her is the town square.

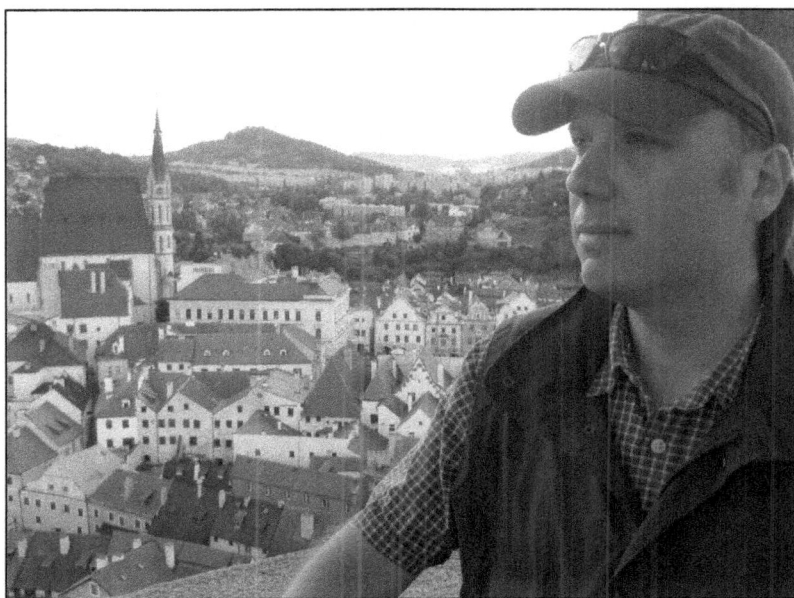

Yours truly in the castle tower, overlooking Český Krumlov.

Český Krumlov central square at night. I was sitting on the bench in the foreground when I saw the shadowy figure for the first time.

One of the narrow streets in Český Krumlov at night.

The window of the toy store where I saw the shadowy figure.

The strange drawing I saw on a wall near where I had an encounter with the shadowy figure.

The statue of Jesus on Lazebnicky bridge.

Chapter Five

A Hazy Shade of Winter

Any great work of art... revives and readapts time and space, and the measure of its success is the extent to which it makes you an inhabitant of that world – the extent to which it invites you in and lets you breathe its strange, special air. [1]
– Leonard Bernstein

Alternate history is a popular genre of fiction which consists of stories set in worlds where events have diverged from what actually happened. A good example can be seen with the Robert Harris novel *Fatherland*, in which the author created an alternate history of the Second World War.

In Harris' version of events the Allied landings on D-Day failed, and by 1964, the year in which the novel is set, Hitler is still in power, locked in a stalemate with the Soviet Union and a cold war with the United States. Dwight Eisenhower retired in disgrace, while Winston Churchill died in exile in Canada and King Edward VIII sits on the throne of the United Kingdom as a Nazi puppet. The plot centers around Hitler's attempt to stop a plucky young American reporter and a German police major from discovering the reality of the Holocaust, which has been successfully covered up. The last thing that the aging Führer wants is for the truth to be revealed on the eve of his summit

---

[1] Leonard Bernstein, "What Makes Opera Grand?" *Vogue*, December 1958, 120 - 121.

134

with President Joseph P. Kennedy.[2]

But as much fun as it may be to read, or even to create, it's all still fiction... right?

Well, maybe not. Some of our brightest scientists now tell us that time travel may indeed be possible, although given the amount of energy it would take it's far beyond our capabilities. This creates all sorts of possibilities when one examines various aspects of what we call the "paranormal". As the late Carl Sagan, the great popular voice of science in the latter half of the Twentieth century, once stated, "There's the possibility that [time travelers are] here and we do see them, but we call them something else – UFOs or ghosts or hobgoblins or fairies or something like that."[3]

Time travel could account for any number of the weird aspects of UFO sightings, for example, or even other paranormal events such as supposed "ghost" encounters. In particular, time travel may provide an answer to the big question: if there is an advanced non-human intelligence interacting with us why doesn't it do so more directly? The simple answer may well be that they aren't able to do anything more than observe, whether through limitations inherent in time travel or as the result of some sort of temporal "prime directive".[4]

But what if things are even more complex than that? What if time travelers *have* been interacting with us? Would we even know about it?

For example, what if future historians, as part of a research project, are endeavoring to create multiple time streams in order to see how

---

[2] Robert Harris, *Fatherland* (London: Random House, 1992).

[3] Carl Sagan, "Carl Sagan Ponders Time Travel," *NOVA*, 10 December 1999. www.pbs.org/wgbh/nova/time/sagan.html.

[4] In the fictional universe of the television series *Star Trek* the Prime Directive was "Starfleet's General Order #1," and as such was the most prominent guiding principle of the space-faring United Federation of Planets. The Prime Directive dictated that there could be no interference with the internal development of alien civilizations.

things would have turned out if "A" had happened instead of "B"? They certainly wouldn't want to run the risk of altering their own time stream – indeed, that probably isn't even an option given the "grandfather paradox," which holds that if you traveled back in time and killed your grandfather then you would never have been born and therefore could never have traveled back in time to kill him. Instead, they would endeavor to create a new time stream that continued on separately from the moment they made a change in the past.[5]

The branching universe hypothesis holds that there are an infinite number of universes, all-together known as the multiverse. If a person travels back in time and changes something, he would create a *new* reality divorced from his own at that point in time onwards. In one world D-Day succeeds and things play out as they have for us, while in another you could wind up with Harris' version of reality as set out in *Fatherland*. As Sagan explained:

> It's still somewhat of a heretical ideal to suggest that every interference with an event in the past leads to a fork, a branch in causality. You have two equally valid universes: one, the one that we all know and love, and the other, which is brought about by the act of time travel. I know the idea of the universe having to work out a self-consistent causality is

---

[5] Carl Sagan on the 'grandfather paradox': "The grandfather paradox is a very simple, science-fiction-based apparent inconsistency at the very heart of the idea of time travel into the past. It's very simply that you travel into the past and murder your own grandfather before he sires your mother or your father, and where does that then leave you? Do you instantly pop out of existence because you were never made? Or are you in a new causality scheme in which, since you are there you are there, and the events in the future leading to your adult life are now very different? The heart of the paradox is the apparent existence of you, the murderer of your own grandfather, when the very act of you murdering your own grandfather eliminates the possibility of you ever coming into existence. Among the claimed solutions are that you can't murder your grandfather. You shoot him, but at the critical moment he bends over to tie his shoelace, or the gun jams, or somehow nature contrives to prevent the act that interrupts the causality scheme leading to your own existence." Sagan, "Carl Sagan Ponders Time Travel."

appealing to a great many physicists, but I don't find the argument for it so compelling. I think inconsistencies might very well be consistent with the universe.[6]

All of which leads one to consider the following question: are we living in one of those realities?[7]

For example, I can picture a future graduate history student working on the following thesis: if an obscure German politician named Adolf Hitler had survived the 1923 beer hall putsch he would have eventually become ruler of Germany and initiated a great war that changed the world. Of course this presupposes that in the future historian's "original" timeline Hitler was killed in 1923, perhaps by a stray bullet when his men were fired upon by the authorities in the streets of Munich. To test his thesis this student pops into the university's "time machine," hits the dial for November 9, 1923, and changes the past when he gets there. The result is that he gets to watch the Holocaust and the Second World War play out in a new reality, which becomes *our* reality, and which my parents and grandparents had to live through.

Imagine the ethical dilemma involved with going back into the past to create this new timeline where Hitler would come to power, or alternatively one wherein he continued in power for almost another year if you wanted to change events in a world where he originally died when Claus von Stauffenberg set of his bomb in the Wolf's Lair in July, 1944.

In the latter case millions more would die. Even worse, imagine a new future where the Nazis somehow managed to snatch victory from the jaws of defeat in 1945, or prolonged the war through the use of new weapons. Would an ethical species allow such experimenting and

---

[6] Ibid.

[7] Sagan stated that, "If we could travel into the past, it's mind-boggling what would be possible. For one thing, history would become an experimental science, which it certainly isn't today. The possible insights into our own past and nature and origins would be dazzling." Ibid.

the creation of a new timeline that might lead to a world with real people who would suffer horribly simply so they could conduct some historical research?[8]

Watching the development of our own timeline, I have little doubt that *we* would do it, so I have no reason to doubt that others would. Given that conclusion, we can only wonder whether someone else, "somewhen" else, has done just that, and here we are today, the result of their ongoing experiment.

Philosopher Nick Bostrom points out other reasons why an advanced civilization might engage in such activity. Once we fix the world and remove all the things that we don't want then we'll have to find "something more inspiring," as Bostrom put it, or something more challenging, as I would phrase it.[9] While Bostrom doesn't go as far into the future as I have in my speculation, to a world where time travel is possible, the principle which he outlines is applicable.

Indeed, with the rise of interactive video games where the player can make more and more decisions and therefore find more and more possible narrative outcomes, we're already seeing people in ever growing numbers in technologically advanced societies playing around with the idea of changing worlds.

I remember playing a *Star Wars* universe X-Box game a few years ago set in the Old Republic. The first time through, which took about a week, the character I played wound up as a Jedi because the choices that I made led him in that direction. Then I played the campaign a second time, made the exact opposite choices, and wound up as a Sith.

The interesting thing is that when I played the game the first time, I

---

[8] Sagan addressed at least part of the ethical dilemma posed by time travel when asked whether he would take advantage of it if it were possible. "I have mixed feelings," he stated. "The explorer and experimentalist in me would very much like it to be possible. But the idea that going into the past could wipe me out so that I would have never lived is somewhat disquieting." Ibid.

[9] Nick Bostrom, "Humanity's biggest problems," *TED Talks*, July 2005. www.ted.com/talks/lang/en/nick_bostrom_on_our_biggest_problems.html.

had formed a sort of "bond" with some of the non-player characters who became my allies. In the second time through I wound up killing most of these "people." In short, I changed their world.

What struck me the most was that I actually felt regret when I went to the dark side, because I was betraying "people" that I had come to like, even though they were just fictional characters in a video game. But I did it anyway because I wanted to see what the outcome would be.[10]

Someday in the future maybe that's exactly what people are doing. Perhaps they're changing the world all the time, and creating all sorts of new worlds, just like we do in video games today. And while the pop histories tend to go for the big picture, with so-called world historical figures, like Hitler, and Lincoln, and Caesar, maybe our future selves are more like those historians who concentrate on social history, where you and I are just as interesting and important in our own ways.

All of this should make one think about the cherished notion of free will. Maybe things that happen to us, both big and small, really do happen for a reason, and we're all just Non-player characters, to borrow a term from the fantasy role-playing game Dungeons & Dragons, in a real-life game of "change the world." Whereas in Dungeons and Dragons you can create and play an 8th level bard, or a 5th level mage, perhaps in the future they can play "lawyer Paul," or "police officer Paul," or "historian Paul," or any of the other paths I could have taken.[11]

Which leads me to wonder whether someone is "playing me" right now.

---

[10] *Star Wars: Knights of the Old Republic*, directed by Casey Hudson (Edmonton: Bioware, 2003). Video game.

[11] I happily admit to being a long-time Dungeons & Dragons player. Once, in my early twenties, while serving as a Dungeon Master at a local tournament, I stood up in a crowded room and yelled, "Damn it, I need more monsters!" – much to the chagrin of the guy who had designed the campaign, and the applause of everyone else.

Maybe they're playing you, too.

All of which takes me back to an evening in February, 2010. I was lying on the Halifax Commons, having fallen on some ice that I hadn't seen in the dark. I was angry as hell because I had spent the whole evening arguing with my friend Ben Stevens about nothing important (he eventually walked out on me, and even then I didn't really blame him – I was more angry at myself than I was at him), and even angrier because I had landed hard and could already feel the pain shooting up my chest despite the anesthetizing effect of the half dozen beers I had consumed.

As I lay there staring up at the stars peeking in and out from beneath the cloud cover, a thought hit me as hard as the ground had.

I should be dead.

Flash back to another cold winter's night, this time in late December, 1985, just after Christmas and just before New Year's. I was out driving around Dartmouth, Nova Scotia, with my oldest pal, Colin White. I was older than my years – for example, when I had showed up that fall to register for my first year at Acadia University, I wore a suit and tie. The senior student who checked me into my residence, who introduced himself to me as "Dude," thought I was having a laugh until my Mom told him that I was serious. I had never had a drink and I had never kissed a girl. In the case of the former, I was still underage, my dad was a judge, and I didn't want to do anything that would embarrass him; in the case of the latter, it just hadn't been a priority. I was a Reach for the Top star, a straight-A high honors student, and a member of my province's National Debating Championship team. I had "better" things to do than party with the teenage hoi polloi.

I seemed like the "Perfect Kid," as much any kid can be "perfect" in the eyes of a parent. But the appearance of maturity and responsibility belied a profound inner recklessness, born of arrogance. I chafed at the boundaries that I felt the mediocrity of my peers had placed on me, and like many kids before me I felt I was indestructible. I hardly ever cracked a book in high school, not because I was lazy but because it all came so naturally to me. My rebellion wasn't flashy, writ in symbolic gestures that showed nothing more than a desire to conform to another system. Any idiot can get their ear pierced, after all. My rebellion was inward and personal, in ways that no-one ever saw.

For example, when you're on the negative side of a debate all you really have to do is understand the opponents' position (i.e. their "plan"), and then prepare to argue against it. Pretty simple, and deadly dull.

Thus, while everyone else was dancing and chatting each other up at the social events at the 1985 High School National Debating Championships in Montreal, I was sitting at a table writing counter-plans on napkins.

What's a "counter-plan," you ask? Well, in short, when the team on the negative side of a proposition put forward a counter-plan they didn't just argue against the affirmative side's plan – they proposed a plan of their own. In doing so, they also took the burden of proof. It was definitely the harder thing to do because it required more preparation.

My partners thought I was nuts, and it probably cost me a few ranking points at the end of the day, but it was worth it all just to see the other side squirm when they suddenly saw their entire plan become moot, and they had to wing it. People would ask me why I liked counter-plans, and I never really told them the true reason: I did it because it was the only way that I could stay interested, because it was something different, and within the context of a national debating championship it was something very risky. Most of all, however, I did it because I could.

Not all of my rebellion was quite as "academic" as constructing debating counter-plans. It often went a lot further than that, in more dangerous ways. But no matter what I did I had always emerged unscathed. As I said, I thought I was indestructible, and I was definitely arrogant.

So there I was on that cold and clear night in late December, 1985, in my Dad's Audi 5000, feeling like the King of the World. I gunned it past the speed limit, headed for an intersection, took the turn far too fast, hit a patch of black ice, and suddenly it was as if time had stopped. It didn't, of course, at least not in the real world, but for me, in that moment, it was like an out-of-body experience. I remember laughing and thinking two things – "cool," and "I can beat this."

And then we went over the hill, and I wasn't laughing anymore. We were sideways and completely out of control, and I remember seeing the tree coming at my side of the car. At that moment, I distinctly recall the realization hitting me like a ton of bricks: I wasn't going to beat this, and it was going to be a really worthless way to die. And then I just closed my eyes and waited for the end.

When the car hit the tree my head jerked forward violently as a large branch smashed through the driver's side window and pushed itself past where my head had been just a second before.

Flash forward to twenty-five years later, lying on the Commons, inebriated, in pain, angry for no good reason... and then it hit me, just as it had hit me many other times since that crash in 1985.

I should be dead.

Somewhere, if there really are alternate universes, I *am* dead. Somewhere, that tree caught my temple as it crashed through the window.

But not in *this reality*.

Ever since that crash I've been in a fitful and slow, but very real, retreat from the arrogance of my youth. I'm still reckless, and I can still be selfish and arrogant, but less so than I once was. I'm not sure I'm a better man now than I was then, but I like to think so, even as I know that I still have a long way to go. The one thing I'm sure of is that I'm a different man than I would have been if the car hadn't gone over the hill that night. Since the moment when the car hit the tree I've felt like I've been living on borrowed time, and I need to make it matter.

If you Google my name you'll find pages and pages about the things

I've done since 1985. I lived in Scotland for a year. I went to law school, and then became a lawyer. I was an RCMP officer for a summer. I was in a couple of rock bands. I was a civil servant. And now I'm a film producer and director. I've been in love, and I've had my heart broken. It's definitely been an interesting ride.

But if you Google the name "Gil Latter" you'll find *one* thing at the top of the search – the Gil Latter Memorial Award at Mt. Allison University, given in memory of one of my best friends who died on his way home one day from Sackville, New Brunswick in a car accident four years after I went over that hill in 1985.

I remember getting the phone call from Colin telling me what had happened like it was just this morning.

My first thought was a simple one – "damn it, no."

After I hung up, I buried my head in my pillow. I wasn't crying – I still haven't cried. Rather, I just wanted to shut the world out, if only for a few moments, and the pillow was the closest thing I had.

As I tried to breathe, another thought crowded its way into my mind – "It could have been me... and maybe it should have been me."

All these years later, I look at our pictures from our high school yearbook, and in Gil's face I see a good young man, gentle, kind and considerate; in mine I see the smirk, and the arrogance in the eyes, and I wonder if the right guy made it.

Every October I drive over to Gil's grave in Dartmouth with the same book, sit down next to the tombstone, and read for a while. [12]

I put a personal audio player on (in the early days it was a cassette "walkman"; now it's an MP3 player), and listen to Simon & Garfunkel – in particular "A Hazy Shade of Winter".

Time, time, time – see what's become of me. [13]

It's always chilly, because of the time of year, but I never feel it. I

---

[12] Albert Camus, *The Stranger*, trans. Mathew Ward (New York: Alfred A. Knopf, 1988).

[13] Paul Simon, "A Hazy Shade of Winter," Perf. Simon & Garfunkel (Columbia, 1966).

always feel warm, and I never feel like I'm alone. As I sit there I like to think that in the alternate universe their Gil Latter is listening to the same song while sitting on the ground somewhere next to my grave.

A quarter of a century ago, I died. And a quarter of a century ago, I didn't. I've been trying to make sense of it ever since, and to explore all of the possibilities that exist in the split second between those two moments in time.

GILBERT LATTER

'Gilby' likes science, girls, weekends, music and ice cream, but says "It's due when?" to homework. Gil remembers the '84 U.N. Assembly most of all. PA wishes you well at med. school.

Gil Latter from our High School yearbook in 1985.

PAUL KIMBALL

Usually just after report cards you'll hear Paul say "It's always darkest before the dawn". He enjoys History, Economics, Politics, and chocolate chip cookies, and hopes to become a lawyer/politician, but dislikes "people who haven't any patience for those of us who walk slowly in the halls".He fondly recalls being a member of the 84-85 Reach For the Top Zuccini Team! Good luck Paul!(Hey Paul, what about the commie's kiss?)

Yours truly from our High School yearbook in 1985.

Chapter Six

The Eternal Now

The insatiable thirst for everything which lies beyond, and which life reveals, is the most living proof of our immortality.[1]
– Charles Baudelaire

When people discuss time travel they almost always talk about it either from the perspective of someone coming to our time from the future or of our traveling back to the past, because those are relatively easy concept to wrap our heads around in terms of the reasons why one might want to make such a trip (as discussed in the previous chapter). But what about the idea of someone traveling *forward* to our time from the past?

It's an intriguing concept, and it's also theoretically possible.[2] The big problem is the most obvious one: if we don't have the technology to travel forward in time, nor can we reasonably imagine having it any time soon, then how could someone in our past travel forward to our time?

The answer is that they couldn't, at least not from our past as we think we know it. But here's the thing – our knowledge of the past is pretty dodgy. We still don't know everything that happened during the

---

[1] Charles Baudelaire, "Theophile Gautier" in *L'Art Romantique*, quoted in Jacques Maritain, *Approaches to God*, trans. Peter O'Reilly (New York: Collier Books, 1962), 80.

[2] Michio Kaku, *Physics of the Impossible: A Scientific Exploration of the World of Phasers, Force Fields, Teleportation and Time Travel* (London: Penguin Books, 2008), 219. Kaku writes, "Time travel to the future is possible, and has been experimentally verified millions of times."

20th century. We know even less about what happened two hundred years ago, and even less still about what happened two thousand years ago.[3] When placed in the context of our planet's entire history the course of recorded *human* history is but a drop in a very large bucket. Even if we think about the time of the dinosaurs, about which we know quite a bit, at least in broad strokes, they still only appeared around 230 million years ago during the Triassic Period. The Earth is over four and a half *billion* years old.

So one then has to ask: how much do we really know about what happened one billion years ago, for example – or maybe even just a million years ago? What if there was, as some people have speculated, and as legend would have it, a civilization on this planet that pre-dates our own, one that was indeed highly advanced, to the point where it had figured out how to travel through time? Maybe human, or maybe something post-human (or "pre-human"). Either way, the very essence of an advanced intelligence.

We might like to think we know how everything happened, but we don't. Anyone who tells you that we would definitely be able to detect remnants of a civilization that inhabited the Earth a billion years ago is dreaming, particularly if that civilization was sufficiently advanced to have taken on a different form beyond the physical. Perhaps they suffered some terrible calamity that wiped them out, or perhaps they chose to "move on".[4]

---

[3] Writing recently about the population of the Roman Empire in the 5th century, for example, historian Adrian Goldsworthy noted that, "We have no reliable statistics for population of the empire before or after it was divided... Archaeological evidence is simply not available in sufficient quantity to permit confident generalisations, and there is always the danger that we will see in it what we expect to see." Goldsworthy, *The Fall of the West*, 274.

[4] The best known "legend" of an advanced civilization destroyed by a natural disaster is Atlantis, first mentioned by Plato around 360 BCE. It was supposed to have existed around 9,000 years before his time. If such a civilization really did exist, was hit by a tsunami or decimated by an earthquake or volcano, and sank beneath the oceans, it is unlikely that we would have found it yet, although every now and then a news item pops up of some group claiming to have discovered the

These are the kinds of ideas that Mac Tonnies bandied about in his controversial final book *The Cryptoterrestrials: A Meditation on Indigenous Humanoids and the Aliens Among Us*. Mac speculated that the UFO phenomenon is caused by a race of indigenous humanoids with whom we share the planet. They're older and technologically superior to us, but are a dying race whose time has passed, while we are the noisy dangerous "new" kids on the block.[5]

Does the cryptoterrestrial hypothesis make any sense? Much of the criticism that has been leveled at the book and Mac's speculative narrative sounds a great deal like this comment by "Anonymous" that was posted at Tony Morrill's *Forteania* blog in 2011:

> Mac's "Cryptoterrestrial Hypothesis" is a dead end. It doesn't further our understanding of the UFO phenomenon and there is no evidence for it. One would think that if Mac was correct that we would have found evidence for a prior advanced civilization, or at least their trash. I mean not even a scrap of plastic. I think it's very safe to dismiss his hypothesis.[6]

My response at Tony's blog when I read this comment was short, and to the point: "For a couple of thousand years," I wrote, "there was no sign of Troy – and then there was, when archeologists finally discovered it. So let's not just fall back on the lazy thinking behind, 'hey, we can't find their trash, so it's simply not possible.'"[7] And Troy

---

fabled city. See, for example, Zach Howard, "Lost city of Atlantis, swamped by tsunami, may be found," *Reuters*, 12 March 2011. http://goo.gl/q0jOu.

[5] Mac Tonnies, *The Cryptoterrestrials: A Meditation on Indigenous Humanoids Among Us* (New York: Anomalist Books, 2010).

[6] Tony Morrill, "Mac Tonnies," *Forteania*, 17 October 2011. www.forteania.blogspot.com/2011/10/mac-tonnies.html#comments.

[7] Ibid. For a good study of the story behind the discovery of Troy, see Susan Heuck Allen, *Finding the Walls of Troy: Frank Calvert and Heinrich Schliemann at Hisarlik* (Berkeley: University of California Press, 1999).

existed just a few thousand years ago. Imagine how difficult it might be to find traces of a civilization that for all intents and purposes disappeared millions of years ago, or longer, particularly if the few survivors made a conscious effort to cover their tracks.

A few other points to consider. First, despite ringing the planet with surveillance satellites, deploying thousands of troops and intelligence agents, and spending billions upon billions of dollars, it took the most powerful nation on Earth a decade to track down Osama Bin Laden. Imagine how long it might take to discover something for which we're not even looking.

Second, about 70.8% of the Earth's surface is covered by water, much of it very deep, accessible only with great difficulty, and largely unexplored. Mac devotes an entire chapter in *The Cryptoterrestrials* to the idea that perhaps the real focus of UFOs, and thus the cryptoterrestrials, lies under the water and not on the land.

"It's probably no coincidence that so many UFOs are reported near large bodies of water," he noted. "Craft can be seen rising from lakes and oceans; sailors observe remarkable wheels of light rotating beneath the hull of their boats – the aquatic equivalent of today's account of 'buzzed' airliners.'"[8]

It's worth noting that the Marianas Trench, the deepest region of the world's oceans, is approximately 2,550 kilometres long with a mean width of 69 kilometres. It reaches a maximum-known depth of about 10.99 kilometres at the Challenger Deep, a small slot-shaped valley in its floor at its southern end, although some unrepeated measurements place the deepest portion at 11.03 kilometres.[9] If Mount Everest, the highest mountain on Earth at 8,848 metres, was set in the deepest part of the Mariana Trench, there would still be 2,150 metres of water left above it.

---

[8] Tonnies, *The Cryptoterrestrials*, 83.

[9] "Scientists map Mariana Trench, deepest known section of ocean in the world," *The Telegraph*, 7 December 2011; William J. Broad, "Filmmaker in Submarine Voyages to Bottom of Sea," *New York Times*, 25 March 2012.

Do we really know everything about what's down there? It's clear that we don't. In October, 2011, for example, news came out that a summer research expedition organized by scientists at Scripps Institution of Oceanography at the University of California, San Diego, had led to the identification of gigantic amoebas, or xenophyophores, in the Marianas Trench. An article in *The Daily Galaxy* noted that the xenophyophores are just the tip of the proverbial iceberg when it comes to considerations of the nature and diversity of life at extreme depths. According to Dhugal Lindsay of the Japan Agency for Marine-Earth Science and Technology, the Dropcam movie which revealed the xenophyophores also depicted the deepest jellyfish observed to date.[10]

In other words, we still have a lot to learn.

"If we're dealing with a truly alien intelligence," Mac concluded in *The Cryptoterrestrials*, "there's no promise that its thinking will be linear. Indeed, its inherent weirdness might serve as an appeal to an aspect of the psyche we've allowed to atrophy. It might be trying to rouse us from our stupor, in which case it's tempting to wonder if the supposed ETs are literally us in some arcane sense."[11]

In the spirit of Mac's thought experimentation, let me throw a scenario out there for you – some speculation about time travel that moves forward, not backward.

One billion years ago a non-human civilization arose on this planet that advanced far beyond the level we have reached in the 21st Century, to a degree where their existence was in some way virtual, not physical. Then, at some point, they merged into a single consciousness.

With their combined intellect they eventually discovered how to travel in time, and possessed the power to make it happen, and so off they went to their future. Not as a physical being, however, but

---

[10] "EcoAlert: Giant Amoebas Discovered at Mariana Trench - Deepest Place on the Planet," *The Daily Galaxy*, 24 October 2011. http://goo.gl/LBFyz.

[11] Tonnies, *The Cryptoterrestrials*, 112.

rather as consciousness – only their thoughts could travel through time. They could interact with beings in the future, including us, but only indirectly – a burning bush that talks, perhaps, or lights in the sky and under the water that baffle us, or maybe something even more complex and interesting that deals with us on a subconscious level. In our dreams, maybe, or maybe through a series of seemingly random events that actually have a meaning when carefully examined.

Once they had finished exploring the future on their home planet perhaps they decided to explore other things. The galaxy perhaps, or maybe other dimensions. In a sense, this would not be dissimilar to what Immanuel Kant imagined in 1755' when he asked, in *Universal Natural History and Theory of the Heavens*:

> Is the everlasting soul for the full eternity of its future existence, which the grave itself does not destroy but only changes, always to remain fixed at this point of the cosmos, on our Earth? Is it never to share a closer look at the rest of creation's miracles? Who knows whether it is not determined that in future the soul will get to know at close quarters those distant spheres of the cosmic structure and the excellence of their dwelling places, which already attract its curiosity from far away? Perhaps that is why some spheres of the planetary system are already developing, in order to prepare for us in other heavens new places to live after the completion of the time prescribed for our stay here on Earth.[12]

And then, when it was all finished, perhaps they returned home for one final journey – a voyage past the "grey wall" that even they could not see beyond, in search of the one thing, when all other things are known, that would still hold a mystery for beings like them. Having seen all that there was to see and experienced all that there was to experience, except for their own mortality, they opened one

---

[12] Immanuel Kant, *Universal Natural History and Theory of the Heavens* (1755), trans. Ian Johnston, available on-line at Vancouver Island University. http://goo.gl/jumgX.

final door and disappeared forever.

Before you dismiss this idea out of hand, ask yourself this – aren't you just the least bit curious about what the future is going to look like? If you had the ability to have a look, wouldn't you use it? I know that I would. Maybe someone else already has – and continues to do so.

Let me leave the subject of time travel by asking the following question about what I would consider its ultimate "paranormal" aspect: What if *we* are the God of the Bible?

One of the central ideas behind God, after all, is that He is eternal – yesterday is today is tomorrow to Him. Religious figures have always spoken about some manifestation of an "eternal now." One of the most notable in my part of the world was Henry Alline, who considered this idea of the "eternal now" to be of fundamental importance when it came to his own direct and transformational experience in the 1770s with what he called "God."

The sudden power of what he termed his spiritual regeneration led him to declare that he had been "ravished with a divine ecstasy" and "wrapped up in God." Most significant was the fact that he described time as having literally stopped for him. God, he wrote, lived in "One Eternal Now," and the "redeemed" inhabited the same place – in a sense, meaning that they could transcend temporal boundaries and travel through time.

In his 1781 theological treatise *Two Mites*, Alline wrote:

> ... with God there never was any such Thing, as before or after, Millions of Ages, before time began, and as many more, after Time is at a Period, being the very same instant; consider neither Time past nor Time to come, but one Eternal NOW; consider that with God there is neither Succession nor Progress; but that with Him the Moment He said let us make Man, and the Sound of the last Trumpet, is the very same instant, and your death as much first as your Birth... with God all things are NOW... as the Center of a Ring, which is as

near the one side as the other.[13]

Historian George Rawlyk put Alline's experience into perspective:

> Conversion, therefore, was... the God-given instrument of telescoping time into the 'Eternal Now.' Regeneration was the process which destroyed artificial time and space and astonishingly transformed, for each individual, the mundane – what Alline described as the world of 'Turnips, Cabbages and Potatoes' – into the cosmic and heavenly – 'the Eternity you once, was, and knew.'[14]

As noted previously, Alline was a Christian mystic. Perhaps like those before him who had opened themselves up to the possibilities of the unknown, he intuitively tapped into the true nature of time – that yesterday really is today, and today really is tomorrow, and tomorrow really is yesterday. In doing so maybe he didn't encounter God so much as he transcended the "artificial time" that we have created for ourselves (or, to look at it another way, imprisoned ourselves within), and discovered something much more interesting and profound.

Science now tells us that time works in much the same way as Alline claimed to have experienced it. It's a realization that may have put us on the path to someday becoming our own God, as we become the true masters of the Eternal Now. At that time we will finally realize the truth of the following observation by philosopher Raoul Vaneigem: "Linear time has no hold over people except in so far as it prohibits them from changing the world, and so forces them to adapt

---

[13] Henry Alline, *Two mites on some of the most important and much disputed points of divinty, cast into the treasury for the welfare of the poor and needy, and committed to the perusal of the unprejudiced and impartial reader* (1781). See also George A. Rawlyk, *The Canada Fire: Radical Evangelicalism in British North America, 1775 – 1812* (Montreal: McGill-Queen's University Press, 1994), 13.

[14] George A. Rawlyk, *New Light Letters and Songs* (Wolfville, Nova Scotia: Lancelot Press, 1983), 10.

to it."[15]

If and when that happens, we may finally discover that *we* are the advanced non-human intelligence we have encountered – "aliens" from the reaches of space to which we have long since journeyed, and the "ghosts" speaking to us from the past we thought we had left behind.

The voices we hear could well be our own, echoing through the very reaches of time itself.

---

[15] Raoul Vaneigem, *The Revolution of Everyday Life,* trans. Donald Nicholson-Smith (London: Rebel Press, 2001), 229. Available on-line at: http://goo.gl/rgSp2.

Chapter Seven

"Met Him Pike Hoses"

The aim of art is to represent not the outward appearance of things, but their inward significance.[1]
– Aristotle

When I was a graduate student in history in the mid-1990s the subject matter of my thesis was 19th century Free Christian Baptists in New Brunswick. The Free Christian Baptists were a denomination founded in 1832, and were among the closest inheritors of Henry Alline's New Light movement. As a result I spent a great deal of time studying Alline's work, as well as that of the people who succeeded him in the late 18th and early 19th centuries and therefore provided a bridge to the Free Christian Baptists. One day while reading through old journals from the period I came across a murder in New Brunswick that really struck a chord with me.

In 1805, three decades after Alline was "ravished by the spirit," a group of people held a series of evangelical revival meetings outside the isolated settlement of Shediac, New Brunswick. The revivals were led by an itinerant preacher named Jacob Peck, who referred to himself as "John the Baptist." He was assisted by a poor local fisherman / farmer named Amos Babcock.

Like many of my own ancestors, Babcock's family had moved to New Brunswick prior to the American Revolution. He had already led a small New Light circle, so when the charismatic Peck arrived in the

---

[1] Aristotle, quoted in Will Durant, *The Story of Philosophy* (New York: Pocket Books, 1953), 73.

Shediac area in early 1805 it was natural that Babcock joined with him in a New Light revival. Things quickly went awry, however, as the revival veered into New Dispensationalist fervor. Under Peck's influence two of the women in Babcock's circle assumed a prophetic role. One of them was Amos' daughter, Mary.

The "New Dispensationalism" preached by Peck was a radical outgrowth of Alline's New Light message. It placed private revelation above any Church authority, ministerial control, and even the Bible. After Alline's death from tuberculosis in 1784 at the age of thirty-six, many of his followers set aside his more mystical beliefs, and his personal asceticism, and began to organize the New Light groups into more structured churches, usually along Baptist or Methodist lines. There was a smaller group, however, that embraced the mysticism inherent in Alline's preaching, but not the personal asceticism. In 1791 these New Dispensationalists began to divide the New Light churches throughout the Annapolis Valley in Nova Scotia. Led by a group of charismatic young preachers, as well as a number of women, their movement quickly spread.

The pastor of the Horton New Light church, John Payzant, at first took a patient attitude to the young people who were formenting this new and even more radical spiritual revolution. He soon discovered, however, that if the original New Lights were the religious equivalent of the Mensheviks in 1917 Russia, the New Dispensationalists were the Bolsheviks.

Lydia Randall, one of the key New Dispensationalists in Horton, claimed to Payzant that she had a vision from the Almighty which had revealed to her that not only were all the orders of the church contrary to the spirit of God, but so was marriage, which came from the devil. She separated from her husband, and began to bring other young women around to her views. The movement spread from the Horton area throughout the Annapolis Valley, and then beyond. The more moderate New Lights became genuinely concerned, as did the secular authorities.[2]

Some of the documented New Dispensationalist activities clearly involved fornication, adultery, and "religious" practices such as women riding on the backs of men. In 1793 at Waterborough, New Brunswick, the preachers John Lunt and Archelaus Hammond introduced their converts to sexual liberation. Rev. Jacob Bailey, a prominent Anglican minister whose own young daughter wound up influenced by the New Dispensationalists (she eventually ran away to Boston), characterized the New Dispensationalists as follows:

Here blue-eyed Jenny plays her part
Inured to every saint-like art
She works and heaves from head to heel
With pangs of puritanic zeal
Now in a fit of deep distress
The holy maid turns prophetess
And to her light and knowledge brings
A multitude of secret things
And as enthusiasm advances
Falls into ecstasies and trances
Her self with decency resigns
To these impulses and inclines
On Jeremy Trim a favorite youth
Who as she sinks into his arms

---

[2] Payzant recorded his impressions of the New Dispensationalists in his journal: "Some said," he wrote, "that all the World would be Saved. Some said that there was no shuch [sic] man as Christ; and all the Christ that there was, was what we felt in ourselves; and therefore why should they hold to Baptism, and the Supper... Many of them gave way to carnal desire, so that their new-plane took a contrary effect, for instead of living so holy as they pretend to, they were light and carnal." John Payzant, *The Journal of the Reverend John Payzant (1749 – 1834)*, ed. Brian C. Cuthbertson (Hantsport, NS: Lancelot Press, 1981), 47 – 55. Payzant was eventually worn out by the disputes with the New Dispensationalists and in 1793 he accepted an offer to become the minister of the New Light congregation in Liverpool, Nova Scotia, well away from the Annapolis Valley and the New Dispensationalists.

Feel through his veins her powerful charms
Grown warm with throbs of strong devotion
He finds his blood in high commotion
And fired with love of this dear sister
Is now unable to resist her.[3]

Full of energy and fervor, exuding in a literal way the kind of sexuality that Alline's preaching had always used as metaphor for the relationship with God, the young and unmarried New Dispensationalist leaders were absolutely convinced that they were divinely ordained instruments for the spiritual transformation of not only Nova Scotia and New Brunswick, but northern New England as well.[4] In the chaotic period following the American Revolution and the settlement of thousands of Loyalists in the Maritime colonies this was dangerous and revolutionary stuff, at least in the eyes of the authorities and the majority of New Lights who wanted to assure the Crown of their loyalty.

It couldn't last, of course. Nothing like the New Dispensationalist movement ever does. By 1797 the fire had died down and the New Dispensationalist leaders were for the most part brought back into line. Indeed, a counter-revolution began, led by former New Dispensationalist preacher Edward Manning, which saw almost the entire New Light movement subsumed within the much more conservative Calvinist Baptist church.

While the leaders and most of their followers had been brought back into the mainstream of the New Light movement, there remained a

---

[3] Public Archives of Nova Scotia, M. G. 1, no. 100, pp. 428 – 431.

[4] Rawlyk, *Ravished by the Spirit*, 77. "Alline made extraordinary use of sexual imagery in order to convey something of the rich emotional texture of conversion. Conversion, for him, was perceived as a spiritual climax, the consummation of an intense love – hate relationship which seemed to be the essence of conviction. For Alline, conversion was, as he often graphically put it, 'being married to Christ'. And it was a 'marriage' to the 'Heavenly Charmer' which would give meaning to all other relationships."

small and scattered group of New Dispensationalists who continued their spiritual revolution at the fringes of colonial society. It was within this tradition that Peck and Babcock operated.[5]

As the revival continued over a period of several days, William Hannington, a neighbor who had been part of Babcock's circle, became disenchanted with the New Dispensationalist turn that Peck and Babcock had taken, particularly when Mary Babcock began to speak about the imminent end of the world. Hannington later recounted that as part of her prophecies, Mary had stated:

> … after this World had Been Drowned Six Years, a Saviour would be Born of a Woman & Laid in a manger in Swaddling Clothes & that the next World would be Be Destroyed By Fire. Mess'rs A Babcock & Peck told me she had said her Father & Mother & all the Children would be saved, But that her Aunt Masa would not.[6]

"Aunt Masa" was Amos' sister, Mercy Hall. This prophecy proved to be her death sentence.

On the evening of February 13th, as a winter storm approached, Babcock met with Hannington, who questioned the direction in which Peck and Babcock had taken the revival and remonstrated with Babcock over the neglect of his farm animals as he had became more and more immersed in prophecy and prayer. Babcock rebuffed Hannington, returned home with his brother Jonathan, and proceeded to grind some grain in a hand mill. As the flour came out of the mill, according to Jonathan, Amos took it in his hand and sprinkled it on the floor, saying that it was "the bread of Heaven." Amos then took off his socks and shoes and went outside into what was a bitterly cold

---

[5] The Babcock story is recounted in James Manning and James Innis, *The Newlight Baptist Journals of James Manning and James Innis*, ed. D. G. Bell. (Hantsport, Nova Scotia: Lancelot Press, 1984). See also "The Babcock Tragedy," *The New Brunswick Magazine*, July – December 1898, 215 – 222.

[6] Manning and Innis, 337. Statement of William Hannington, 13 Feb. 1805.

evening.

As he trudged through the snow around their ramshackle house he cried out, "The world is to end! The world is to end!"

He then looked up at the sky, and yelled, "The stars are falling! It will be but a few minutes before they are here!"

He went back inside and arranged his family in order against the wall.

"I am the angel Gabriel," he said. "You need not be afraid."

He told his wife to keep her eyes on him at all times or else he would "run her through." When she looked away he struck her with his fist. He then turned to his two young sons and proclaimed them "Gideon's men," after which he took his youngest child into his arms, and blew into the 3 year old's mouth so hard that according to his brother "it was almost strangled." He then threw the child "with great force across the house against the Logs." Fortunately, the child survived, but there was worse to come.

Amos took a knife, sharpened it on a whetstone, and walked over to his sister, Mercy.

"Take off your dress," he told her, "and get on your knees and prepare for death, because your hour has come."

Whether it was because she was scared for her life, she didn't really believe that her brother would harm her, or she willingly accepted what was about to happen because she believed that the end of days really was upon them, is impossible to say, but Mercy Hall did as Amos commanded.

Amos then turned to his brother Jonathan and ordered him to take his clothes off as well. As was the case with Mercy, he complied.

Amos walked over to the window and stared outside, as if waiting for something to happen, or perhaps receiving his final orders. Either way, after several moments he turned away from the window and proceeded to dance about the room with the knife in his hand. Suddenly he made several feints at his brother, striking him in the hand. As Jonathan recoiled from his superficial wound Amos spun around and "flew across" the house towards Mercy. With three savage thrusts of the knife, he fulfilled at least part of his daughter's prophecy. Mercy Hall, blood gushing from her wounds, collapsed and died on the spot.

Amos' brother didn't wait around to see who was going to be next. He rushed to the door and fled into the cold winter's night, completely naked. He made his way through the snow to the house of the nearest neighbor, Joseph Poirier, which was approximately a quarter of a mile away. Poirier gave the terrified Jonathan some clothes and then they headed to the home of Hannington. After Jonathan related what had happened Hannington and Poirier, along with two of Poirier's sons, proceeded to the Babcock home to investigate.

When they arrived they found the family in shock and Amos Babcock pacing about the room with his hands clasped, muttering to himself. Hannington told the two Poirier boys to restrain him. Babcock snapped to attention and tried to resist, but the Poiriers overpowered him even as he turned to his young sons and screamed, "Gideon's men, arise!" They stood up to help their father but were compelled by Hannington to sit down again. Amos Babcock was tied up and then Hannington began the search outside for Mercy Hall's body, which was no longer in the house.

As the darkness of the night began to give way to the morning light Hannington and Poirier discovered the disemboweled body of Amos' sister buried in a snow drift outside the house.[7]

Hannington placed Babcock under arrest and took him to the home of Amasa Killam, who had also been involved in the New Light revival until it had veered off into New Dispensationalism. When Babcock saw that his brother had given a statement describing what

---

[7] Ibid., 346. The report of Gideon Palmer, the coroner for the County of Westmoreland, makes for grisly reading. He described the wounds to Mercy Hall as follows: "In and upon the pit of the stomach between the breasts... one mortal wound of the breadth of two inches and of the depth of six inches; in and upon the right side of the belly between the hip and short ribs... one mortal wound of the length of six inches and of the depth of five inches; in and of the back part of the head... one other mortal wound of the length of three inches and of the depth of half an inch."

had happened, he cried out: "There are letters to Damascus! Send them to Damascus!" He became so violent that he had to be restrained on a bed, with his arms fastened securely to the floor.

Before anything more could be done a violent winter storm hit the area. It lasted for three days, after which Hannington and several others put a strap around Babcock's arms and placed him on a light one-horse sled. They put their snow-shoes on and hauled Babcock by hand through the woods to the county jail at Dorchester. It was a twenty-six mile trek.

Babcock was indicted for murder a few months later, ironically on the same day that Jacob Peck was brought to book by the worried authorities for "blasphemous and seditious language."[8]

Solicitor-General Ward Chipman, who prosecuted Babcock, clearly thought that he was delusional, but in 1805 that was no bar to a guilty verdict and a capital sentence. Babcock was convicted and hanged.[9]

Flash forward almost two hundred years to the early 1970s when I was a kid, around five, maybe six. I can distinctly remember lying on the couch at home reading a book and then suddenly getting a feeling in the pit of my stomach like I was falling from a great height. I could actually feel the wind rushing around me as the velocity increased,

---

[8] Peck's indictment charged that he was "a profane wicked and blasphemous man, and a wicked and base Imposter and perverter of the sacred Scriptures of the New Testament" who sought to "terrify and deceive divers of the liege subjects of His majesty... with false denunciations of the Judgments of Almighty God and to bring the Christian religion and the doctrines thereof into derision and contempt." He was never prosecuted.

[9] In his opening address, Chipman stated, "If ignorant and weak minds by indulging in reveries of this kind, imbibe such principles and act upon them, however conscientious they may pretend to be, they must be answerable for all their conduct and suffer punishment for their crimes... such delusion will by no means lessen their guilt."; Chipman papers, vol. 19, Lawrence Collection, Public Archives of Canada. Chipman later became a justice of the Supreme Court, and is considered by historians to be one of most influential early leaders of the colony of New Brunswick. Phillip Buckner, "Chipman, Ward," *Dictionary of Canadian Biography Online*. www.biographi.ca/009004-119.01-e.php?&id_nbr=2802.

and then it would stop as suddenly as it had begun.

It didn't feel *as if* I was falling – it felt like I was *really falling*. It was a frightening sensation, and it happened repeatedly.

As I grew older the experience stopped happening, and I stopped thinking about it. But other experiences replaced it. One of them was a particular dream that I had many times when I was eleven or twelve. In the dream I always wound up killing someone with a knife in what appeared to be a frontier setting. It wasn't someone I knew in the real world, but it was always the same person in my dream, a young woman. The dream was so vivid that there were actually days when I went to school wondering to myself if I had really killed someone and repressed the memory.

Like the falling sensation this dream eventually stopped happening, and for years I forgot about it. It wasn't until I started looking into the paranormal, and considering what might be possible beyond the "normal" world in which we're told we live, that I recalled these earlier experiences (and others), and wondered if they might in some way be indicative of past lives. In the example of falling, could this be a holdover from a previous life where I had fallen to my death? Where the dream is concerned, maybe it was a holdover memory of a past life where I had indeed killed someone, a link through time still embedded in my subconscious.

Years later when I discovered the tragic case of Amos Babcock and Mercy Hall, the thought occurred to me that perhaps *I* was Babcock in a previous life, falling through the trapdoor with the hangman's noose around his neck. Furthermore, perhaps someone I knew now was once Mercy Hall. At the very least, maybe I had experienced something similar in a past life, which was why the Babcock case resonated with me.

Which leads me, in a very circuitous way, to the subject of reincarnation, and its possible relationship to an advanced non-human intelligence.

The concept that the soul or spirit returns to live in a new body after death, either as a human being or in some traditions perhaps as an animal or plant, is a central tenet of many of the world's major religious belief systems, particularly Hinduism and Buddhism. It was also promoted by many of the ancient Greek and Roman philosophers, who called it *metempsychosis* (or as the character of Molly Bloom famously mispronounces it in James Joyce's classic novel *Ulysses*, "met him pike hoses").[10] It can also be found in most aboriginal cultures.[11]

Reincarnation is rejected, however, by the orthodoxies of Christianity, Judaism and Islam, the belief systems that stem from the Old Testament. In the West it's most often associated with celebrities such as Shirley MacLaine and the television talk show circuit, although in the past few decades it's begun to receive more serious consideration, if not necessarily acceptance, within the mainstream.

Geddes MacGregor, for example, who was Dean of the Graduate School of Religion and Distinguished Professor of Philosophy at the University of Southern California, examined reincarnation in his book *Reincarnation in Christianity: A New Vision of the Role of Rebirth in Christian Thought*. He concluded that Christian doctrine and reincarnation are not mutually exclusive belief systems.

"Each reincarnation," wrote MacGregor, "is, of course, a

---

[10] In ancient Greece, the concept of reincarnation was most closely associated with Plato. See Plato, *Plato's Republic*, trans. G. M. A. Grube (Indianapolis: Hackett Publishing Company, 1974), 239-263. In Plato's view, the number of souls was fixed, and they transmigrated from one body to another. "If someone," he concluded, "whenever he comes to live here on earth, pursues philosophy soundly, and the lot of the choice does not place him among the last, he is likely to be happy here, according to the message received from the other world, and his journey from here to there and back again will not be along the rough path below the earth, but along the smooth and heavenly." Ibid., 261. James Joyce's *Ulysses* is available online at Project Gutenberg. www.gutenberg org/ebooks/4300.

[11] See, for example, Ian Stevenson, "Characteristics of Cases of the Reincarnation Type among the Igbo of Nigeria," *Journal of Asian and African Studies*, Vol. 21, No. 3 - 4 (July 1986): 204 - 216. There are, of course, significant differences between how each of these varying traditions view reincarnation, but they all share a common acceptance of the central idea of a rebirth into a new life.

resurrection... [which] can now be seen as a continuing process in which every rebirth gives us a new capacity for walking closer and closer with God."

MacGregor then raised the possibility of a special evolutionary leap that I find quite intriguing.

"At the end of every aeon," he conjectured, "there might well be... a unique step in the infinite pilgrimage toward God. I cannot know; but what I can know of my past, and even of the moral and spiritual development in my own life on earth suggests to me that such 'leaps' might occur at the end of every age of cosmic history."[12]

Notable figures in the past have also taken reincarnation seriously within Western society. David Lloyd George, for example, told his friend Lord Riddell that, "The conventional Heaven, with its angels perpetually singing, etc., nearly drove me mad in my youth and made me an atheist for ten years." As he grew older, he continued, his perspective broadened and his opinions changed, until he came to the conclusion that, "We shall all be reincarnated and that hereafter we shall suffer or benefit in accordance with what we have done in this world."[13]

The Scottish novelist John Buchan, who wrote *The Thirty-Nine Steps* and later served as Governor-General of Canada after he had been made the Lord Tweedsmuir, described his own experience in which he hinted at past lives. "I find myself in some scene which I cannot have visited before and which is perfectly familiar," he wrote. "I know that it was the stage of an action in which I once took part

---

[12] Geddes MacGregor, *Reincarnation in Christianity: A New Vision of the Role of Rebirth in Christian Thought* (Wheaton, IL: The Theosophical Publishing House, 1978), 172 - 173. For MacGregor, Christ still had a role to play when one considers the idea of reincarnation. "Christ may be seen," he wrote, "as Christians have always seen him, as providing me with the conditions for freeing myself."

[13] George Allardice Riddell, *Intimate Diary of the Peace Conference and After, 1918 - 1923* (London: Victor Gollancz, 1933), 123.

and am about to take part again."[14]

I've had experiences similar to Buchan's. In 1987 I spent my third year as an undergraduate in college on exchange at the University of Dundee in Scotland. As soon as I got off the plane at Prestwick I felt an immediate affinity for Scotland that has continued ever since. There were certain places that I visited where I felt at home, as if I had been there before (St. Andrew's was definitely one; Inverness was another). I've traveled to many other places since then but I've never felt a connection quite like the one I've always felt with Scotland. It was a feeling that was as strong as ever when I went back in 2009 with Holly Stevens. As I wandered about the Highlands, and visited the ancient standing stone circle at Lochbuie, and the ruins on the Isle of Iona, it all seemed familiar to me in the same way that it had twenty years before.

For most within Western society, however, the views outlined by Canadian author Tom Harpur on the subject of reincarnation in his best-selling book *Life After Death* remain the norm. Harpur examined reincarnation, and ultimately rejected it. "I have serious doubts about the value of a belief which tells me I have lived many times before when I haven't the slightest glimmering of a memory of any of it," he wrote. "It's fine to say we're in a kind of cosmic school, where we learn successive lessons about life and gradually purify ourselves. But if I can't remember a single thing from all of this, of what use are these lessons and who is the 'I' who is supposed to be the student?"[15]

"Since memory is an essential part of what makes me me and you

---

[14] John Buchan, *Memory Hold-the-Door* (London: Hodder & Stoughton London, 1940), 122. Tweedsmuir travelled widely in Canada, and he instituted the Governor General's Literary Awards. A year after Tweedsmuir's death in 1940, Prime Minister William Lyon MacKenzie King, who as was noted earlier had a profound interest in spiritualism, continued to think of Tweedsmuir as being one of "the three men who spiritually were closer to me than any other." See "Behind the Diary: A King's Who's Who Biographies, John Buchan, 1st Baron Tweedsmuir (1875-1940)" Library and Archives Canada, 31 March 2002. http://goo.gl/VSXO5.

[15] Tom Harpur, *Life After Death* (Toronto: McClelland & Stewart, 1991), 107.

166

you," he concluded, "I cannot see in what sense we remain the same person through repeated incarnations, or what possible good it does to be told that we have lived before."[16] This focus on lack of memory of past lives is central to the Western critique against reincarnation. However, there are a number of answers that address the concerns raised by Harpur in a way that I find compelling.

August Strindberg, for example, in *Zones of the Spirit*, presented the following dialogue between a pupil and a teacher:

> The pupil asked: "Why is one not informed of one's Karma from the beginning?" The teacher answered: "That is pure pity for us. No man could endure life if he knew what lay before him. Moreover, man must have a certain measure of freedom; without that he would only be a puppet."[17]

This makes perfect sense when you think about it. Who would want to go through life with all of the memories from previous incarnations? Indeed, most of us have enough trouble getting through our current lives with the memories we have accrued here. Adding memories from other lives, particularly if they were painful memories, would make a new life unbearable. They would represent the kind of emotional "baggage" that many people in this life try to leave behind, often through years of therapy.

Arthur Conan Doyle echoed Strindberg when he wrote in *The History of Spiritualism*, "We may point out that such remembrance would enormously complicate our present life, and that such existences may well form a cycle which is all too clear to us when we come to the end of it, when perhaps we may see a whole rosary of lives threaded upon one personality."[18]

---

[16] Ibid., 108.

[17] August Strindberg, *Zones of the Spirit: A Book of Thoughts* (New York: G. P. Putnam's Sons, 1913), 51.

[18] Arthur Conan Doyle, *The History of Spiritualism, Vol II* (London: Cassell and

The concept of "one personality" is intriguing, and ties into the idea that there is much more for us than just the individual. I've been known to say while discussing religion and philosophy with friends over a couple of drinks that "Jesus was a communist." My point is that the focus on the individual that is the hallmark of Western society is like picking one piece of a very large, complex puzzle, and putting it forward as the key to our existence, when that piece is ultimately meaningless without all of the other pieces joined together. In my opinion, the "Kingdom of Heaven" is properly understood, if such a thing actually exists, as being *all of us*, linked together, whether here or in the great beyond.

There's also the possibility that the memories *are* there, but we have to open ourselves up to them and make a conscious effort to access them. Maybe we can still hear the echoes as young children, before we are fully acclimated into this life and while we have a closer proximity to the last one.

Perhaps this world is just a stage in our development. When we die it's possible that we have the opportunity to go on to the next, more advanced stage. Many people have described seeing the "white light" during what have become known as near death experiences, where a sort of doorway opens that we can go through. This could well be the moment of transition to the next stage of our development, which I'm convinced would be a collective consciousness where we leave our individuality behind and become one with each other in a being that would be by its very nature empathic, and therefore moral.[19]

Accordingly, people who have done evil in this world wouldn't get in to the next one but would be returned for another go around (which

---

Company, 1926). Available on-line at Classic Literature Library. www.classic-literature.co.uk/scottish-authors/arthur-conan-doyle/the-history-of-spiritualism-vol-ii/, 67.

[19] I highly recommend the podcast *Skeptiko* with host Alex Tsakiris, who has recorded dozens of episodes on the question of near death experiences with some of the world's foremost researchers. Alex Tsakiris, *Skeptiko: Science at the Tipping Point*. www.skeptiko.com.

might explain why I'm here writing this, and you're reading it, instead of experiencing the "great link," to borrow a term from *Star Trek: Deep Space Nine*). Further, there are many of us who would still be anchored to the idea of the individual, and therefore wouldn't want to advance to this new level of development as part of a more enlightened group consciousness. Those types would also come back for another kick at the can in the hope that they would slowly come to see that they are part of something greater than themselves. As Victor Hugo observed, "The whole creation is a perpetual ascension, from brute to man, from man to God. To divest ourselves more and more of matter, to be clothed more and more with spirit, such is the law."[20]

Ultimately, the idea of reincarnation provides us with grist for the speculative mill when it comes to an advanced non-human intelligence. For example, what if such as intelligence is actually our collective consciousness – in essence, the portion of humanity that has grown up and reached the next level? It may exist as a being that is immortal, timeless, and virtually all-knowing, because it would embrace the entirety of human experience. This could be the quantum consciousness about which some scientists have started to speculate.[21]

---

[20] Victor Hugo, *Victor Hugo's intellectual autobiography: (Postscriptum de ma vie); being the last of the unpublished works and embodying the author's ideas on literature, philosophy and religion* (New York: Haskell House Publishers, 1971), 269.

[21] Stuart Hameroff, who is well known for his work with physicist Roger Penrose in trying to develop a model for quantum consciousness, stated in a 2005 interview that, "I'm not an idealist, like Bishop Berkeley or Hindu approaches, in which consciousness is all there is. Nor am I a Copenhagenist in which consciousness causes collapse (and chooses reality from a number of possibilities). But somewhere in between. Consciousness exists on the edge between the quantum and classical worlds. I think more like a quantum Buddhist, in that there is a universal proto-conscious mind which we access, and can influence us. But it actually exists at the fundamental level of the universe, at the Planck scale." See Greg Taylor, "The Quantum Mind of Stuart Hameroff," *The Daily Grail*, 21 January 2005. www.dailygrail.com/Interviews/2005/1/Quantum-Mind-Stuart-Hameroff. The entire quantum conversation is an interesting scientific sideshow, but we're still far from

Perhaps this collective consciousness can inspire and even guide those who have not yet become a part of it, but it chooses to do so in a way that allows the individual to come to an acceptance of the true collective nature of humanity in their own time, just as parents don't force someone to marry a particular person anymore. But they can still make the introduction, and set up some "chance" meetings between two people, and maybe that's what the advanced non-human intelligence does in the various ways that it interacts with us, as it tries to lead us to a "marriage" with ourselves (in this case, "post-human" or "post-individual" as opposed to "non-human" intelligence would perhaps be a better way of looking at things). As a result, maybe we do indeed "remember" past lives, but in an oblique or abstract way, through synchronicities, déjà vu, dreams, and other "hints." Even things such as the UFO phenomenon and ghosts could be part of the memory process. As discussed previously, they could be harbingers that give us a clue that there is something more than "this."

One could go even further and imagine that at death, even if an individual accepted the nature of this collective being, he or she might choose to return to gain further experience which would eventually enhance the collective consciousness. Our existence could be a symphony that is constantly being written, with each life that we live a new note added to the whole. In a sense, we could be similar to honeybees, moving back and forth from the hive with the nectar – the "honey" for us would be experience that would enhance the collective.

This is a subject that the great French author Honoré de Balzac wrote about in his novel *Seraphita*. The main character is a perfectly

---

developing anything beyond a very basic understanding of consciousness. Indeed, little has really changed since 1868, when T. H. Huxley wrote, "What consciousness is, we know not; and how it is that any thing so remarkable as a state of consciousness comes about as the result of irritating nervous tissue, is just as unaccountable as the appearance of the Djin when Aladdin rubbed his lamp." See T. H. Huxley and W. J. Youmans, *The Elements of Physiology and Hygiene: A Textbook for Educational Institutions* (New York: D. Appleton & Co., 1868), 178.

androgynous being born to parents who by the doctrines of Emanuel Swedenborg have transcended their humanity in much the same way that the "post-individual human" collective consciousness could be the ideal culmination of the human experience. In the novel, Balzac wrote:

> All human beings go through a previous life in the sphere of Instinct, where they are brought to see the worthlessness of earthly treasures, to amass which they gave themselves such untold pain! Who can tell how many times the human being lives in the sphere of Instinct before he is prepared to enter the sphere of Abstraction, where thought expands itself on erring science, where mind wearies at last of human language? For, when Matter is exhausted, Spirit enters... Then follow other existences – all to be lived to reach the place where Light effulgent shines. Death is the post-house of the journey.[22]

He continued by observing that, "A lifetime may be needed merely to gain the virtues which annul the errors of man's preceding life... the virtues we acquire which develop slowly within us, are the invisible links which bind each one of our existences to the others – existences which the spirit alone remembers, for Matter has no memory of spiritual things." For Balzac, thought alone held the tradition of the past lives. "The endless legacy of the past to the present," he concluded, "is the secret source of human genius."[23]

The most compelling evidence to me that there may indeed be something to the idea of reincarnation comes from the research of Canadian doctor and child psychiatrist Ian Stevenson, who spent decades examining thousands of children around the world who claimed to recall past lives.

---

[22] Honoré de Balzac, *Seraphita*, trans. Katharine Prescott Wormely. (Pennsylvania State University, 2002), 114. http://goo.gl/UQ3Q4.

[23] Ibid.

Stevenson had a long and successful career in psychiatry, including a term as the Chair of the Department of Psychiatry and Neurology at the University of Virginia. He focused on young children because they would be less likely to have been exposed to the details of a dead person's life. As I noted previously, if we *have* lived lives before this one, it also seems to make sense that any echoes in the new one would be strongest in the very young. Like the rock I tossed into the Vltava River, the ripples will be more pronounced at the moment of impact, and then slowly dissipate as they get further from the point of origin.

Stevenson employed a rigorous methodology, which he explained in 1989 as follows:

> In the study of spontaneous paranormal phenomena we must usually interview and cross-question informants about events that have happened before we arrive on the scene. In principle, the methods are those that lawyers use in reconstructing a crime and historians use in understanding the past. Having the best account possible of the events in question one considers one by one the alternative explanations and tries to eliminate them until only the single most probable one remains. One then tries with further observations to confirm or reject the initially preferred explanation. In addition, series of apparently similar phenomena are searched for recurrent features that may provide clues to causative conditions and processes of occurrence.[24]

"The study of spontaneous cases of extrasensory perception," he added, "sometimes needs defending against the disapproval of those who have come to equate science with the controlled conditions that laboratories can offer and naturalistic situations cannot. Here the first

---

[24] Ian Stevenson, "Some of My Journeys in Medicine," The Flora Levy Lecture in the Humanities, Vol. 9 (Lafayette: The University of Southwest Louisiana, 1989). www.medicine.virginia.edu/clinical/departments/psychiatry/sections/cspp/dops/publ icationslinks/some-of-my-journeys-in-medicine.pdf.

point to make is that some important phenomena, such as the weather, volcanoes, fossils, earthquakes, and meteorites, do not occur in laboratories under controlled conditions, and yet we study them with scientific methods. We do this because science is not a physical location."[25]

What Stevenson discovered in a typical case of the reincarnation type showed the following features: 1) Starting in years 2–4 the child spontaneously narrated details of a previous life. 2) The volume and clarity of statements from the child increased until ages 5–6, when the child talked less about them. 3) By age 8, remarks about previous life generally ceased. 4) Unexpected behavior unusual for a child but concordant with behavior of the deceased person occurred, such as phobias for guns or special interests and appetites. 5) In many cases the child had a birthmark or congenital deformity that corresponded in location and appearance to the body of the previous personality. A high number of reincarnated personalities reported violent death, to which the child alluded. 6) In some cultures the individual who "reincarnates" predicted his or her next incarnation and sometimes appeared in a dream to the expectant mother of the child to announce an intention to reincarnate in the baby. 7) After the age of 10 these child subjects usually developed normally.[26]

Stevenson's work never managed to gain widespread acceptance in the scientific community, largely because he couldn't offer any physical evidence to support claims of reincarnation (the same argument used against the UFO phenomenon and ghosts).[27] But he

---

[25] Ibid.

[26] Remi Cadoret, "European Cases of the Reincarnation Type," *American Journal of Psychiatry*, Vol. 162, No. 4: 823.

[27] There were notable exceptions. In 1977, the *Journal of Nervous and Mental Disease* devoted most of one issue to Stevenson's work. In an editorial, psychiatrist Eugene Brody wrote, "Our decision to publish this material, which may appear to some outside the limits of scientific inquiry, recognizes the scientific and personal credibility of the authors, the legitimacy of their research methods, and the conformity of their reasoning to the usual canons of rational thought." Eugene

compiled a large body of research that for an objective observer must at the very least raise questions. For example, in one celebrated case a boy in Beirut described being a 25-year-old mechanic who died after being hit by a speeding car on a beach road. Witnesses said the boy gave the name of the driver as well as the names of his sisters, parents, and cousins, and the location of the crash. The details matched the life of a man who had died years before the child was born, and who was apparently unconnected to the child's family. Stevenson always sought alternative explanations, but repeatedly came across cases like this where none could be found.[28]

Stevenson himself was cautious in his conclusions. As Dr. Jim Tucker noted in a review of Stevenson's work, he always emphasized that no single case offered evidence that compelled a belief in reincarnation, and he was adamant that the term "proof" not be used for the evidence he had accumulated or even hoped to find. Nonetheless, Stevenson considered reincarnation to be the best explanation for the stronger cases that he had investigated, and he took a dim view of the narrow-mindedness of much of modern science when it came to subjects such as reincarnation.[29]

"For me," he stated in 1989, "everything now believed by scientists

---

Brody, "Research in Reincarnation and Editorial Responsibility," *The Journal of Nervous and Mental Disease*, Vol. 165, No. 3 (September 1977): 151. In the same issue, psychiatrist Harold Lief commented: "While I withhold final judgment on the content and conclusions of my friend's study of telepathy, xenoglossy, and reincarnation, I am a 'true believer' in his methods of investigation. Stevenson's writing and research reports are the work of a man who is methodical and thorough in his data collection and clear and lucid in their analysis and presentation." Stevenson, concluded Lief, was either "making a colossal mistake, or he will be known as 'the Galileo of the 20th century.'" Harold Lief, "Commentary on Dr. Ian Stevenson's 'The Evidence of Man's Survival After Death'," Ibid., 171.

[28] Tom Shroder, "Ian Stevenson: Sought to Document Memories of Past Lives in Children," *Washington Post*, 11 Feb. 2007.

[29] Jim B. Tucker, "Ian Stevenson and Cases of the Reincarnation Type," *Journal of Scientific Exploration*, Vol. 22, No. 1 (2008): 41.

is open to question, and I am always dismayed to find that many scientists accept current knowledge as forever fixed. They confuse the product with the process."[30]

Even Carl Sagan, who set out to debunk Stevenson's work, was forced to conclude that it was worthy of consideration. In *Demon Haunted World* he noted that the claims "that young children sometimes report details of a previous life, which upon checking turn out to be accurate and which they could not have known about in any other way than reincarnation" represented a phenomenon for which he could not offer an explanation. Of course, this was not an admission by Sagan that he believed in reincarnation. Rather, he was simply conceding that it was an idea "that might be true," and which had what he considered "at least some, although still dubious, experimental support."[31]

This brings me back to Michio Kaku and the example of the e-mail he used in answer to my question about a galactic conversation. He might have had it right, but perhaps he applied it in the wrong way. Yes, there could indeed be a message, and the information in the message is broken up into all sorts of little pieces, just like we do with e-mails. The mistake that Kaku might have made, however, is in seeing the message as something for us, or about us, or beyond us, when it may well be that the message *is* us. Perhaps *we* are the information, and slowly, over the course of time, the message is being re-assembled into its whole.

One final thought about reincarnation. Most of us think of it within the context of a human coming back as another human, but what if it's really a process of constant evolution, from the lowest form of life to the most advanced? Perhaps we begin as something like a paramecium and work our way up through myriad lifetimes until we hit the human stage, which is the final step on the staircase of

---

[30] Stevenson, "Some of My Journeys in Medicine."

[31] Carl Sagan and Ann Druyan, *The Demon-Haunted World: Science as a Candle in the Dark* (New York: Random House, 1995), 302.

individuality before we enter the door at the top and move into that collective phase of consciousness.

This might explain the affinity we have for pets, or why some people seem drawn to certain animals. In 1955, for example, the music critic Howard Taubman related how Finnish composer Jean Sibelius had considered this idea. "As a boy," wrote Taubman, "Sibelius wandered in the wilderness of his native province of Hame. Birds always fascinated him. 'Millions of years ago, in my previous incarnation,' he once told Jala [his son-in-law], 'I must have been related to swans or wild geese, because I can still feel that affinity.'"[32]

Philosopher Thomas Nagel examined the idea of consciousness and experience in his classic article, "What Is It Like To Be a Bat." It was impossible, in his view, for a human being to truly imagine what it would be like to be a bat, or any other animal. "I am restricted to the resources of my own mind," he wrote, "and those resources are inadequate to the task. I cannot perform it either by imagining additions to my present experience, or by imagining segments gradually subtracted from it, or by imagining some combination of additions, subtractions, and modifications. To the extent that I could look and behave like... a bat without changing my fundamental structure, my experiences would not be anything like the experiences of those animals."[33]

If we are meant to have a complete range of experiences then it would make sense that this would include not just the human experience but experience as other forms of life, including animals. As Nagel observed, "Even if I could by gradual degrees be transformed into a bat, nothing in my present constitution enables me to imagine what the experiences of such a future stage of myself thus metamorphosed would be like. The best evidence would come from

---

[32] Sylvia Cranston and Carey Williams, *Reincarnation: A New Horizon in Science, Religion and Society* (Pasadena, CA: Theosophical University Press, 1993), 340.

[33] Thomas Nagel, "What Is It Like To Be A Bat?" *The Philosophical Review*, Vol. 83, No. 4 (Oct., 1974): 435-450, 439.

the experiences of bats, if we only knew what they were like."[34] In other words, to understand the bat, we would have to become the bat. And so maybe we have.

Or perhaps maybe we *do*. Instead of viewing reincarnation as a stairway with humanity located at the top, maybe humanity sits at the bottom. We begin there and work our way through the other creatures, from cats to dogs to bats to the "lowly" paramecium.

Something to consider the next time we sit down for a turkey dinner, or a Big Mac, or pay for tickets to watch Michael Vick play football in our Society of the Spectacle.[35]

---

[34] Ibid.

[35] Vick was a Pro-Bowl caliber quarterback in the National Football League when he was convicted for his involvement in an illegal dog-fighting ring. He served 21 months in prison, after which he returned to professional football, where he is now the multi-million dollar starting quarterback for the Philadelphia Eagles.

John Buchan, 1st Baron Tweedsmuir, Governor-General of Canada from 1935 until 1940. "I find myself in some scene which I cannot have visited before and which is yet perfectly familiar." (Photo: Yousuf Karsh, Yousuf Karsh fonds / Library and Archives Canada, Accession 1987-054 – public domain)

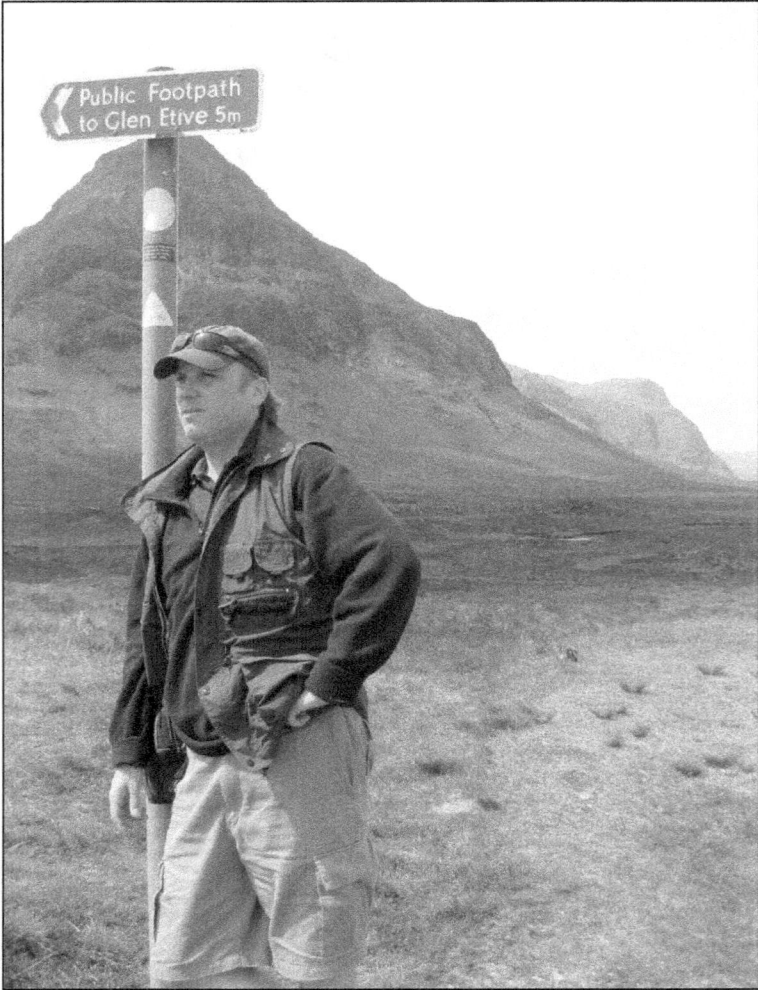

Yours truly in the Highlands of Scotland, 2009. Scotland was a land I immediately felt a connection to when I first arrived there as a student in 1987, as if I had lived there before.

Chapter Eight

The Observer Effect

I'm interested in trying to explore what I think is the truth at a given time in my life, and part of the process of being honest is – in my mind – talking about the idea that you're watching a movie. You're sitting here watching a movie. And I like that. It appeals to me intellectually, and also in a way I can't even explain.[1]
– Charlie Kaufmann

My best friend Peter Black was a master at the "come hither" look. He could sit in a bar, stare at a girl in a certain way, and in most instances he would establish a contact that led to a conversation at the very least.

I remember once betting him a pint of beer that he couldn't get a particular girl to notice him.

"Make it a pitcher of Stella Artois," he deadpanned, "and I'll have her and her friend at our table in ten minutes."

That seemed to be too good a deal to pass up because while I didn't think he could do it, the girl's friend was cute and I never had a problem playing wingman. So I took the bet, on the off chance that Peter could actually make it happen.

Less than seven minutes later I was ordering him a pitcher of beer and buying a couple of drinks for the girls, who had come over to our table without Peter saying a word to them, or motioning, or anything like that. He just looked at them in that certain way of his and by doing so he changed the course of events. It wasn't something that I

---

[1] Charlie Kaufmann, "Charlie Kaufmann on Synecdoche, New York," *Rotten Tomatoes*, 22 October 2008. http://goo.gl/EAJdc.

could do myself, because I would almost always look away at the pivotal moment. Even if I didn't look away, I could never quite read the "signs."[2]

We can see the basic principle that observation changes behavior manifest itself in our own lives each and every day. The example of Peter and the girl in the bar is amusing, but a far more concrete and pervasive example comes from my own work as a documentary filmmaker, where the first rule of thumb is that as soon as you point a camera at someone you invariably change their behavior. People react to being observed.

Many documentary filmmakers tend to look down on "reality" television as a kind of abomination. They contend that it isn't an accurate representation of "reality." It's true that such shows are heavily scripted, whether in the field or in the edit suite. Even if they weren't, however, how could one expect someone on a show like *Survivor* or *Pawn Stars* or *Ghost Hunters* to behave the same way he normally would without a camera crew following him around?

But what some of my holier-than-thou colleagues in the documentary world won't tell you is that documentaries are no different. When I was filming *Stanton T. Friedman is Real* in 2001, for example, there were in many cases marked differences between how Friedman, the man who re-discovered the Roswell UFO case in the late 1970s, interacted with people when the camera was on, and how he interacted with them when it wasn't. There were also a number of planned shots that we set up of Friedman. In one instance, for example, we had him walk down the middle of a deserted road. When we ran through the shots beforehand Friedman acted normally, because he knew the camera wasn't on. When we ran it for the camera, his gait changed, as did his expression. He knew he was being "observed" and he altered his behavior accordingly.

Another good example of how the observer effect changes reality within a documentary production can be seen in the work of J. D.

---

[2] Indeed, years later I wrote a song about the experience. Paul Kimball, "Semaphore," Perf. Mike Trainor (2011). http://goo.gl/3Mwf8.

Johannes. A former Marine, Johannes directed *Outside the Wire*, a series of documentaries about the Iraq War and the subsequent occupation of that country.[3] As a result, he spent a significant amount of time in the field with American troops. He wrote about the potential impact of the observer effect on both his filmmaking and the soldiers with whom he was embedded.

"How much did my presence with a camera documenting the event modify the event?" Johannes asked candidly. He recounted one particular sequence in the film *Danger Close*, where a soldier made a dangerous run across a roof while addressing the camera, and concluded that the soldier may not have done so if Johannes had not been present and filming. "My presence with a television camera changed the event," he wrote.[4]

Modern news reportage is similarly impacted by observation. In the riots that followed the loss by the Vancouver Canucks in the 2011 Stanley Cup finals, some people in the streets of Vancouver engaged in destructive behavior precisely because they knew that they were being filmed. If the cameras hadn't been there, it's likely that at least some of them wouldn't have taken part in the mayhem. Conversely, there are myriad cases where the presence of a news crew in a war-zone has prevented people from committing atrocities.

We constantly change our behavior based on our interactions with others, or simply based on being observed, even if it's only the feeling of being watched.[5] All that "reality" television does is create a different "reality" than the one which might have existed had the cameras not been there. In this critical sense it's no different than any

[3] J. D. Johannes, "J. D. Johannes: About the Director," *Outside the Wire*. http://outsidethewire.com/about-the-director.html.

[4] J. D. Johannes, "Observer Effect, Uncertainty Principle & War Correspondence," *Outside the Wire*. http://goo.gl/AcpWN.

[5] Observers are increasingly artificial in nature, like the pervasive video cameras that we see on almost every street corner in most cities these days. We've become a surveillance society, which I consider to be a very troubling development.

"traditional" documentary. Both are based on an observed "reality," and the filmmaker's ultimate presentation and interpretation of that "reality."

The intriguing question is whether one can actually *control* the change induced by the observer effect and therefore influence people's behavior, as opposed to generating a random effect that changes their behavior in unpredictable ways.

In other words, do we ride the wave, or does the wave ride us?

For example, Peter wanted a *particular* result when he looked at the girl in the bar. Accordingly, he looked at her in a particular way. If it had been someone like me who was less adept at "the look," the likelihood of getting the desired result would have been much lower.

I think it's possible that the observer effect doesn't just apply to the paranormal, but that it could form the core of what it's all about.

When we look at UFO cases, for example, I think we can discern a pattern indicative of an advanced non-human intelligence interacting with us and then observing our reactions, just as we do when we take a laser pointer and run the light along a wall to amuse a cat.[6]

A case like one that occurred here in Nova Scotia in 1976 seems to fit this pattern. An RCMP constable was called to investigate strange lights in the sky above a house in Lower Sackville, a suburb of Halifax. When he arrived the lights were still there. He checked with the local airports and they had no record of anything in that area. The officer's report included the following description:

> With the aid of the complainants' binoculars I noticed three unidentified flying objects. All of them were round in shape and had red flashing lights on the bottom and also a flashing white light. There was a stable green light which appeared to

---

[6] A number of writers have used this analogy, most recently the late Mac Tonnies. Mac played the game with his own cats: "All the while I'm controlling the red dot, I'm taking pains to make it behave like something intelligible... I make it 'climb,' 'jump,' and scuttle when cornered. This sense of physicality seems to be the element that makes chasing the laser so engaging – both for the cats and for me." Mac Tonnies, *The Cryptoterrestrials,* 21 – 22.

be located inside the objects. At this time the objects were stationary; however, I noticed that they began to move and when they did, the lights changed to a turquoise color. As the objects began to move, their altitude became greater. There was no sound or smell. The sky was clear at this time.

He observed the lights for a prolonged period during which time neither he nor the other witnesses heard anything out of the ordinary. "I might add," he wrote later, "that there is no possibility at all that what I saw might have been stars or even another planet as I was looking through the binoculars and therefore, would have been able to tell the difference."

The constable then went next door to see if the neighbors had seen anything, which is standard procedure. What he discovered were a husband and wife who had been hiding in their bedroom, scared out of their wits by a loud, persistent roaring noise unlike anything that they had heard before. They told the officer that they felt the source of the strident noise was something hovering low over their suburban home. The husband, who was employed by the Department of National Defence as a naval architect, was certain that it wasn't anything like a helicopter or conventional aircraft, with which he was well familiar. Then, in a final twist, they informed the officer that the noises had ended at the very moment he had knocked on their door.[7]

To describe what happened as "not normal" would be an understatement. These were credible witnesses who experienced the same event but in completely different ways. One couple was terrorized by an abnormally loud sound that shook their entire house, while at the same time their neighbors were watching strange and unexplained lights in the sky next door with the police officer. It is the epitome of a "high strangeness" incident.[8]

---

[7] Quoted in Paul Kimball, "High Strangeness in Halifax," *The Other Side of Truth*, 19 October 2005. http://goo.gl/2KRaj.

[8] "High strangeness" is a term most often associated with scientist and UFO researcher Jacques Vallee, who believed that UFO researchers, particularly the ones

184

In many ways the Lower Sackville case drives home the point that Mac Tonnies made at the end of my 2007 documentary *Best Evidence: Top 10 UFO Sightings*, when he stated:

> Whatever UFOs might ultimately prove to be, and we might never find out, it seems to me that they are definitely worth scientific consideration if for no other reason than they affect how we think and how we perceive our universe. They apparently have been recurring throughout time, and they have infringed upon our belief systems to the point where we now think of the alien as something very specific. If for no other reason than understanding how our mind reacts to the presence of a possible "other" in our midst, I think it's imperative that we understand UFOs and what they are. If, on the other hand, they are physical objects, or para-physical objects, which might be the case, and I don't think that we have the proper vocabulary for that yet frankly, I think that it's doubly important that we understand what these things are, because if they are real, if they are craft of some sort, if they are disinformation devices, then it seems to me that what they are doing is influencing the way we think, influencing our mythologies and our collective way of knowing ourselves, and I think that's a pretty sacred thing to be messing with. It would certainly behoove us to understand what we're dealing with.[9]

---

convinced that UFO reports indicated proof of extraterrestrial visitation, often overlooked or downplayed those aspects of UFO reports which seemed to represent "absurd behavior" – or "high strangeness" – that couldn't be related to actual phenomena. "This argument," he wrote, "can be criticized as an anthropocentric, self-selected observation resulting from our own limited viewpoint as 21st century Homo Sapiens trying to draw conclusions about the nature of the universe." Jacques F. Vallee and Eric W. Davis, "Incommensurability, Orthodoxy and the Physics of High Strangeness: A 6-Layer Model for Anomalous Phenomena," *Jacques Vallee*, 24 October 2003. www.jacquesvallee.net/bookdocs/Vallee-Davis-model.pdf.

[9] *Best Evidence: Top 10 UFO Sightings*, directed by Paul Kimball (Halifax: Redstar

I've quoted Mac in full because for me his statement stands as the perfect summation of why the UFO phenomenon remains a genuine and compelling mystery. I'm convinced that something is happening in the skies above us. I can present case after case after case that show there is something real to the UFO phenomenon that has defied our best attempts at prosaic explanation, and which seems to exhibit signs of advanced non-human intelligence.

A good example can be seen with the UFO case that was overwhelmingly selected as the strongest in terms of evidence by the researchers I polled for *Best Evidence*. On July 17, 1957, the six man crew of a United States Air Force RB-47 aircraft, which was outfitted with state-of-the-art electronic countermeasures and detection equipment, including electronic intelligence stations manned by highly trained electronic warfare officers nicknamed "ravens" or "crows," was literally tailgated by something that continues to defy explanation to this day.[10]

The plane was flying out of Forbes Air Force base in Kansas. The crew was on a training mission to shake down the aircraft and test out its sophisticated components. They detected and recorded on wire recorders and tape recorders the electronic signals, radar-like in nature, that came from the same direction and location as a UFO that followed them as they flew over Louisiana, Texas, Mississippi and Oklahoma for more than two hours that night.

Films, 2007). Television. Available on-line at: http://beyonderstv.com/paulkimball-media/paul-kimballs-real-world-films/best-evidence-top-10-ufo-sightings/.

[10] James E. McDonald, "Science in Default: Twenty-Two Years of Inadequate UFO Investigations," The 134th meeting of the American Association for the Advancement of Science (Boston, 27 December 1969). Available on-line at: http://goo.gl/uKjQ7. The RB47 case was extensively investigated by McDonald, at the time a highly respected professor of atmospheric sciences at the University of Arizona. After interviewing all of the RB47 crew members, he concluded: "What is of greatest present interest is the point that here we have a well-reported, multi-channel, multiple-witness UFO report, coming in fact from within the Air Force itself… conceded to be unexplained."

I interviewed Lieutenant Colonel Bruce Bailey for the film. Bailey was a highly decorated veteran of the United States Air Force who served as a "raven" on RB-47s at the height of the Cold War.[11] After he retired he became an author. Among his books are *Flying the RB47*, an historical study of the RB-47s and the men who flew them, and *We See All: A Pictorial History of the 55th Strategic Reconnaissance Wing 1947-1967*.[12] He knew the crew involved in the 1957 incident, and described them as follows:

> The crew involved in the UFO incident was one of the top crews in the wing. They were instructors and evaluators in the standardization division and were highly respected. They had the most experience and the best training. The aircraft commander, in fact, Lewis Chase, he made a landing after take-off when one of the outboard engines froze up and broke off and broke the wing off there, and he brought the aircraft back in. That attests to his skill as a pilot. In the back-end, the three "crows" back there were the most experienced, and they trained all of the new "crows" coming into the wing. Provenzano and McClure trained me when I came in, as a matter of fact. Eventually these guys were not on the same crew because they had so much experience and knowledge that they were put on separate crews and became three instructors and evaluators within the wing.[13]

As the RB-47 flown by these experienced men moved over Texas, Major Chase contacted radar operators at Duncanville Air Force

---

[11] By the time of his retirement, Bailey had been awarded the Bronze Star, the Distinguished Flying Cross several times, and wore the Combat Crew badge.

[12] Bruce Bailey, *Flying the RB47* (Bruce Bailey, 2000); Bruce Bailey, *We See All: Pictorial History of the 55th Strategic Reconnaissance Wing 1947-1967* (Bruce Bailey, 1982).

[13] *Best Evidence*.

Station in Texas, who confirmed that their radar had also detected the UFO. The UFO continued to play "tag" with the RB47, which had left its scheduled flight path to pursue the object, until the aircraft began to run low on fuel and turned to head home. The UFO followed the RB47 until the signal finally faded as the crew approached Oklahoma City.

In his report on the encounter, the Director of Intelligence of the 55th Strategic Reconnaissance Wing stated that he had "no doubt the electronic D/F's coincided exactly with visual observations by a/c [aircraft commander] numerous times, thus indicating positively the object being the signal source."[14]

Despite all of the evidence, Project Blue Book concluded that the object was an ordinary civilian jetliner. In doing so they failed to explain the ongoing nature of the incident over several states, the appearance and disappearance of the object, both visually and on radar and electronic countermeasures equipment, and how the Duncanville radar station failed to distinguish between a civilian aircraft that was almost a thousand kilometers away from the RB47, and a UFO.[15]

According to researcher Brad Sparks, the case is unique because it's "the only time in history that radio or radar signals have been detected and recorded from a UFO. Not just using radar to bounce signals off a UFO. We actually detected something that the UFO seemed to be

---

[14] James E. McDonald, "UFO Encounter I: Sample Case Selected by the UFO Subcommittee of the AIAA," *Astronautics & Aeronautics* (July 1971): 70.

[15] The Project Blue Book explanation was also at odds with the Electronics Branch of the United States Air Force's Air Technical Intelligence Center, which was Project Blue Book's parent organization. It reviewed the case and concluded that, "There is such a mass of evidence which tends to all tie in together to indicate the presence of a physical object or UFO," and that it was "difficult to conclude that nothing was present, in the face of visual and other data presented." See: Brad Sparks, "Case Update : RB-47 case, July 17, 1957, Mississippi-Louisiana-Texas-Oklahoma," *National Investigations Committee on Aerial Phenomena*, 7 August 2008. www.nicap.org/reports/rb47_update_sparks.htm.

sending out."[16]

This indication of intelligence made the Project Blue Book explanation even more absurd, as did the fact that this wasn't the only time an RB47 encountered a UFO. Lieutenant Colonel Bailey recounted his own similar incident:

> We were flying a mission during the Cuban Missile Crisis, where we flew a mission every day to go down and take a good, close look at Cuba and to identify any site that should fire on a U2 or any US vessel or aircraft. On this mission, we would fly down to New Orleans and hit a tanker right over the Gulf of Mexico, out of New Orleans, get filled up with fuel, and then head on to Cuba. Well, on this mission, shortly after completing our air re-fueling, we had some aircraft or something come up, a bright light, and intercept us. Ground control was tracking it, they could copy it too. It wasn't with us that long, probably a total of ten minutes, but that was broken in the middle with a gap of about two minutes when it went away. The differences in our experience and the other crew in 1957 was our equipment in the back end. All we got was noise. It just wiped us out. We didn't get any intelligible signals at all.[17]

---

[16] *Best Evidence*. Sparks' analysis was based on the complete files of the 1968 Condon committee, which had been thought lost, the complete files of Project Blue Book, James McDonald, the National Investigations Committee on Aerial Phenomena, and the Aerial Phenomena Research Organization, as well as portions of Philip Klass' files, and scientific, technical, and historical data from Boeing, General Electric, American Airlines, National Climatic Data Center, National Geophysical Data Center, Electromagnetic Compatibility Analysis Center, Naval Intelligence Command, Air Force Archives, Air Training Command, and Aerospace Defense Command (formerly Air Defense Command). For a recent attempt at a rebuttal, see Tim Printy's various articles on the case at *Sunlite* 4, No. 1 (January – February 2012): 5 – 38. http://goo.gl/cTFDe. Lieutenant Colonel Bailey didn't find it compelling, and neither do I – but judge for yourselves.

[17] Ibid.

When asked what it was that he and his crew encountered over the Gulf of Mexico in 1962, Bailey could only offer the same conclusion reached by Major Chase and his crew five years earlier:

> Unidentified flying object is what would explain it, I guess. The crew up front could see it. We had no windows in the "crow" compartment, so we couldn't see anything. But they could see it, and what they saw jibed with what ground control was reporting, and the navigator could also track it on his radar. It all tied together. There was something there, and it had a capability far greater than anything we could do.[18]

We talk about ourselves as witnesses, or sometimes as experiencers, when confronted with something like what happened to the people in Lower Sackville, or the crew of the RB47, that seems to be outside our range of understanding. But what are we witnessing or experiencing, and why? And while we are watching "them" (or "it," as the case may be), it is clearly under conditions that "they" control, at least to the extent of initiating contact – much like my friend Peter did at the bar, or a documentary director does just before the camera rolls. We may be witnesses, but "they" are the ultimate observers.

While one could see incidents such as these as some sort of experiment by an advanced non-human intelligence, in the same way that we run rats through mazes, I think that given the wide range and interactive nature of paranormal events it's reasonable to speculate – as I have throughout this book – that we could be something more important to them, and that any interaction with such an intelligence has a potentially greater purpose.

It is at this point that we must pause to consider the question that I think is central to any examination of the paranormal as it relates to our observation by, and interaction with, an advanced non-human intelligence: if "they" do indeed exist, what do they see when they look at us?

---

[18] Ibid.

Chapter Nine

The Other Side of Truth

"Between truth and the search for it, I choose the second."[1]
- Bernard Berenson

In October, 2006, I put together a one-day conference called the New Frontiers Symposium here in Halifax, Nova Scotia, which featured a wide range of speakers, including Stan Friedman, Nick Redfern, Greg Bishop and the late Mac Tonnies. During his thought-provoking lecture on "post-humanism," Mac asked a critical question as he pondered whether we would make it to a post-human future (or any future, for that matter): "does humanity deserve to survive?"[2]

The only thing more provocative than his question, which drew more than a few raised eyebrows from the crowd, was his answer, which he gave after a short, thoughtful pause.

"I don't know," he said quietly.

When I look at the world today, much less at the whole of human history, I'm forced to agree with Mac. We've done some amazing things in our relatively short time as a sentient species on this planet. We built great cities, crossed the oceans and then the skies, split the atom, and eventually made our way to space. But to what end, and at

---

[1] Bernard Berenson, quoted at "Quotes by Berenson," *Long Wharf Theatre*, accessed 24 August 2012, http://www.longwharf.org/old-masters-quotes-berenson-and-duveen; "Bernard Berenson Art Quotes," *The Painter's Keys*. http://quote.robertgenn.com/auth_search.php?authid=2868.

[2] Nick Redfern, "New Frontiers Symposium, Canada, 2006," *Fortean Times*, 2006. http://www.forteantimes.com/features/fbi/13/new_frontiers_symposium_canada_2006.html.

what cost?

I've been to Los Angeles many times. I consider it one of the great cities of the world, but the problem is that it's really only great for a privileged few. Poverty and homelessness are visible everywhere – except, perhaps, in the poshest neighborhoods like Beverley Hills, where the police work very hard to make sure that the dark side of our society is kept at a safe distance, as if the poor were the zombies in George Romero's *Land of the Dead*.

And then there's the question of how we "acquired" the land upon which we built this great city and all the others like it in North America. Our ancestors committed the kind of genocide against the indigenous population that would have given even Slobodan Milosevic pause. Of course, we remember the native Americans through our sports teams, like the Atlanta Braves, Cleveland Indians, Edmonton Eskimos, Kansas City Chiefs, and, as the apotheosis of offensiveness, the Washington Redskins. It would be as if aliens from Mars arrived here tomorrow, wiped out the majority of the human population, and then hundreds of years later "commemorated" us by naming a couple of their "foosball" teams the Zeldergarb Pinkskins and the Zolatarin Terrans.

When I visit Los Angeles I stay with my friend Greg Bishop, who lives in a predominantly Jewish neighborhood. The Los Angeles Museum of the Holocaust is a couple of blocks away from his house, and there's a nice statue on the corner of Fairfax Avenue and Beverley Boulevard in memory of Raoul Wallenberg, the Swedish diplomat who saved tens of thousands of Jews during the Second World War.[3]

Unfortunately, the fact that we have memorials for something like this at all reminds us of who we *really are* as a species, and it's not a pretty picture. For every Wallenberg, how many were there who actively participated in the Holocaust? Perhaps worse still, how many

---

[3] Wallenberg is one of my personal heroes. For an excellent study of his life, see John Bierman, *Righteous Gentile: The Story of Raoul Wallenberg, Missing Hero of the Holocaust*, rev. ed. (London: Penguin Books, 1996).

simply looked away – and not just in Germany?[4]

If the Holocaust was just an isolated incident in human history perhaps we could rationalize it in some way, but it's not. Each case is of course unique in its specific details, but they all stand as signposts along an incremental continuum of horror, violence, and oppression, often perpetrated by people who were once victims themselves. For example, we can see the same pattern of behavior, in principle if not in scale, being repeated in the Middle East today, only now the roles have been reversed. It is the Israelis who wield the cudgel of systemic violence and degradation towards other human beings, who are themselves far from blameless. Indeed, if one was to write an accurate history of the human race, "Far From Blameless" would be a most fitting title.

This is the big picture. But there are myriad smaller signs that we haven't progressed one iota as a species throughout our history, each of which fits as a brick in the foundation upon which the edifice of horror has been built.

The Romans had gladiators? Well, so do we. There are differences, of course. Roman gladiators sometimes died in combat, whereas our gladiators die years later, beset by myriad medical problems incurred in the name of entertainment, broken shells of the men and women that they once were and could have been. We call them professional football players, or hockey players, or mixed martial arts fighters, or whatever, and elevate them to the status of gods, with a far larger audience and much more lucrative compensation than the Roman gladiators ever enjoyed, but the modus operandi remains the same, even as it has been extended into almost all aspects of our lives.

---

[4] One of the more shameful episodes was the refusal by Cuba, the United States, and Canada to allow the *MS St. Louis* to land in 1939. The ship was carrying 937 German Jewish refugees, of whom it is estimated a quarter eventually died at the hands of the Nazis after they were forced to return to Europe. See "Voyage of the St. Louis," U.S. Holocaust Museum. http://goo.gl/y8lm2; see also Gordon Thomas and Max Gordon Witts, *Voyage of the Damned: A Shocking True Story of Hope, Betrayal and Nazi Terror* (London: JR Books, 2009).

The bread and circuses of ancient Rome have become in our modern world what the French political philosopher Guy Debord described as *The Society of the Spectacle*. First published in 1967, Debord's treatise has only grown in relevance in the years since. He outlined the development of a modern society in which authentic social life has been replaced with its representation.

"In societies where modern conditions of production prevail," wrote Debord, "all of life presents itself as an immense accumulation of *spectacles*. Everything that was directly lived has moved away into a representation."[5]

Debord described the spectacle as the mechanism by which a sort of never-ending present is created and maintained. On the surface it entertains, but in reality the quality of life is impoverished, with a diminishment over time of the thirst for knowledge and authentic experience. This in turn has led to the loss of our authentic selves. We are encouraged to consume as opposed to create.

It's a theme I addressed in a poem called "Scene from a Mall" that I wrote a couple of years ago whilst standing near the "food court" of a local shopping mall just before Christmas, which is perhaps the ultimate manifestation of the modern spectacle.

> Time stops by the 3rd floor railing
> next to the food court
> (no real food actually served),
> as I endure the grey glop mush of
> mediocrity which passes for the
> human race these days,
> the screens of their blackberries
> the only illumination they'll ever know.
> If they all dropped dead
> no one would miss them,
> least of all themselves...

---

[5] Guy Debord, *The Society of the Spectacle*, Chapter 1: 1. Available on-line at: http://library.nothingness.org/articles/SI/en/pub_contents/4.

an inconspicuously conspicuous mass of
conspicuously inconspicuous consumerites,
legions of the lackluster
for the new Imperium.

In 2007, I wrote another poem on this subject, which I called "The New Frontier":

Soul grifters...
time drifters –
no longer heavy lifters,
Independence,
but no longer independent,
faces like the aftermath
of a nuclear weapons test.
The irradiated chickens
(half lives and half wits)
have come home
to roost
on the new frontier –
pick a channel
and watch them
cluck.

"The images detached from every aspect of life," observed Debord, "fuse in a common stream in which the unity of this life can no longer be re-established. Reality considered *partially* unfolds, in its own general unity, as a pseudo-world *apart,* an object of mere contemplation. The specialization of images of the world is completed in the world of the autonomous image, where the liar has lied to himself. The spectacle in general, as the concrete inversion of life, is the autonomous movement of the non-living."[6]

It should come as no surprise that even our wars are trending towards this non-reality. "Smart" bombs are delivered by drone

---

[6] Debord, Chapter 1: 2.

aircraft controlled by soldiers in a distant location who watch it all on a video screen. Soon even our mass murder will no longer be authentic, which will no doubt make it that much easier to commit, and to ignore. We are not encouraged to think; rather, we are trained to obey.[7]

It's true that there's another side of the ledger, where we can find great composers, authors, philosophers, spiritual leaders, painters, humanitarians, and peacemakers, all of whom have worked to enhance the human condition in their own way. But I would argue that these men and women are *the exception rather than the rule*, and they are not the exemplars celebrated by our society. We remember MacArthur, Patton and Rommel, and have created a cult of personality around current military leaders like David Petraeus (and professional soldiers in general), but if you ask people to identify Dag Hammarskjöld, the great diplomat and peacemaker who served as Secretary General of the United Nations until his death in a plane crash in 1961 while trying to negotiate a cease-fire in the Congo, you would be sorely disappointed.[8] Mozart and Bach take a back seat to the pop tart du jour, while arts programs in schools are cut so that kids can be taught about business. More than ever, people have become as disposable as the commodities that they consume.

When I think it all over I come to the conclusion that Mac was

---

[7] The proliferation of film and television programming related to zombies in recent years should also come as no surprise. Shows like *The Walking Dead* and films such as *28 Days Later* are in many ways like looking in a metaphorical mirror. Perhaps somewhere deep in their subconscious viewers realize that they have far more in common with the zombies than they do with the plucky heroes who fight them.

[8] Hammarskjöld was the Secretary General of the United Nations from 1953 until his death in a 1961 airplane crash in the Congo. He's another one of my heroes. See: Foote, Wilder, ed., *Servant of Peace: A Selection of the Speeches and Statements of Dag Hammarskjöld, Secretary-General of the United Nations 1953-1961* (New York, Harper & Row, 1962); Dag Hammarskjöld, *Markings*, trans. Leif Sjöberg and W. H. Auden (New York: Ballantine, 1984); and Brian Urquart, *Hammarskjold* (New York: Alfred A. Knopf, 1972), which I consider to be the definitive biography of Hammarskjöld.

probably more understanding than I am. Where he answered that he didn't know whether or not we deserve to survive as a species, I would answer that I *do* know. As a species, we *do not deserve* to survive. To paraphrase the songwriter Morrissey: "We just haven't earned it yet, baby."

When we watch sci-fi monsters such as the Daleks, or the Borg, or the Cybermen, we do so knowing that they aren't real, and so even though they might scare us they can't actually hurt us. We further comfort ourselves with the idea that we could never be like them. And that's where we're wrong. If we want a vision of our present, and our future – the "modern man," if you will – we can find it by looking in the past.

Albert Speer was Hitler's Minister of Armaments from 1942 onwards, and for much of the 1930s and early 1940s he was the closest thing that Hitler had to a friend. He was tried at Nuremberg in 1945 and 1946, and found guilty of war crimes and crimes against humanity. He was sentenced to 20 years imprisonment at Spandau prison, a term which he served in full.

At his trial Speer was the one Nazi leader who admitted at least a sense of general responsibility for the crimes of the regime. He was always very careful, however, to deny direct knowledge of the greatest crime of all – the Holocaust. If it had been shown that he knew about the extermination of the Jews he surely would have been hanged, which is the fate that befell his underling Fritz Sauckel, the man who rounded up the labor that Speer used to keep the factories running.

In the years that followed his release Speer published a number of books, including the best-selling memoir *Inside the Third Reich*, which told his side of the story and which was accepted by many historians as a reasonably accurate and candid version of events. However, his claims not to have known about the Holocaust became more controversial as the years went along and new information surfaced, particularly about his presence at the Posen Conference on October 6, 1943, where Reichsführer-SS Heinrich Himmler gave a speech to Nazi leaders in which he detailed what was happening in the concentration camps and the killing fields of eastern Europe. Speer was mentioned several times in the speech, and Himmler seemed to address him directly.

In *Inside the Third Reich*, Speer mentioned his own address to the officials (which took place earlier in the day), but he didn't mention Himmler's speech. He later claimed that he left before Himmler took the podium. However, Speer recalled that on the evening after the conference many Nazi officials were so drunk that they needed help boarding the special train which was to take them to a meeting with Hitler. Speer claimed that in writing *Inside the Third Reich* he had confused an incident that happened at another conference at Posen a year later with the conference in 1943, a claim which strained credulity on such an important point. To the end of his life, he maintained that he didn't know about the Holocaust, and that he was not at Posen for Himmler's speech.[9]

Gitta Sereny, in her book *Albert Speer: His Battle With Truth*, concluded that Speer must have known about the Final Solution at least by the time of the Posen conference whether or not he was actually present at Himmler's speech. She based this judgment on extensive conversations with Speer, analysis of his published and unpublished writings, and interviews with Speer's family and colleagues. In Sereny's view, Speer's acknowledgment of his guilt as a Nazi and his complicity in crimes of which he claimed to be unaware was part of a complex process by which he evaded acknowledgment of the full truth.[10]

The matter was finally resolved in 2007 with the publication of a letter that Speer had written to the widow of a Belgian resistance

---

[9] Paul L. Montgomery, "Albert Speer Dies at 76; Close Associate of Hitler," *New York Times*, 2 September 1981. Montgomery wrote that "Speer was the only Nazi leader to admit his guilt," which demonstrated just how successful Speer's campaign at public rehabilitation had been.

[10] Gitta Sereny, *Albert Speer: His Battle With Truth* (New York: Random House, 1995).

fighter in 1971. Speer wrote, "There is no doubt - I was present as Himmler announced on October 6, 1943 that all Jews would be killed." Even after this admission, however, he continued to equivocate. "Who would believe me that I suppressed this," he added. "That it would have been easier to have written all of this in my memoirs?"[11]

I have always found Speer fascinating, not because I bought into the myth of the "good Nazi" that he peddled for so many years and which so many people seemed to accept, but because an examination of the extent of Albert Speer's complicity in the Holocaust, and his "struggle with the truth," as Sereny termed it, leads to an even bigger and more important question: what did the average German know? And that in turn is a question that leads to *us*.

It's easy now to look back at the Nazis and say that it was *then*, and *there*, and *they* were a singular kind of evil. We look at the architects of the war and the Holocaust, men like Hitler, Himmler, and Heydrich, who have assumed an almost cartoon-like quality over the decades, and comfort ourselves with the thought that, like the Borg or the Daleks, it could never happen to us.

But people like Hitler are the exception. History has shown us, time and again, that people like Speer are the rule. He was bright, educated, and filled with ambition. He was the thoroughly modern man who enabled the monsters to flourish. It was probably the key factor that saved his life at Nuremberg. Compared with an uneducated thug like Sauckel, or a pure killer like Heydrich's successor, Ernst Kaltenbrunner, Speer looked normal because he *was* normal. Subconsciously, he reminded the Western judges of themselves. They could convict him, and they could sentence him to prison, but they couldn't bring themselves to hang him because they couldn't bring themselves to see him for who he really was. In the end, he was their kind of Nazi.

That was their tragic mistake. Without Speer and millions like him

---

[11] Kate Connolly, "Letter proves Speer knew of Holocaust plan," *The Guardian*, 13 March 2007. Available on-line at: http://goo.gl/JP6aN.

there would have been no Nazi regime, no Second World War, no Holocaust. He was not less guilty; he was the *most* guilty of them all – not because he was the kind of monster that hides in the shadows, but because he was the kind of monster that lives within us all.

When one looks at the life and career of Albert Speer the central issue is not what he knew, or even what he wanted to know, but what he *did not* want to know. Then we have to ask ourselves what happens when everyone in government, and industry, and our society in general, acts like Speer. What happens when people just don't want to know anymore?

That's the question that we confront every day, particularly in the Society of the Spectacle in which we live, where we have enough nuclear weapons to destroy the planet many times over. In such a world it isn't the next Adolf Hitler against whom we need to be on guard; it's the next Albert Speer, looking back at each of us in the mirror.[12]

The 20th century belonged to the likes of Speer. The First World War, the Second World War, the Armenian genocide, the Russian Civil War, the Chinese Civil War, the Holocaust, the Killing Fields of Cambodia, the Vietnam War, Soviet collectivization, the Iran – Iraq War, the Spanish Civil War, the Great Leap Forward, the Congo conflict, the Rwandan genocide, the Korean War... it was a never-ending story that has continued unabated into the 21st century. Indeed, as I write this, the war-hawks in Washington are pushing for a new war with Iran, even as troops are being pulled out of Iraq and Afghanistan after a decade of war and occupation.[13]

---

[12] As Laurence Rees wrote, the Nazis brought into the world an awareness of what technologically advanced human beings are capable of "as long as they possess a cold heart. Once allowed into the world, knowledge of what they did must not be unlearned. It lies there - ugly, inert, waiting to be rediscovered by each new generation." Laurence Rees, *Auschwitz: The Nazis and the 'Final Solution'* (London: BBC Books, 2005), 302.

[13] Brian Montopoli, "Romney, Gingrich at GOP debate: We'd go to war to keep Iran from getting nuclear weapons," *CBS News*, 12 November 2011.

If so many people have been killed then someone must have been doing the killing. And if people were doing the killing then many more people must have approved of it, or at the very least done nothing to stop it. Of course none of this really addresses all of the people who have died as a result of general day-to-day poverty, disease and malnutrition that could have been prevented if we as a species adhered to a different set of priorities. Violence comes in many forms. Then there's the fact that the vast majority of wealth is owned and controlled by a very small group of people.[14] Of course, this ignores the issue of how we define "wealth" and "value" in the first place – as things, as opposed to ideas. And on it goes.

The only reasonable conclusion that can be drawn from all of this is that we humans are violent, selfish, and cruel, and that these are traits which we celebrate and reward on a regular basis. We have become the embodiment of the banality of evil.

The saving grace is that I firmly believe we can be so much more. The human condition is not immutable; it's something that *we* have created over the course of our history, and that means that it's something we can change in the future. Saul Bellow wrote about this theme in his novel *Henderson the Rain King*. The eponymous main

---

http://www.cbsnews.com/8301-503544_162-57323686-503544/romney-gingrich-at-gop-debate-wed-go-to-war-to-keep-iran-from-getting-nuclear-weapons/.

[14] In the United States wealth is highly concentrated in a relatively few hands. As of 2007, the top 1% of households (the upper class) owned 34.6% of all privately held wealth, and the next 19% (the managerial, professional, and small business stratum) had 50.5%, which means that just 20% of the people owned a remarkable 85%, leaving only 15% of the wealth for the bottom 80% (wage and salary workers). In terms of financial wealth (total net worth minus the value of one's home), the top 1% of households had an even greater share: 42.7%. As C. William Domhoff, Professor of Sociology at the University of California at Santa Cruz, concluded in 2007, "Since financial wealth is what counts as far as the control of income-producing assets, we can say that just 10% of the people own the United States of America." C. William Domhoff, "Who Rules America: Wealth, Income and Power," *Who Rules America*, September 2005, updated March 2012. http://www2.ucsc.edu/whorulesamerica/power/wealth.html.

character learns that a man can, with effort, have a spiritual rebirth when he realizes that spirit, body and the outside world can live in harmony. In order to achieve this, however, we have to stop the cycle of violence:

> "Brother raises a hand against brother and son against father (how terrible!) and the father also against son. And moreover it is a continuity-matter, for if the father did not strike the son, they would not be alike. It is done to perpetuate similarity. Oh, Henderson, man cannot keep still under the blows.... A hit B? B hit C? – we have not enough alphabet to cover the condition. A brave man will try to make the evil stop with him. He shall keep the blow. No man shall get it from him, and that is a sublime ambition."[15]

We must become neither "takers" nor "leavers" as envisioned by author Daniel Quinn in his novel *Ishmael* – we must become *sharers*.[16] We must learn to keep the blow, or at least aspire to do so, even if we may never completely succeed. Our future depends on it. It's imperative that we begin to look at ourselves as an advanced non-human intelligence would see us – as members of the human race who share this world with other creatures both big and small, all of us floating through time and space together on what Carl Sagan famously called this "pale blue dot".[17]

This might all sound a bit "new agey" to some readers, but to those

---

[15] Saul Bellow, *Henderson the Rain King* (New York: Avon, 1976), 181.

[16] Daniel Quinn, *Ishmael: An Adventure of the Mind and Spirit* (New York: Bantam Books, 1991).

[17] As Sagan observed, "There is perhaps no better demonstration of the folly of human conceits than this distant image of our tiny world. To me, it underscores our responsibility to deal more kindly with one another, and to preserve and cherish the pale blue dot, the only home we've ever known." Carl Sagan, *Pale Blue Dot: A Vision of the Human Future in Space* (New York: Ballantine Books, 1997), 7.

202

who would see it that way I ask one simple question: isn't it time for a "new age" given how the "old age" has worked out for us and our fellow inhabitants of this fragile world? As Dag Hammarskjöld said, "Is life so wretched? Isn't it rather your hands which are too small, your vision which is muddied? You are the one who must grow up."[18]

The questions we have to address are simple: who are we, and even more importantly, *who do we want to become*? Regardless of whether the advanced non-human intelligence are visitors from some other planet, or live amongst us, or come from another dimension, or another time, or represent a supernatural "parent" of some sort, I think it's safe to assume that they're waiting for us to come up with an answer.[19] Even if they exist only in our imagination the questions remain. Indeed, if we *have* created this concept of an advanced non-human intelligence, perhaps the motivating factor has been our own guilty conscience, both as individuals and as a species.

In the preceding pages, I have explored the idea that the paranormal is art, in varying manifestations, created by an advanced non-human intelligence for our benefit. Artistic expression has always been one of the primary mechanisms we use as social commentary. It has been the prism through which we look at ourselves in ways as varied as the plays of Sophocles and Aeschylus in ancient Greece through to the three-chords-and-the-truth blasts of punk rock that began in the mid 1970s. The artist has stood as both reporter and analyst, critic and performer, in the ongoing exploration of the nature of the human condition.

While art may reside at the fringes of our consciousness at any

---

[18] Hammarskjöld, *Markings*, 41.

[19] I consider it safe to make this assumption because any civilization technologically advanced enough to get "here" from "there" would be technologically advanced enough to conquer and / or destroy us in short order if it wished to do so. After all, Hernán Cortez conquered the Aztec Empire with just 500 men, and the God of Abraham laid waste to the planet with the Great Flood. See Buddy Levy, *Conquistador: Hernan Cortes, King Montezuma, and the Last Stand of the Aztecs* (New York: Bantam Dell, 2008).

given moment, it remains timeless in a way that is unique. It forms a continuum of understanding and evolving awareness that stands in opposition to the continuum of violence and horror we create (and often celebrate) in our day to day lives. It is the true epitome of human potential and accomplishment. As Jean-Luc Goddard said, "Art attracts us only by what it reveals of our most secret self."[20]

What we call the paranormal could be serving the same purpose. It could be designed to remind us that we don't sit at the top of the mountain; indeed, that we haven't even established a base camp yet. The Irish artist Francis Bacon observed that the job of the artist is always to "deepen the mystery."[21] Perhaps whatever intelligence is behind the paranormal is doing just that. It wants us to look up at the lights in the sky and to think about the mysteries and puzzles around us as a form of artistic expression designed to challenge us and to make us think about who we are, where we have been, and where we are going.[22]

As Stella Adler observed, "Life beats down and crushes the soul, and art reminds you that you have one."[23] In the end, I think that's exactly the message a non-human intelligence is trying to communicate to us through its "art".

---

[20] Jean-Luc Goddard, *Goddard on Goddard*, ed. Tom Milne (New York: Da Capo Press, 1972), 31.

[21] Francis Bacon, quoted in Larry Chang, ed., *Wisdom for the Soul: Five Millenia of Prescriptions for Spiritual Healing* (Washington: Gnosophia Publishers, 2006), 57. The remark was originally made in the *Sunday Telegraph* in 1964.

[22] My good friend Greg Bishop touched upon this idea in 2007 when he wrote, "The non-human intelligences knocking at our collective consciousness may have no other message than 'look,' or 'think,' or perhaps even 'you don't know everything.' Ultimately, what the UFO subject does is throw a mirror in front of us and ask us to look at what we are, and how we perceive our reality, which is one of the things that great art is supposed to do." Greg Bishop, "UFOs as a Cosmic Art Exhibit," *UFO Mystic*, 29 September 2007. http://www.ufomystic.com/2007/09/29/ufo-art-2/.

[23] Stella Adler, quoted in *Stella Adler on America's Master Playwrights*, ed. Barry Paris (New York: Alfred A. Knopf, 2012), xi.

204

I return to my friend Mac, and his final words in *The Cryptoterrestrials*, written shortly before he died. The future was still very much at the forefront of his thoughts.

"Sometimes I fear that we've reached a critical threshold." he wrote. "For Earth and its teeming billions of passengers, the end is always nigh; for too long we've relied on blind luck and narrow escapes. Despite brushes with cataclysm and the rigors of evolution, we've survived – but only barely."

Despite our grim past, however, and our flawed nature, he saw the same possibilities for escape from our existential trap that I do.

"Although I harbor serious reservations about humanity's ability to make the evolutionary cut, I'm not without hope," he concluded. "Our potential as genuine cosmic citizens challenges the imagination and stretches conceptual boundaries to dizzy extremes."[24]

I'm convinced that this challenge to our imagination, and the prospect for liberation that it holds, is exactly what the "paranormal" is all about, and why it matters so much.

"Art," pronounced Pablo Picasso, "washes away from the soul the dust of everyday life."[25]

What remains is the other side of "truth" – the world not as we have been told it is, but as we are being encouraged to imagine it could become.

---

[24] Tonnies, *The Cryptoterrestrials*, 113.

[25] Pablo Picasso, quoted in *Dictionary of Quotations*, 3rd ed., ed. Connie Robertson (Hertfordshire, UK: Wordsworth Editions, 1998), 325.

Yours truly in June, 2009, at the Small Fortress in Terezin, Czech Republic. The fortress served as a Gestapo prison during the Second World War. Approximately 32,000 people arrived at the fortress, most of whom were later sent to various concentration camps. 2,600 were executed, starved, or succumbed to disease there. Of the 15,000 children sent there it's estimated that only 1,500 survived. Part of a continuum of horror that we must face every time we look in the proverbial mirror as a reminder to strive for a better future.

Chimpanzee at the Los Angeles Zoo, June 2009. We aren't the only inhabitants of this planet and yet we often act like it. How would an advanced non-human intelligence view our treatment of our fellow non-human Earthlings?

Conclusion

It's All in the Hearing

"It is when we all play safe that we create a world of utmost insecurity. It is when we all play safe that fatality will lead us to our doom. It is in the 'dark shade of courage' alone that the spell can be broken."[1]
- Dag Hammarskjöld

Back in the 1990s Peter Black and I used to drink "on occasion." We would spend those late evenings and early mornings discussing all things metaphysical, mystical and philosophical (we still do this, but far less frequently, alas). Our conversations ranged from Marxism to Christian mysticism to ghosts to Aleister Crowley and many points in between, off to the side, and over the proverbial fence. From time to time we would light a little fire in the center of the room and try to commune with the elder gods, should they exist in some form and still be in the practice of accepting calls. To this day, I'm not sure that we ever got an answer, but that wasn't the point – it was enough for us to have the imagination to ask the questions.

As a musician in the years after law school I took many of these conversations and used them as springboards for my songwriting. I wasn't the only one drawing upon a wide variety of literary influences for musical inspiration back then, however. Another of my best friends, John Rosborough, fronted an aptly-named band called The Fourth Wall, with which my various bands frequently shared a bill.

---

[1] Dag Hammarskjöld, *Public Papers of the Secretaries-General of the United Nations, 1956 – 1957*, eds. Andrew W. Cordier and Wilder Foote (New York: Columbia University Press, 1973), 142.

Like me he looked to the Beats for inspiration, as well as earlier philosophers, mystics and poets such as William Blake. *Beltane Born*, the title of his band's one full-length CD release, gives a hint to some of the more mystical elements of John's writing.[2]

John now works in the film and television industry here in Halifax, and from time to time he still plays with The Fourth Wall. Over the years we've spent a fair bit of time together on the road, mixing work with adventure, and a fair bit of personal discovery. I recall one time, while we were in Puerto Rico filming *Fields of Fear*, when the two of us wandered out into the Old Town section of San Juan one night, chatting about life and how to live it as we made our way from one bar to another and then down a couple of interesting alleyways as well. Always the professionals, we somehow still made the 9 am call time the next morning.

One of my favorite stories happened on a trip we took to Las Vegas in 2003 with my brother and two other friends. One night, after John and I had been "politely" asked to leave the Rio Casino for some minor infraction of the rules, we continued on to the Sand Dollar Blues Lounge while the others went back to the hotel. The Sand Dollar, like a lot of places in Las Vegas, either doesn't have windows or keeps them well covered so that the customers lose track of time. When we got there it was roughly 2:00 am and the place was completely deserted with the exception of the bartender and a woman in her late 40s of questionable repute who was perched on a stool across from him. John and I settled in for a drink or two at a table well away from the "lady of the evening" and had an invigorating conversation about Kerouac, Bukowski, and all sorts of other things.

After what seemed like a short while we decided to head back to the hotel, at which point we discovered three things: first, that it was after 9:30 am; second, that one or two drinks had actually been several; and third, that the Sand Dollar Blues Lounge was a lot farther from our hotel on the Strip than it had seemed at 2:00 am in the taxi we took to

---

[2] The Fourth Wall, *Beltane Born* (Halifax: The Fourth Wall, 1993). Selections available on-line at: http://www.myspace.com/thefourthwallhfx/music.

get there. We could have called a taxi to get back, but we decided that it would be an adventure to walk to the hotel along the very busy highway. It probably wasn't the smartest thing we've ever done, and we were baking like leather-wrapped chickens on a rotisserie spit as we made our way back, shielding our eyes from the glaring sun like vampires and dodging traffic like raccoons as we walked. But it was fun because it was an experience that we *lived*.

The moments that define our lives come in many different shapes and sizes. In November, 2007, I flew Mac Tonnies up to Halifax for the premiere of *Doing Time*, the play we had written together.[3] After the first performance we went out for a drink with the cast. The actors bailed on us after maybe an hour, so Mac and I had a couple more drinks, railed at the lack of respect that the younger generation had for we "old-timers," and then went for a walkabout around Halifax.

We eventually made our way down to the waterfront where we found a perch on one of the piers and stared out at the harbour, with the buoy lights bouncing up and down on top of the restive black water.

It was cold and the wind whistled past us, almost like a song, as we sat there for five or six minutes. Neither of us said a single word – we just took all of it in. I looked over at Mac after what seemed like a particularly chilly gust, and while I could spend an hour sitting on a pier staring at the night (and have, many times), I figured maybe he had had enough.

"Want to head back?" I asked.

He shook his head, just a bit, and said, "No. This is perfect." And so we remained at the end of the pier for another forty-five minutes or so, intermittently breaking the comfortable silence of friends to talk

---

[3] Paul Kimball and Mac Tonnies, *Doing Time* (Halifax: Redstar Films Limited, 2007). Available on-line at: http://goo.gl/Du1cB. See also Kate Watson, "Semaphore Theatre Company's Sci-Fi Hit," *The Coast*, 30 November 2007. Watson wrote: "A highly entertaining mystery… The story is classic sci-fi but you don't have to be a fan of the genre to enjoy *Doing Time*. In a season that has already had a banner crop of shows, *Doing Time* still manages to stand out."

about the state of our love lives (or what passed for them at the time).

Since Mac passed away in October, 2009, I've wandered down to that pier more than once late at night. I sit on the same bench we occupied back in 2007 and listen to the wind whisper as if I was listening to him breathe. Who knows? Maybe he *is* whispering to me, sending a message in the most abstract way possible. That would be just like him.

All of which is my way of saying, by way of conclusion, that I firmly believe we demonstrate our willingness to open ourselves up to possible contact with an advanced non-human intelligence through our actions as much as anything else. After all, if we don't make the effort to visit an art gallery, or go to a concert or play, we'll never see or hear what's been created by the performers and artists. So too, I think, with the "paranormal." At some level, perhaps even one that we're not aware of within our subconscious, we must "purchase a ticket" for the show that's on offer.

As William Blake famously wrote, "The road of excess leads to the palace of wisdom; for we never know what is enough until we know what is more than enough."[4]

Or, as John said to me once in San Juan, "I hear music and laughter. C'mon – let's see what's down this alley."

If there is an advanced non-human intelligence out there (or, as I've speculated, perhaps a "post-human" or "post-individual" intelligence), I'm convinced that the place we'll find it is "on the road." In my own way, that's where I've been travelling over the years through my work in music, film and television, and most importantly in my life experiences and search for adventure and knowledge.

Many years ago, when I was "young and carefree, famous among the barns, in the sun that is young once only," I wrote a song for my old band called "It's All in the Hearing."[5] I include an excerpt from it

---

[4] William Blake, quoted in "Thoughts on the Business of Life," *Forbes.com.* http://thoughts.forbes.com/thoughts/waste-william-blake-the-road-of.

[5] The words I've quoted here come from Dylan Thomas' "Fern Hill," one of my

here as my final statement of purpose, in the spirit of Blake and the Beats, and all of my other fellow travelers over the years. Let it serve as a signal, to whomever or whatever might be listening, that I remain on the road, always open to new thoughts, ideas and experiences, always aware that the journey really is the destination… and always searching for the artist within us all.

> Picturesque faces locked in timeless smiles,
> Long hollowed spaces, barren for miles,
> Searching for something, somewhere beyond,
> Searching for someone who's already gone,
> 'cause they've seen it, just listen to them –
> It's all in the hearing.[6]

favorite poems. I included it as part of my personal write-up in my yearbook entry when I graduated from Acadian University in 1989. Of course, after this reflective quote from Thomas I cheekily added, "See you all at 24 Sussex Drive," which is the official residence of the Prime Minister of Canada. It's the yin and yang of my personality for which I'll always be trying to find a balance.

[6] Paul Kimball, "It's All in the Hearing," Perf. Tall Poppies, *Tall Poppies - All Points in Between* (2012). http://youtu.be/6WCFf3TC-eo.

Selected Bibliography

What follows this note is a selected list of the books that were influential in formulating the ideas contained in *The Other Side of Truth*. It is by no means exhaustive, nor does it include specific government documents, archival resources, newspapers, journals, or web-based material, all of which can be found in the footnotes (some of the website URLs have been shortened from the original in order to facilitate formatting). All websites were last accessed on 24 September, 2012.

I recommend *The Daily Grail* (dailygrail.com) and *The Anomalist* (anomalist.com) for daily general information and news on many of the subjects contained in this book; also, the radio show *Radio Misterioso* (radiomisterioso.com), the podcasts *Strange Days Indeed* (virtuallystrange.net/ufo/sdi/program) and *Binnall of America* (binnallofamerica.com), and the long-running magazine *The Fortean Times* (forteantimes.com), as sources of informed discussion about the "paranormal" and related subject matters. I also recommend three blogs: (1) Nick Redfern's *Nick Redfern's World of Whatever* (nickredfernfortean.blogspot.com), where you can follow Nick's often zany adventures; (2) *The Posthuman Blues* (posthumanblues.com), written by the late Mac Tonnies until his untimely death in 2009, a treasure trove of original thought; and (3) *The UFO Iconoclasts* (ufocon.blogspot.com), the home of the controversial but thought-provoking commentator / provocateur Rich Reynolds. All three are valuable repositories of interesting observations about the weird world around us and within us.

My own writing on the subject over the years can be found at my old blog *The Other Side of Truth*, which is no longer updated but continues to exist in cyberspace (redstarfilms.blogspot.com). Most of my films, new writing, and my occasional podcasts can be found at my personal website (beyonderstv.com) and my company's website (redstarfilmtv.com).

- Paul Kimball, 25 September 2012

Adams, James Luther. *Paul Tillich's Philosophy of Culture, Science, and Religion*. New York University Press, 1965.

Alline, Henry. *The Life and Journal of The Rev. Mr. Henry Alline*. Eds. James Beverly and Barry Moody. Lancelot Press Limited, 1982.

_____. *The Sermons of Henry Alline*. Ed. George A. Rawlyk. Lancelot Press Limited, 1986.

Baggini, Julian. *The Duck that Won the Lottery, and 99 Other Bad Arguments*. Granta Books, 2008.

Bellow, Saul. *Henderson the Rain King*. Avon, 1976.

Bentley, G. E. Jr. *The Stranger from Paradise: A Biography of William Blake*. Paul Mellon Centre for Studies in British Art, 2003.

Bishop, Greg, ed. *Wake Up Down There: The Excluded Middle Collection*. Adventures Unlimited Press, 2000.

Blake, William. *William Blake: The Complete Illuminated Books*. Thames & Hudson, 2001.

_____. *The Complete Poetry & Prose of William Blake*. 2nd. Ed., Ed. David V. Erdman. Anchor, 1997.

Booth, Marin. *A Magick Life: The Life of Aleister Crowley*. Coronet Books, 2000.

Boyd, Malcolm. *Bach*. Oxford University Press, 2001.

Brunvand, Jan Harold, ed. *American Folklore: An Encyclopedia*. Garland Publishing, 1996.

Breisach, Ernst. *Introduction to Modern Existentialism*. Grove Press, 1962.

Burroughs, William. *The Western Lands*. Viking, 1987.

_____. *The Wild Boys: A Book of the Dead*. Grove-Atlantic, 1992.

Camus, Albert. *The Myth of Sisyphus*. Trans. Hamish Hamilton. Penguin Books, 1975.

_____. *The Stranger*. Trans. Mathew Ward. Alfred A. Knopf, 1988.

Charters, Ann, ed. *The Portable Beat Reader*. Penguin Classics, 2003.

Clarke, David, and Andy Roberts. *Phantoms of the Sky: UFOs - A Modern Myth*. Robert Hale, 1990.

_____. *Twilight of the Celtic Gods: Exploration of Britain's Hidden Pagan Traditions*. Blandford Press, 1996.

Coleman, Loren. *Mysterious America: The Ultimate Guide to the Nation's Weirdest Wonders, Strangest Spots, and Creepiest Creatures*. Paraview Pocket Books, 2007.

Collier, James Lincoln. *The Making of Jazz: A Comprehensive History*. Dell Publishing Co., 1978.

Condon, Edward U. *Scientific Study of Unidentified Flying Objects*. Bantam Books, 1969.

Cooke, Mervyn. *Jazz*. Thames and Hudson, 1999.

Creighton, David. *Ecstasy of the Beats: On the Road to Understanding*. Dundurn Press, 2007.

Creighton, Helen. *Bluenose Ghosts*. Nimbus Publishing, 1994.

_____. *Bluenose Magic: Popular Beliefs and Superstitions in Nova Scotia*. The Ryerson Press, 1968.

Damon, S. Foster. *A Blake Dictionary: The Ideas and Symbols of William Blake*. Brown, 1988.

Debord, Guy. *The Society of the Spectacle*. Trans. Donald Nicholson-Smith. Zone, 1995.

Dmytryk, Edward. *On Filmmaking*. Focal Press, 1986.

Dole, George F., and Stephen Larsen. *Emanuel Swedenborg: The Universal Human and Soul-Body Interaction*. Paulist Press, 1984.

Downing, Barry H. *The Bible and Flying Saucers*. 2nd ed. Marlowe & Company, 1997.

Ellwood, Robert S. *Tales of Light and Shadows: Mythology of the Afterlife*. Continuum, 2010.

Fante, John. *Ask the Dusk*. Harper Perennial Modern Classics, 2006.

Fest, Joachim C. *Hitler*. Weidenfeld and Nicolson, 1974.

Feyerabend, Paul. *Against Method: Outline of an Anarchist Theory of Knowledge*. New Left Books, 1975.

_____. *Conquest of Abundance: A Tale of Abstraction Versus the Richness of Being*. Ed. Bert Terpstra. University of Chicago Press, 1999.

Frye, Northrop. *Fearful Symmetry: A Study of William Blake*. Princeton University Press, 1969.

Ginsburg, Allen. *Allen Verbatim: Lectures on Poetry, Politics, Consciousness*. Ed. Gordon Ball. McGraw-Hill, 1974.

_____. *Collected Poems: 1947 – 1980*. Harper & Row, 1984.

Greene, Brian. *The Elegant Universe: Superstrings, Hidden Dimensions, and the Quest for the Ultimate Theory*. Vintage Books, 2000.

_____. *The Fabric of the Cosmos: Space, Time, and the Texture of Reality*. Vintage, 2005.

Guiley, Rosemary Ellen. *The Encyclopedia of Witches and Witchcraft*. 2nd. ed. Checkmark Books, 1999.

Hall, Richard. *The UFO Evidence, Volume II: A Thirty Year Report*. Scarecrow Press, 2001.

_____, ed. *The UFO Evidence*. National Investigations Committee on Aerial Phenomena, 1964.

Hammarskjöld, Dag. *Markings*. Trans. Leif Sjoberg and W. H. Auden. Alfred A. Knopf, 1964.

Hancock, Graham. *Supernatural: Meetings with the Ancient Teachers of Mankind*. Rev. Ed. The Disinformation Company, 2007.

Harpur, Tom. *Life After Death*. Toronto: McLelland & Stewart, 1991.

_____. *Living Waters: Selected Writings on Spirituality*. Thomas Allen Publishers, 2006.

Hawking, Stephen. *A Brief History of Time*. Bantam, 1988.

_____. *The Universe in a Nutshell*. Bantam, 2001.

Hesse, Hermann. *Demian*. Harper Perennial, 1999.

Hook, Sidney, ed. *Religious Experience and Truth: A Symposium*. New York University Press, 1961.

Hopke, Richard H. *There Are No Accidents: Synchronicity and the Stories of Our Lives*. Riverhead Books, 1997.

Hoss, Rudolph. *Death Dealer: The Memoirs of the SS Kommandant At Auschwitz*. Da Capo Press, 1996.

Huxley, Aldous. *The Doors of Perception and Heaven and Hell*. Harper Perennial Modern Classics, 2009.

_____. *Huxley and God: Essays on Religious Experience*. Ed. Jacqueline Hazard Bridgeman. The Crossroad Publishing Company, 2003.

_____. *Moksha: Aldous Huxley's Classic Writings on Psychedelics and the Visionary Experience*. Ed. Michael Horowitz. Park Street Press, 1999.

_____. *The Perennial Philosophy: An Interpretation of the Great Mystics, East and West*. Harper Perennial Modern Classics, 2009.

Hynek, J. Allen. *The UFO Experience: A Scientific Inquiry*. Henry Regnery Company, 1972.

Hynek, J. Allen, and Jacques Vallee. *The Edge of Reality: A Progress Report on Unidentified Flying Objects*. Regnery, 1975.

James, William. *The Varieties of Religious Experience: A Study in Human Nature*. The Modern Library, 2002.

Jung, C. G. *Dreams*. Trans. R. F. C. Hull. Princeton University Press, 1974.

_____. *Jung on Synchronicity and the Paranormal*. Ed. Roderick Main. Routledge, 1997.

_____. *Synchronicity: An Acausal Connecting Principle.* 2nd ed. Trans. R. F. C. Hull. Princeton University Press, 1981.

Kaku, Michio. *Parallel Worlds: A Journey Through Creation, Higher Dimensions, and the Future of the Cosmos.* Anchor Books, 2006.

_____. *Physics of the Future: How Science Will Shape Human Destiny and Our Daily Lives by the Year 2100.* Doubleday, 2011.

_____. *The Physics of the Impossible: A Scientific Exploration into the World of Phasers, Force Fields, Teleportation, and Time Travel.* Anchor Books, 2009.

_____. *Visions: How Science Will Revolutionize the 21st Century.* Anchor Books, 1998.

Kaufmann, Walter. *Critique of Religion and Philosophy.* Princeton University Press, 1979.

_____. *From Shakespeare to Existentialism.* Princeton University Press, 1980.

_____. *Discovering the Mind, Volume One: Goethe, Kant, and Hegel.* Transaction Publishers, 1991.

_____. *Discovering the Mind, Volume Two: Nietzsche, Heidegger, and Buber.* Transaction Publishers, 1992.

_____. *Discovering the Mind, Volume Three: Freud, Adler and Jung.* Transaction Publishers, 1992.

_____, ed. *Existentialism from Dostoevsky to Sartre.* Rev. Ed. New American Library, 1975.

Kerouac, Jack. *Big Sur.* Penguin, 1992.

219

_____. *Lonesome Traveler*. McGraw Hill, 1960.

_____. *On The Road*. Viking, 1957.

_____. *The Dharma Bums*. Viking, 1958.

Knox, Ronald A. *Enthusiasm: A Chapter in the History of Religion*. 1950. University of Notre Dame Press, 1994.

Kurzweil, Ray. *The Age of Spiritual Machines: When Computers Exceed Human Intelligence*. Viking, 1999.

_____. *The Singularity Is Near: When Humans Transcend Biology*. The Viking Press, 2005.

Leary, Timothy. *The Psychedelic Experience: A Manual Based on the Tibetan Book of the Dead*. Citadel, 2000.

Lester, David. *Is There Life After Death? An Examination of the Empirical Evidence*. McFarland & Company, 2005.

Levi, Primo. *Survival in Auschwitz*. Touchstone, 1995.

MacGregor, Geddes. *Reincarnation in Christianity: A New Vision of the Role of Rebirth in Christian Thought*. Theosophical Publishing House, 1978.

MacKillop, James. *Dictionary of Celtic Mythology*. Oxford University Press, 1998.

Manning, James, and James Innis. *The Newlight Baptist Journals of James Manning and James Innis*. Ed. David G. Bell. Lancelot Press, 1984.

Maritain, Jacques, *Approaches to God*. Trans. Peter O'Reilly. Collier Books, 1962.

Martin, Bernard. *The Existentialist Theology of Paul Tillich*. College and University Press, 1963.

Mera, Steve. *Paranormal Insight: A concise study of the strange and profound*. Blurb, 2011.

_____. *Strange Happenings: Memoirs of a Paranormal Investigator*. Blurb, 2010.

Moseley, James W., and Karl T. Pflock. *Shockingly Close to the Truth*. Prometheus Books, 2002.

Neufeldt, Ronald W., ed. *Karma and Rebirth: Post Classical Developments*. State University of New York Press, 1986.

Neumann, Erich. *Art and the Creative Unconscious*. Trans. R. F. C. Hull. Princeton University Press, 1971.

_____. *The Origins and History of Consciousness*. Trans. R. F. C. Hull. Princeton University Press, 1970.

Palmer, Michael. *Paul Tillich's Philosophy of Art*. Walter de Gruyte, 1984.

Pflock, Karl T. *Roswell: Inconvenient Facts and the Will to Believe*. Prometheus Books, 2001.

Pinchbeck, Daniel. *Breaking Open the Head: A Psychedelic Journey into the Heart of Contemporary Shamanism*. Broadway Books, 2003.

Poulin, Jacques. *Volkswagen Blues*. Babel, 1996.

Progoff, Ira. *Jung, Synchronicity, and Human Destiny: C.G. Jung's Theory of Meaningful Coincidence*. Three Rivers Press, 1987.

Quinn, Daniel. *Ishmael: An Adventure of the Mind and Spirit*.

Bantam, 1995.

_____. *The Story of B: An Adventure of the Mind and Spirit.* Bantam, 1996.

Radin, Dean. *The Conscious Universe: The Scientific Truth of Psychic Phenomena.* HarperOne, 1997.

_____. *Entangled Minds: Extrasensory Experiences in a Quantum Reality.* Paraview Pocket Books, 2006.

Rawlyk, George A. *The Canada Fire: Radical Evangelicalism in British North America, 1775-1812.* McGill-Queen's University Press, 1994.

_____. *Henry Alline: Selected Writings.* Paulist Press, 1988.

_____. *Ravished by the Spirit: Religious Revivals, Baptists and Henry Alline.* McGill-Queen's University Press, 1984.

Rawlyk, George A., ed. *The New Light Letters and Spiritual Songs, 1778-1793.* Lancelot Press, 1983.

Redfern, Nick. *Contactees.* New Page Books, 2009.

_____. *Final Events and the Secret Government Group on Demonic UFOs and the Afterlife.* Anomalist Books, 2010.

_____. *Memoirs of a Monster Hunter: A Five Year Journey in Search of the Unknown.* The Career Press, 2007.

_____. *The Real Men in Black: Evidence, Famous Cases, and True Stories of These Mysterious Men and their Connection to UFO Phenomena.* New Page Books, 2011.

_____. *Three Men Seeking Monsters: Six Weeks in Pursuit of*

Werewolves, Lake Monsters, Giant Cats, Ghostly Devil Dogs, and Ape-Men. Pocket Books, 2004.

Redfern, Nick, and Andy Roberts. *Strange Secrets: Real Government Files on the Unknown*. Pocket Books, 2003.

Rees, Laurence. *Auschwitz: A New History*. Public Affairs, 2005.

Rutkowski, Chris A. *A World of UFOs*. Dundurn Press, 2008.

Sadler, Dave. *Paranormal Reality: Ghosts, UFO's and Pussy Cats*. Blurb, 2010.

Sagan, Carl. *Billions & Billions: Thoughts on Life and Death at the Brink of the Millennium*. Ballantine Books, 1998.

_____. *Broca's Brain: Reflections on the Romance of Science*. Ballantine Books, 1986.

_____. *Cosmos*. Ballantine Books, 1985.

_____. *The Dragons of Eden: Speculations on the Evolution of Human Intelligence*. Ballantine Books, 1986.

_____. *Pale Blue Dot: A Vision of the Human Future in Space*. Ballantine Books, 1997.

_____. *The Varieties of Scientific Experience: A Personal View of the Search for God*. Ed. Ann Druyan. Penguin, 2007.

Sagan, Carl, and Ann Druyan. *The Demon-Haunted World: Science as a Candle in the Dark*. Random House, 1995.

Sanford, John A. *Soul Journey: A Jungian Analyst Looks at Reincarnation*. Crossroad Publishing, 1991.

Sartre, Jean-Paul. *No Exit (and Three Other Plays)*. Vintage Books, 1955.

Scharlemann, Robert P. *Reflection and Doubt in the Theology of Paul Tillich*. Yale University Press, 1969.

Schopenhauer, Arthur. *On the Suffering of the World*. Trans. R. J. Hollingdale. Penguin Books, 1970.

Schuchard, Marsha Keith. *William Blake's Sexual Path to Spiritual Vision*. Inner Traditions, 2008.

Sereny, Gitta. *Albert Speer: His Battle With Truth*. Knopf, 1995.

Simpson, Jacqueline, and Steve Roud. *A Dictionary of English Folklore*. Oxford University Press, 2000.

Speer, Albert. *Inside the Third Reich*. Simon & Schuster, 1997.

Steiger, Brad. *Out of the Dark: The Complete Guide to Beings From Beyond*. Kensington, 2001.

Strassman, Rick. *DMT: The Spirit Molecule: A Doctor's Revolutionary Research into the Biology of Near-Death and Mystical Experiences*. 3rd Ed. Park Street Press, 2000.

Strassman, Rick, et al. *Inner Paths to Outer Space: Journeys to Alien Worlds through Psychedelics and Other Spiritual Technologies*. Park Street Press, 2008.

Sturrock, Peter A. *The UFO Enigma: A New Review of the Physical Evidence*. Aspect: 2000.

Swedenborg, Emanuel. *Divine Love and Wisdom*. A & D Publishing, 2007.

_____. *Life on Other Planets*. Trans. John Chadwick. Swedenborg Foundation, 2006.

_____. *Swedenborg's Journal of Dreams: The Extraordinary Record of the Transformation of a Scientist into a Seer*. Trans. James John Garth Wilkinson. Swedenborg Foundation Publishers, 1986.

Tanizaki, Junichiro. *In Praise of Shadows*. Trans. Thomas J. Harper and Edward G. Seidensticker. Charles E. Tuttle, 1988.

Tillich, Paul. *The Courage to Be*. Yale University Press, 2000.

_____. *The Eternal Now*. SCM Press, 2002.

_____. *The New Being*. Charles Scribner's Sons, 1969.

Tonnies, Mac. *After the Martian Apocalypse: Extraterrestrial Artifacts and the Case for Mars Exploration*. Paraview Pocket Books, 2004.

_____. *The Cryptoterrestrials: A Meditation on Indigenous Humanoids Among Us*. Anomalist Books, 2010.

_____. *Illumined Black and Other Adventures*. Phantom Press Publications, 1995.

Vallee, Jacques. *Confrontations: A Scientist's Search for Alien Contact*. Ballantine Books, 1990.

_____. *Dimensions: A Casebook of Alien Contact*. Contemporary Books, 1988.

_____. *Passport to Magonia*. Neville Spearman, 1970.

Vallee, Jacques, and Chris Aubeck. *Wonders in the Sky: Unexplained Aerial Objects from Antiquity to Modern Times*. Tarcher, 2010.

Vallee, Jacques, and Janine Vallee. *Challenge to Science: The UFO Enigma*. Ballantine Books, 1974.

Vaneigem, Raoul. *The Revolution of Everyday Life*. 2nd ed. Trans. Donald Nicholson-Smith. Rebel Press, 2001.

Watson, Steven. *The Birth of The Beat Generation: Visionaries, Rebels, and Hipsters, 1944 – 1950*. Pantheon, 1995.

Wright, Robert. *The Evolution of God*. Little, Brown and Company, 2009.

_____. *Nonzero: The Logic of Human Destiny*. Vintage, 2001.

_____. *The Moral Animal: Why We Are The Way We Are*. Pantheon, 1994.

_____. *Three Scientists and Their Gods: Looking for Meaning in the Age of Information*. HarperCollins, 1989.

INDEX

234

About the Author

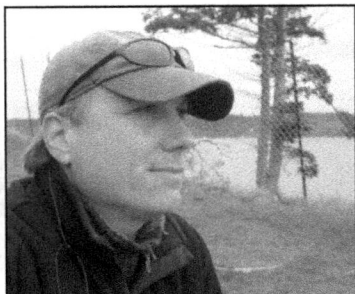

After winning multiple scholarships and awards - including the University Medal in History at both Acadia University and the University of Dundee, and the CLB Award at Dalhousie Law School - Paul Kimball graduated from Acadia in 1989 with an Honors Degree in History and in 1992 from Dalhousie with a law degree. From 1992 until 1997, Paul was a musician, songwriter and producer during the heyday of the Halifax indie music scene. In late 1997 he moved to the film and television industry, working as the Program Administrator at the Nova Scotia Film Development Corporation and a consultant for several provincial governments before he founded the Halifax-based production company Redstar Films in 1999. He has since had work commissioned by a wide variety of networks and distributors, including the CBC, Space, TVNZ, Vision TV, Bravo, Content Films, and B7 Media. His films include the documentaries *Stanton T. Friedman Is Real*, *Best Evidence: Top 10 UFO Sightings*, *Denise Djokic: Seven Days Seven Nights*, *Synchronicity*, and *Fields of Fear*, the television series *The Classical Now* and *Ghost Cases*, and the feature films *Eternal Kiss* and *Damnation*. He has served as the Treasurer and President of the Nova Scotia Film and Television Producers Association, a member of the Nova Scotia Film Advisory Committee, and was a founding member of the Motion Picture Industry Association of Nova Scotia. His paranormal-themed blog, *The Other Side of Truth*, has been read by over 1,000,000 people since its creation in 2005, and he has appeared on myriad radio and television programs over the past decade to discuss his films, including *Coast to Coast*, *The X-Zone*, *Binnall of America*, *Radio Misterioso*, *Night Fright*, *The Paranormal Podcast*, and *Strange Days Indeed*. He has written for various magazines, including *Phenomena* and *Alien Worlds*, and spoken at a number of conferences in Canada, the United States, and the United Kingdom. Paul lives in his hometown of Halifax, Nova Scotia, where he continues to enjoy chocolate chip cookies, the zen of the vanilla milkshake, and slow walks to nowhere in particular.

www.ingramcontent.com/pod-product-compliance
Lightning Source LLC
Chambersburg PA
CBHW060233050426
42448CB00009B/1423